Katuan
Wadayt

KU-099-785

Applied EI

Applied EI

The Importance of Attitudes in Developing Emotional Intelligence

Tim Sparrow and Amanda Knight

(2006)

Chichester

JOSSEY-BASS
A Wiley Imprint
www.josseybass.com

Copyright © 2006   John Wiley & Sons Ltd, The Atrium, Southern Gate, Chichester,
West Sussex PO19 8SQ, England

Telephone (+44) 1243 779777

Under the Jossey-Bass imprint, Jossey-Bass, 989 Market Street, San Francisco CA 94103-1741, USA
www.jossey-bass.com

Email (for orders and customer service enquiries): cs-books@wiley.co.uk
Visit our Home Page on www.wiley.com

All Rights Reserved. No part of this publication may be reproduced, stored in a retrieval system or
transmitted in any form or by any means, electronic, mechanical, photocopying, recording, scanning
or otherwise, except under the terms of the Copyright, Designs and Patents Act 1988 or under the
terms of a licence issued by the Copyright Licensing Agency Ltd, 90 Tottenham Court Road, London
W1T 4LP, UK, without the permission in writing of the Publisher. Requests to the Publisher should
be addressed to the Permissions Department, John Wiley & Sons Ltd, The Atrium, Southern Gate,
Chichester, West Sussex PO19 8SQ, England, or emailed to permreq@wiley.co.uk, or faxed to (+44)
1243 770620.

Designations used by companies to distinguish their products are often claimed as trademarks. All
brand names and product names used in this book are trade names, service marks, trademarks or registered trademarks of their respective owners. The Publisher is not associated with any product or
vendor mentioned in this book.

This publication is designed to provide accurate and authoritative information in regard to the subject
matter covered. It is sold on the understanding that the Publisher is not engaged in rendering professional services. If professional advice or other expert assistance is required, the services of a competent
professional should be sought.

Other Wiley Editorial Offices

John Wiley & Sons Inc., 111 River Street, Hoboken, NJ 07030, USA

Jossey-Bass, 989 Market Street, San Francisco, CA 94103-1741, USA

Wiley-VCH Verlag GmbH, Boschstr. 12, D-69469 Weinheim, Germany

John Wiley & Sons Australia Ltd, 42 McDougall Street, Milton, Queensland 4064, Australia

John Wiley & Sons (Asia) Pte Ltd, 2 Clementi Loop #02-01, Jin Xing Distripark, Singapore 129809

John Wiley & Sons Canada Ltd, 22 Worcester Road, Etobicoke, Ontario, Canada M9W 1L1

Wiley also publishes its books in a variety of electronic formats. Some content that appears in print
may not be available in electronic books.

Library of Congress Cataloging-in-Publication Data
Sparrow, Tim.
    Applied EI : the importance of attitudes in developing emotional intelligence / Tim Sparrow and
Amanda Knight.
        p.   cm.
    Includes bibliographical references and index.
    ISBN-13: 978-0-470-03273-2 (cloth : alk. paper)
    ISBN-10: 0-470-03273-1 (cloth : alk. paper)
    1. Employees – Coaching of.   2. Emotional intelligence – Study and teaching.   3. Attitude
(Psychology)   4. Adaptability (Psychology)   5. Management – Psychological aspects.   I. Knight,
Amanda, 1964-   II. Title.
    HF5549.5.C53S67   2006
    658.3'82 – dc22   2006016611

British Library Cataloguing in Publication Data

A catalogue record for this book is available from the British Library

ISBN 13 978-0-470-03273-2 (HB)
ISBN10 0-470-03273-1 (HB)

Typeset in 11/15pt Goudy by SNP Best-set Typesetter Ltd., Hong Kong
Printed and bound in Great Britain by TJ International Ltd, Padstow, Cornwall, UK
This book is printed on acid-free paper responsibly manufactured from sustainable forestry
in which at least two trees are planted for each one used for paper production.

It is not your aptitude, but your attitude that determines your altitude.
Zig Ziglar

To the CAEI Steering Group – David, Jo, John, Matt, Maureen and Richard. For your support, commitment and energy. Thank you.

Contents

Who this book is for

This book is aimed at three categories of people.

(1) Anybody, private individual or member of an organisation, who wants to

enhance their personal effectiveness in the world and their life outcomes, and/or to

improve the quality of their personal relationships, and/or to

improve their health, both physical and emotional, and/or to

increase their happiness, and who

understands that developing their emotional intelligence is the royal road towards the achievement of these aims.

(2) Anybody who has organisational responsibility for performance improvement; in other words, anyone who has managerial responsibilities of any kind. (The more senior you are, the more your organisation will benefit if you take on the lessons of this book.)

(3) Anyone whose role is to facilitate personal or organisational change, including management consultants, personal or management development specialists, coaches (both executive coaches and life coaches), counsellors and psychotherapists.

While these three categories are conceptually distinct, we hope that in practice they will overlap, that those with the responsibility for performance improvement (2) will also want to make the shift for themselves (1). And even more that those whose job is to facilitate change (3) will also want to embark on personal change (1): they will not be effective change facilitators unless they do so.

How to use the book

This book grew largely out of our nine month course for professional EI practitioners, and like that course is ideally designed to be started at the beginning and then gone through until the end. However, we recognise that different people have different priorities, and in particular that busy managers may be tempted to go straight to sections of Part 3 "Applying Emotionally Intelligent Attitudes" which have particular implications for them or for their organisation. We have therefore attempted to make this possible by introducing summary reviews of the foregoing theory into the various chapters of Part 3. So, if you find yourself coming across repetitions of the basic models, please note that this is deliberate and for a purpose. By all means skip the repetitions if you want to.

Introduction

We believe the exploration of the notion of emotional intelligence to be the most significant event in the fields both of personal development and of management theory in the last twenty years. Properly understood and applied, we believe it to have the potential both for transforming individual people's life experience, their health, happiness and success, and for transforming the effectiveness of work organisations.

The last ten years have seen a growing acceptance of the importance of emotional intelligence as a significant variable in determining organisational outcomes. However, as with any new field, there is a variety of conflicting views about the nature of what is being talked about, and indeed about what we need to do about it. We meet a lot of people who are at the point of saying: this is obviously important, but what exactly is it, and what do I need to do about it? It is those questions that we address in this book.

The main thing that distinguishes the view of the Centre for Applied Emotional Intelligence (see page 297), which is what is outlined here, from other approaches to the subject is that we see emotional intelligence neither as an intellectual capacity, nor as an aspect of personality, nor as just another term for soft skills. But rather it is a characterisation of our habitual stance towards self and the world, which is determined largely by the attitudes we hold. The happy result of this fact is that it is entirely changeable and developable. Hence its importance: it is highly influential of our personal and organisational outcomes, and it is something we can do something about.

What it is that we need to do all depends on where we – or our team and our organisation – are now. Hence we need to understand the various different aspects of emotional intelligence, how to measure them and how to develop them. All of that is set out in this book, and we hope that it will facilitate readers to embark on, or to pursue, a successful programme of personal and organisational change.

We wish you all success in the enterprise.

Tim Sparrow
Amanda Knight
June 2006

Acknowledgements

The chief acknowledgement that we each need to make is to the other. Luckily our strengths are complementary. Tim has been the originator of much of the theoretical development that is contained in this book. However, if Tim has been the thinker, Amanda has been the feeler and the doer: it is she who has ensured that the thinking is accessible, that the book has been created, and that it has taken the form that it has.

Both of us wish to acknowledge the contribution of the Centre for Applied Emotional Intelligence's partners: Jo Maddocks (Tim's co-designer of the *ie*™ and the *ie*™) and John Cooper of JCA Occupational Psychologists of Cheltenham, and Matt King of Activate Training in Lymington in the New Forest, specialists in outdoor experiential learning.

As are all writers on the subject, we are indebted to Daniel Goleman for having popularised the idea of emotional intelligence in the 1990s and for having pursued his development of the theory so energetically and so creatively. We are also grateful to Dr Alex Concorde for her contribution to our understanding of the physical basis of emotional intelligence, and for her endorsement of this book.

Individually, we each of us have more debts to acknowledge than can fully be enumerated here. Tim particularly wants to thank Dr Elizabeth Morris, the Principal of the School of Emotional Literacy, and professors Maria Gilbert and Charlotte Sills who introduced him to Transactional Analysis – and to the idea of personal change – for their contributions to his thinking. Amanda wishes to thank in addition Ian Havelock-Stevens, Stephen Bray and David Hand for their mentorship, and the following people for their unconditional love and support: Sheila (Mum), John (Dad), Marilyn, Pip, Louise, Anne, Caroline, Darci, and Neil.

Also thanks to Mike Wilman for facilitating the introduction to Wiley, and to Francesca and the team for delivering the final product.

The material in this book has been endlessly refined by the reactions to it of successive generations of students on our Certificate course in Applied Emotional Intelligence practitionership, and of delegates on our EI development programmes. We are indebted to them all.

PART I

How Our Attitudes Underpin Our EI

1

Why EI now?

The ever-increasing pace of change

We live in a world where change has to be taken for granted, and where the rate of change appears to be increasing steadily (though probably the rate at which it is increasing is itself increasing). This is due to the effects of a combination of factors:

- advances in technology, particularly information and communication technology;
- globalisation;
- the Internet;
- breakdown of cultural and, since the end of the cold war, political barriers, leading to more rapid exchange of ideas;
- the spread of literacy and higher education;
- greater openness to the contribution of different cultures;
- the decline of conservative institutions, such as the extended family, and authoritarian regimes.

Learning to live with change, to embrace it and not to be frightened by it is a task for us all, and involves not so much cognitive abilities as appropriate feelings and attitudes.

Leadership, too, requires a new approach. As business strategists such as Dr Lynda Gratton of the London Business School and Professor Richard

Scase of the University of Kent are predicting, tomorrow's leaders will need to cope with more demanding customers and a more discerning employee base. The leaders of the future will need to be facilitators – leaders who enable others to develop their own leadership and potential. They will also be collaborative leaders, highly skilled in developing and sustaining mutually beneficial partnerships and able to influence and lead non-employees and stakeholders. These both require a new set of skills and attitudes for leadership – emotionally intelligent skills and attitudes.

A crisis of meaning

For most of the history of mankind people have been overwhelmingly preoccupied with what Maslow would call safety and survival needs: warding off physical threats, getting enough to eat and drink and bringing up the next generation. With the coming of the Industrial Revolution, people went to work to get money to house and feed themselves. It is just over 100 years since Thorstein Veblen published his book on *The Theory of the Leisure Class*, and in developed countries the majority of the population is now relatively leisured – or could be if they chose to be. Many people are no longer prepared to exchange hours of boring drudgery and partial loss of liberty for cash.

For many years this exchange has been fostered by the triumph of Western materialism: people wanted more and more, often for purposes of conspicuous consumption, and for that they needed more and more money. Increasing material wealth has not brought in its train increasing happiness: having too little money may make you anxious and unhappy, but above a basic minimum having more will not make you happier. The triumph of materialism in the West to date has, therefore, been an empty triumph, and, coinciding as it has with a decline in adherence to revealed religion, has led to a psychological revolution: the evolution of humanism.

Humanism posits the human being, with his/her needs and aspirations, as the central value of our society and as the solution to the crisis of meaning which has assailed Western culture ever since the abandonment of the selfish materialism of the "me" generation at the end of the twentieth century. Nowadays, many people seek to spend their lives not just earning money for themselves at whatever personal cost, but working in accordance with their values, which include the promotion of a society in which human rights are completely realized: the right to health, education, freedom, spirituality, search for the meaning of life and an existence with dignity. As well as seeking work which accords with their values, educated employees in particular – those belonging to what economists and sociologists would traditionally have called the white-collar and managerial class – seek work that fosters their self development, that allows them to grow towards what they could possibly be. In Maslow's terms, they seek opportunities for self actualisation at work. We take a look in Chapter 5 at how we can create more meaning in our working lives through developing our emotional intelligence.

The arrival of EI

The history of emotional intelligence is most easily set out in tabular form:

Table 1.1 *The history of Emotional Intelligence.*

1920 ~ Edward Thorndike first talked of a "Social intelligence"

1940 ~ David Wechsler, the father of IQ, discussed the "Non intellective aspects"

1966 ~ Leunen published a paper on emotional intelligence and emancipation

1974 ~ Claude Steiner published his first article on Emotional Literacy

1983 ~ Howard Gardner's first work on Multiple Intelligences was published

1986 ~ Wayne Payne used the phrase "emotional intelligence" in an unpublished thesis

1990 ~ Peter Salovey & Jack Mayer announced their emotional Intelligence theory

1995 ~ Daniel Goleman published the first of his emotional intelligence books

And here we are, some ten years on from Daniel Goleman's acclaimed book, and emotional intelligence hasn't gone away. In fact there are more and more books, articles and references being made about EI now than there ever have been – this book included!

So why has it stood the test of time? Briefly because of the connection between levels of emotional intelligence and levels of performance, particularly in senior jobs: anyone interested in performance improvement (and who isn't?) needs to be interested in emotional intelligence. (We address the connection between EI and performance more specifically on page 22.)

Furthermore, EI hasn't just passively "stood the test of time" in the sense of proving not to be a short-lived flash in the pan; as the years pass it is coming to be seen as more and more important.

This is, in summary, because the changes in society and work organisation which have taken place over recent years, and which are continuing, mean that there are new requirements of today's and tomorrow's organisation leaders and members, and they all demand emotional intelligence.

Figure 1.1 sets out the societal changes and the new organisational requirements to which they are giving rise.

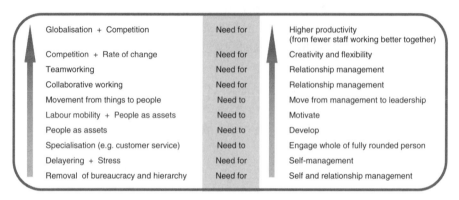

Globalisation + Competition	Need for	Higher productivity (from fewer staff working better together)
Competition + Rate of change	Need for	Creativity and flexibility
Teamworking	Need for	Relationship management
Collaborative working	Need for	Relationship management
Movement from things to people	Need to	Move from management to leadership
Labour mobility + People as assets	Need to	Motivate
People as assets	Need to	Develop
Specialisation (e.g. customer service)	Need to	Engage whole of fully rounded person
Delayering + Stress	Need for	Self-management
Removal of bureaucracy and hierarchy	Need for	Self and relationship management

Figure 1.1 *Societal changes and the associated new organisational requirements.*

None of these new or enhanced requirements is technical; they all involve aspects of emotional intelligence.

Why is EI the answer?

Our answers to this question lie in this book, but here is an overview.

Traditionally, people were employed largely for their muscle power – to do physical things. Increasingly during the second half of the last century they were employed for their brain power – to do mental things. But the new requirements of organisations and their leaders listed above, which translate into new requirements of their employees by the leaders of organisations in the 21st Century, require that people bring their whole selves to work rather than just their muscles and/or their brains. Similarly, employees want the fulfilment of involving and developing their whole selves, rather than just their muscles and/or their brains, at work.

Our sense of ourselves is largely tied up with our feelings, and this development entails the recognition of organisation members as being feeling beings as well as thinking beings. Similarly, our values are related to our feelings and attitudes, not just our thoughts and ideas. Again, employees who are value-driven need to be recognised as being feeling beings as well as thinking beings. Since emotional intelligence is about integrating feeling and thinking, it is clear that developing EI in organisations, in teams, in managers and in employees is the appropriate response to these developments.

From management's point of view, the above changes have led to a significantly increased need in themselves and their employees for effective self management and relationship management, which, as we shall see later, are two key EI processes; for creativity and flexibility, both aspects of EI, and consequently to the need to consider staff as fully rounded human beings, to develop them, to motivate them and to lead them rather than just manage them, all part of the emotionally intelligent approach to organisation management.

To boil it all down to one statement: emotional intelligence is highly correlated with performance, and since we are all in the business of performance improvement, we all need to focus on emotional intelligence.

Reference

Veblen, T. (1994) *The Theory of the Leisure Class*, Dover Publications. First published in 1899.

2

IQ and EI

A word about the term EQ. In the early days of the study, and the promotion, of emotional intelligence, this label was adopted by those who wished to persuade what they thought would be a sceptical, and largely male, audience of the "hard" and respectable nature of the concept. By creating an acronym of Emotional Quotient they created a term that enabled EI, or as they labelled it EQ, to be put in the same frame as cognitive intelligence, or IQ.

EI testers then set about creating questionnaires to help you ascertain your EQ score, by which you could measure "how emotionally intelligent you are compared with other people", just as your IQ score measures how cognitively intelligent you are compared with other people.

But the creation of a single score of EQ involved suggesting that our emotional intelligence can be reduced down to just one thing, by which we can then be compared with other people. Which is not the case: our EI is made up of a multitude of components, each of which we can have to varying degrees and each one of which represents a different aspect of the way we handle or use feelings. To reduce this down to one score, a single number, misses the point and only serves to give us yet another measure by which we can judge ourselves or others.

In this book which outlines the model of emotional intelligence adopted by the Centre for Applied Emotional Intelligence (CAEI), we demonstrate how meaningless it is to attempt to represent our emotional intelligence with a single score.

The two sides of emotional intelligence

To begin with, we can divide the supposedly unitary concept of emotional intelligence into two: the *intrapersonal* and the *interpersonal*, as shown in Figure 2.1.

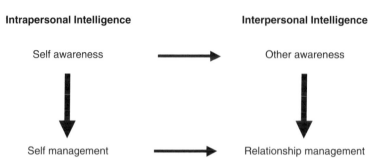

Figure 2.1 *Managing our relationships with ourselves and others.*

The arrows in this model represent causation. The chief causal connections are downwards: we can only manage ourselves effectively to the extent that we are self aware, and we can only manage our relations with others effectively to the extent that we are aware of them and their feelings. The bottom horizontal arrow is fairly obvious: I can only manage my relationship with you effectively to the extent that I can manage myself. If every time you say something that irritates me I lose my temper and bop you on the nose, then it is unlikely that we will have a good relationship. The top horizontal arrow is perhaps a little more esoteric. It refers to the fact that we use our body as a source of information, non-cognitive information, about other people ("hunches", "gut feelings", "instinctive reactions", "intuition"), and to the extent that we are unaware of what our body is telling us we will also be unaware of the other. (The exceptions appear to be sociopaths and conmen: highly aware of others but not in touch with themselves.)

The three-layered cake

In order to understand how to measure emotional intelligence properly, we need first to understand what is being measured.

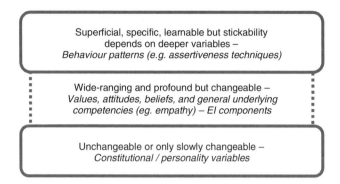

Superficial, specific, learnable but stickability
depends on deeper variables –
Behaviour patterns (e.g. assertiveness techniques)

Wide-ranging and profound but changeable –
*Values, attitudes, beliefs, and general underlying
competencies (eg. empathy) – EI components*

Unchangeable or only slowly changeable –
Constitutional / personality variables

Figure 2.2 *The three-layered cake.*

Imagine we are like a three-layered cake – a Victoria Sandwich – with a layer of sponge on the top and on the bottom and a juicy, fruity layer in between (Figure 2.2)! The top layer represents the overt part of us: what we do. This is relatively easily changed: we can go on a training course and be taught new patterns of behaviour – such as being more assertive, for example. However, whether these newly learned behaviours are retained and integrated into our repertoire of behaviour, whether they "stick", depends on the impact of deeper variables underneath. In our example of assertiveness, if we don't believe we are as important as other people are, then it will be difficult consistently to stick up for our rights, even if we have learned how to do so.

In the bottom layer of the cake are to be found the relatively fixed parts of ourselves, whether inborn or the result of very early learning: our personality (personality being an abstraction from behaviour which is constant over time). The acquired, rather than inherited, aspects can change, although this may be a drawn-out process involving many years of psychotherapy or personal development.

Finally we have the juicy bit in the middle! This is where the essence of our emotional intelligence resides. It is made up of our beliefs, our values, our attitudes, sometimes expressed in our habits. Also, some underlying general competencies like the capacity to empathise. These are wide-ranging and profound (like the bottom layer) but also changeable if we want (like the top layer). This is the area that we focus on in this book, although what lives here also has associated with it certain personal and interpersonal skills which live in the top layer.

Emotional intelligence, because it addresses primarily the middle layer as well as the top one, therefore cannot be reduced to "soft skills".

Furthermore, EI, as we have already seen, is composed of two complementary aspects: *intra*personal intelligence (to do with our relationship with ourselves) and *inter*personal intelligence (to do with our relationships with others). "Interpersonal skills" only looks at one of these, and therefore misses half the point.

Contrariwise, "personality" is unchangeable, or very difficult to change: it refers to things in the bottom layer of our cake, e.g. being an introvert or an extravert. Whereas emotional intelligence refers to things in the middle layer, and all the components of emotional intelligence are changeable and developable. Emotional intelligence is not the same as personality: it is about how we *manage* our personality.

Of course, our "three-layered cake" model is pretty crude and schematic: in practice the three layers are not separate, unrelated boxes; there are things which straddle the boundaries. For example, for the general population the capacity to empathise belongs in the middle layer and is changeable, but in the case of individuals with Asperger's or another condition in the autistic spectrum it may well be that their difficulty with feeling empathy is more fixed, to do with the way their brain is wired, and therefore belongs in the bottom layer. In general, however, as a conceptual aid, the three-layered cake model helps bring clarity to what is often a muddled and confusing area.

Where do the ideas come from?

When Daniel Goleman's book *Emotional Intelligence: Why it can matter more than IQ* was first published in 1995, it went straight to the top of the *New York Times* Non-fiction Bestseller list and stayed there for six months, which no book had ever done before. Why was this? Because people were ready for an idea like this, and one of the reasons why they were ready was a number of research advances that had been published and popularised in the preceding fifteen to twenty years.

Let us consider these under three headings.

- Educational research and the multiple intelligences (see immediately below).
- Brain research, brain imaging and connections between the prefrontal cortex and the amygdala (see False fact no. 4 later in this chapter).

- Psychoneuroimmunology and connections between the body and the brain, and the effects of stress on both of these (see Chapter 5).

First, let us have a look at the previous understanding of the nature of intelligence, which these developments have begun to impact.

Four false "facts" about intelligence

As well as the misplaced emphasis on the supposed unitary nature of emotional intelligence and the generation of a single figure to summarise it, the other great drawback of the use of the label "EQ" was that it encouraged people to import into the field of emotional intelligence all the false ideas prevalent about intelligence summed up in the idea of "IQ". Four of these in particular were an impediment to a proper understanding of the nature of emotional intelligence.

False fact no. 1

Intelligence is one thing that you have more or less of, i.e. IQ.

Harvard Professor of Education emeritus Howard Gardner and his multidisciplinary team began publishing their research into the nature of intelligence in the 1980s. This work made two significant shifts in previous understanding. First, they found intelligence not to be a single unitary factor but a bundle of related factors. They described not human intelligence but multiple human intelligences, as listed in Table 2.1. Each of the intelligences they identified had to meet eight stringent criteria, including having its own area within the brain where it is housed and activated and being able to vary independently of other intelligences.

The concept of our multiple intelligences is being used quite widely now in education, promoting the attitude that what's important is not how smart we are but how we are smart. It is still true that our education system very much focuses on the need to be able to read, write and add up, and the syllabus primarily teaches skills to develop our IQ. But Howard Gardner's work is helping us see that our IQ is just the tip of the iceberg; research is now showing that we need more than just our IQ in life to be effective and successful.

Table 2.1 *Howard Gardner's multiple intelligences.*

• Verbal / Linguistic • Logical / Mathematical	Cognitive intelligences, i.e. **IQ**
• Visual / Spatial • Musical / Rhythmic • Bodily / Kinaesthetic	Specialist intelligences
• Intrapersonal • Interpersonal	Personal intelligences, i.e. **EI**
• Naturalistic • *Spiritual / Existential*	Later additions to the original 7

The other shift in thinking which derived from this work is an encouraging one: that each of these intelligences is not fixed, at birth or before, but is capable of being developed during life.

Note that "*Spiritual/Existential*", as well as being a later addition, unlike the others does not seem to be localised to a particular segment of the brain; it involves the whole brain and so is put in italics. We should make it clear that while the identification of the intelligences in the table is due to Gardner, the groupings they have been put into are our own.

Although Gardner himself did not equate the sum of his intrapersonal and interpersonal intelligences with emotional intelligence, a concept which was popularised after the initial publication of his work, we see them as being equivalent, hence the division we have already made of emotional intelligence into its two components of intrapersonal and interpersonal intelligence.

Table 2.2 *Intrapersonal intelligence.*

• Being intelligent in picking up what is going on inside us and doing what we need to do about it.	What you need for effective self management, including:
• Helps us make sense of the things we do, the thoughts we have, the feelings we feel – and the relationships between them all.	• mood management • self motivation • dealing with setbacks • using your intuition • managing your energy • dealing with stress
• With it you can learn how to stay in charge of yourself and your emotions.	• avoiding depressions and addictive behaviour.

The far from exhaustive list of aspects of self management in the right-hand side of Table 2.2 may need some expansion and explanation.

Mood management

For those who doubt the possibility of mood management we recommend *The Good Mood Guide* by Ros and Jeremy Holmes. We are referring here to what Neurolinguistic Programming (NLP) calls "state management" – NLP has some useful tools to help us do this effectively.

Self motivation

Self motivation demands intrapersonal intelligence because to motivate ourselves we need to be good at picking up the cues from our body that tell us what we like and what we don't, what turns us on and what alienates us.

Dealing with setbacks

"Dealing with setbacks" is common language for what, in psychological jargon, is called emotional resilience. That demands intrapersonal intelligence because we need to pick up the bodily cues that tell us what we need in such situations of adversity, and there is often a physical element to the support that we need.

Using your intuition

Insofar as intuition is concerned, there is a common fallacy that women have more intuition than men. We do not believe this to be the case, but it is true that men do not use their intuition as much as women tend to. They seem on the whole to spend more time not just in their heads but in their cortex, being cognitive, and to pay less attention to the intuitive information available to them from their bodies and from their limbic system.

Managing your energy

"Managing your energy" means making sure that your body has what it requires for you to perform well. Tim used to be so lacking in intrapersonal intelligence that, for example, it took someone else to point out to him that when he got dehydrated he got short tempered and the quality of his thinking deteriorated. Having recognised the truth of this, he is now careful to drink enough at all times. For many people it is about food rather than drink: they need to monitor their bodies so that they ensure that they eat regularly enough to avoid their blood sugar plummeting so that they feel tired and energy-less.

Dealing with stress

Stress avoidance and handling stress are both key aspects of self management and they both demand intrapersonal intelligence. Each person experiences slightly different things as more or less stressful, each person has a different series of bodily signals that appear at increasing levels of stress and each person needs different things to handle their stress effectively at various levels of intensity. We therefore each of us need to be in touch enough with our bodies to know what stresses us, to pick up and be able to assess the significance of our stress signals and to know what we need to help us deal with various levels of stress (see Chapter 5).

Avoiding depression and addictive behaviour

Lastly, depression and addiction are symptoms that the body, or our self, is not getting what it needs. Addiction, whether to drugs, drink, sugar, chocolate or work, is an inappropriate way to respond to the body's needs. It doesn't work, so we need more and more of what we are addicted to in order to dull the pain of not getting what it is we really need. Depression is a consequence of the person being deprived of what it is they need, in emotional terms. If we are intrapersonally intelligent, pick up the bodily signs that tell us what it is we need and then ensure that we get it, we will not need to resort to substance abuse and we will not get depressed, thus avoiding two of the greatest scourges affecting people's wellbeing in the Western world.

And now for the other side of the coin, interpersonal intelligence.

Table 2.3 *Interpersonal intelligence.*

• Being intelligent in picking up what is going on in other people and between people and doing what we need to do about it.	What you need for effective relationship management, including: • motivating others • leading others • developing others • collaborating with others • confronting others • facilitating relationships between others.
• Helps us tune into other people, empathise with them, communicate clearly with them, inspire and motivate them and understand our relationships with them and the relationships between them.	
• With it you can inspire other people, develop their trust in you very quickly, create a team that performs rather than storms and is effective and creative.	

The examples of effective relationship management in Table 2.3 are perhaps a bit more self explanatory, but it should be acknowledged that you can't really motivate other people beyond the carrot and stick level. If you really want others to be truly motivated so as to contribute their energy and their creativity, then what you have to do is to help them motivate themselves and obviously you need to be interpersonally intelligent to do that, because you need to pick up what it is that turns them on or turns them off.

It should also be noted that being interpersonally intelligent does not mean being all lovey-dovey. You need interpersonal intelligence to collaborate effectively with others and get them to collaborate with you, certainly. But you also need to be interpersonally intelligent to have an effective confrontation with someone else.

Insofar as "facilitating relationships between others" is concerned, this applies not just to professionals, like mediators and couples counsellors, but more generally to all parents who have more than one child and to team leaders and all managers who have more than one subordinate.

Similarly, "developing others" involves not just management development specialists but all managers, all teachers, all parents, all sports coaches, and so on.

False fact no. 2

Intelligence is fixed; you are born more or less clever or stupid and remain that way for the rest of your life.

This is the optimistic version. In practice it is worse than that: many aspects of cognitive intelligence seem to peak at around 20 years of age and then to decline year by year after that. However, analyses of emotional intelligence test data show that the opposite seems to be true of emotional intelligence, which appears to continue to rise throughout the years of working life – it seems we naturally develop our emotional intelligence through the University of Life. The growth is not steady: the biggest jump appears to be between the average emotional intelligence of people in their twenties and those in their thirties. It seems to us that this is likely to be the result of parenthood: there is nothing like having young children to force you to learn how to manage yourself and your relationships more effectively!

This rise in EI test scores with age chimes in with our belief that all the aspects of emotional intelligence are not fixed but are changeable and developable. It also helps us to answer a question put by some sceptics: "If EI is so important, how come nobody had noticed it or given it a name before the 1990s?" Of course, emotional intelligence is not a new thing: human nature is no different now from what it was before Daniel Goleman wrote his first book. "Emotional Intelligence" is just a new label for old-fashioned virtues previously ignored by psychologists, educationalists and HR professionals, although recognised by the man or woman in the street: *wisdom* and *maturity*.

Wisdom and maturity naturally grow as we get older, provided we learn the lessons that our life experience offers us. So, if to a degree this happens naturally for most of us, why bother pro-actively to develop our emotional intelligence? Quite simply, there is no need to wait for life to dish out its lessons when you can create your own learning opportunities and speed up the process, thereby experiencing more of your potential more of the time and getting more out of your life. The real challenge in our pursuit of growth as human beings is to create our own change, rather than waiting for circumstances or other people to force change upon us. Also, pro-actively developing our EI will lead to a greater increase in it than merely picking up the lessons that the University of Life offers us.

A large aspect of this life-learning experience is, in fact, unlearning. Most of us in our childhood come to some overgeneralised conclusions in response to the way the grown-ups treat us that we continue to live by in adulthood, even though they no longer apply – perhaps they never did, because a lot of what adults tell children is not true, and what we worked out for ourselves we did with our childish brains on the basis of very limited experience. So, if we are told "I want never gets", or "Speak when you are spoken to", or were treated cruelly by a man with red hair, we may go through life not asking for what we want, being passive and not initiating interactions and terrified of all redheads, however mild and benevolent. A lot of these patterns are unconscious but nonetheless powerful for that, probably more so because it means that they escape conscious examination and review. These false beliefs and unhelpful patterns we call, after Timothy Gallwey, *interferences*.

Timothy Gallwey started off as a tennis coach who achieved remarkable success in getting very unathletic, unsporty, unconfident people to play a reasonable game of tennis. He managed this because he tumbled to the fact that their main problem was not that their capacity, their potential, was limited, but that they prevented themselves from reaching their potential by espousing a lot of limiting beliefs. ("I'm no good at sports." "I have hopeless eye–hand coordination." "I'm the wrong shape." "No-one in my family can play tennis properly." And so on.) The route to success lay not so much in addressing their technical deficiencies, but in dismantling these internal "interferences" as he called them. He communicated his learning in the book *The Inner Game of Tennis* and followed that up with *The Inner Game of Golf* and a whole series of best-selling "Inner Game" books. The core of his approach is summed up in the equation:

$$P = p - i, \quad \text{or} \quad \text{Performance equals potential minus interference.}$$

We believe this applies to functioning with emotional intelligence just as much as it does to sports. In fact more so, since the physical and technical requirements for emotionally intelligent functioning are minimal. All of us have the potential. Unfortunately, most of us have, at least to start with, lots of powerful interferences too.

Be warned that this belief distinguishes our approach to EI, and our beliefs about it, from those of many others. You may come across a number of EI specialists who see emotional intelligence as being like any traditional aspect of intelligence – relatively fixed and perhaps inborn. As they see it, your only hope of being emotionally intelligent, just as it is of being clever, is to choose your parents well. And you will also come across EI specialists (this time coming from the gang of psychologists who call themselves personality theorists rather than intelligence theorists) who believe that EI is a trait, or at best a bundle of traits, that are relatively fixed, perhaps inborn, parts of someone's personality.

The $P = p - i$ equation has significant implications for those of us who seek to raise our own emotional intelligence and/or to facilitate others to raise theirs. First, and happily, it means that we are not embarking on a wild goose chase: we *can* increase our performance, our effectiveness, by diminishing our interferences. And similarly for other people. Indeed, it is our belief that although there are no doubt individual differences in potential for being emotionally intelligent – for example, introverts are likely to be more self-aware and extraverts likely to be more aware of others – such differences in individual potential are completely swamped by the differences in the nature and strength of people's interferences. So, for practical purposes, in most cases we can take the potential for granted and concentrate solely on the interferences.

Second, it means that different people are likely to have different interferences. This is not entirely true, since cultural interferences will be fairly general: a couple of generations ago probably most parents, and most nannies, told the children in their charge "I want never gets." But it is true enough to mean that the route to be followed by somebody to raise their emotional intelligence will be relatively unique. Blanket prescriptions of one sheep dip for all will not do the business. It will be important to make an individual diagnosis (effectively of the nature and the strength of the individual's interferences) before the appropriate route to change can be identified. Hence the importance of measuring EI, that is to say the various components of EI, in each individual to provide a base line to start from and to identify the route to the goal.

Third, since, as we have seen, a lot of these interferences are unconscious, an early part of the process of dismantling interferences will be bringing them into conscious awareness. We are in the realm of the process illustrated in Figure 2.3. The problem with this is that the first step, moving from unconscious incompetence to conscious incompetence, can be very discouraging and seem like a step backwards, when really it is the first step in the right direction. Then the second step, from conscious incompetence to conscious competence can seem – to begin with – very false and artificial and can require a considerable amount of attention and energy. Lastly, the third step from conscious to unconscious competence, since it involves changing an ingrained habit and, in IT terms, changing the default setting, will take some time and many repetitions, say three weeks or more. Still, with support, it can all be done!

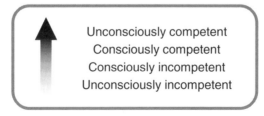

Figure 2.3 *The route to the goal.*

False fact no. 3

(Cognitive) intelligence determines success in life.

Part of most of us seems to subscribe to this idea, yet at the same time all of us, we suspect, are aware of many counter-instances. On the one hand, of people who are very brainy and "clever" but whose personal and professional lives are a shambles; on the other hand, of people who without being exactly stupid are never going to be rocket scientists but who are extremely happy and successful.

So, if being clever is not the key factor, what is? You will not be surprised to learn that we believe that emotional intelligence is the key, and that health, happiness and success are generated by EI and two related factors: self esteem and self confidence (Figure 2.4).

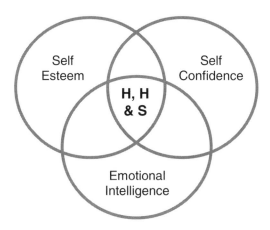

Figure 2.4 *A model for health, happiness and success.*

To understand this model, you need to appreciate the distinction between self esteem and self confidence. Self esteem (the same concept we shall later refer to as "self regard", or "I'm OKness") we define as our attitude towards our *being*, whereas self confidence (highly correlated with, but not the same as, self esteem/self regard and also highly correlated with our sense of personal power – one of the aspects of EI we can measure) we conceive of as our attitude towards our *doing*. "Health" here refers not only to our emotional health but to our physical health too: high emotional intelligence, self esteem and self confidence will mean that we are less likely to get stressed, less likely to get depressed or commit suicide, less likely to have accidents owing to inattention or recklessness, less likely to abuse our bodies with drugs or alcohol or sugar or food in general, less likely to present as what doctors call a "Type A" personality and be liable to high blood pressure, heart attacks and strokes, and our immune system is likely to be in much better nick, so that we suffer less from infections of various kinds.

The connection between good life outcomes and emotional intelligence is not surprising when you consider the following syllogism:

1. Emotional intelligence is composed of intrapersonal intelligence and interpersonal intelligence.
2. Intrapersonal intelligence is what you need for effective self management.
3. Interpersonal intelligence is what you need for effective relationship management.
4. Effective self management plus effective relationship management leads to effective overall performance.
5. Therefore, emotional intelligence leads to effective performance.

Obviously there are some jobs where the need for emotional intelligence is greater than others: all jobs involving a significant element of person management and/or leadership, all jobs involving direct contact with the public (therefore, other things being equal, service jobs rather than production jobs), all sales jobs, all jobs involving development of others (all management jobs again, all jobs in education, in HR and training, consultancy) and so on and so on. But in the end it is hard to think of a job where emotional intelligence is not one of the determinants of success: whatever our job we have to manage ourselves and in the vast majority of jobs we also have to manage relationships, with colleagues, with bosses, with subordinates, with customers, with the general public, with suppliers, and so on. Professional hermits (and they are not very common these days) may be immune from the need for relationship management but not really anybody else. So, in short, emotional intelligence is an important determinant of performance, to a greater or lesser degree, in all jobs. And also in no job at all: since we are talking about health and happiness as well as about success, we are inevitably talking about life outcomes as a whole as well as job performance.

False fact no. 4

Intelligence / thinking is separate from, and liable to be undermined by, feelings.

This goes back to Descartes and his "cogito ergo sum" – "I think, therefore I am" – see Antonio Damasio's fascinating book *Descartes' Error* (1994). In its traditional, say nineteenth century, form this fallacy was put forward in a highly, if on the whole implicitly, sexist way. Effectively: intelligence / thinking is superior and belongs to men but it is liable to be undermined by feelings, which are inferior and belong to women. Thanks to recent developments in brain science we now know this to be entirely false.

It has been understood for twenty years or so that anatomically we have a triune brain: a reptilian brain stem, a mammalian midbrain or emotional brain, and a primate neocortex or thinking brain (Figure 2.5).

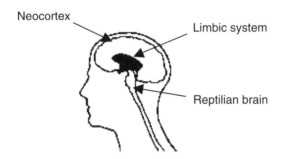

Figure 2.5 *The human triune brain.*

With the advent of techniques of brain imaging, we are beginning to understand the brain's physiology as well as its anatomy; to understand it in process as well as in structure. Thus, our assertion that most human beings are capable of acting with emotional intelligence boils down to an assertion that in most human beings there is potentially good communication between the thinking brain (the prefrontal cortex) and the feeling brain (the limbic system of the midbrain, including the amygdala). This is indeed the case, and, as so often, it is the exception that proves the rule. Antonio Damasio in *Descartes' Error* tells a tragic story of a well-functioning and successful man who had to have surgery for a brain tumour, which turned out to lie just between the midbrain and the cortex. The good thing about this location was that Damasio was able successfully to excise the cancer without impairing either the patient's thinking or his feeling. But in the process of the surgery the connections between cortex and midbrain were severed, with the result that the patient was (since emotional intelligence is about thinking about feeling and feeling about thinking) rendered surgically completely emotionally unintelligent. The first way this showed itself was in a complete inability to take decisions, which is an evaluative process involving feeling applied to the results of thinking. Overall, the results were disastrous: the patient's life was saved but his effectiveness as a human being was destroyed. Within nine months he was divorced and had lost his job.

EI / EQ / IQ

In all these respects, therefore, emotional intelligence, despite having been saddled for a period with the label EQ, does not fit in with the popular notions of IQ. Like cognitive intelligence, it is comprised of two of the multiple intelligences which Gardner and his team identified, but different ones: intrapersonal and interpersonal intelligences as opposed to verbal / linguistic and logical / mathematical intelligences. (And, as we shall see later, it can be broken down into many more subdivisions.) A person's EI is not fixed and does not, under normal circumstances, decline through the life course: it tends to grow as people learn and mature. Far from cognitive intelligence being the main determining factor in life outcomes, EI seems to have much more influence. And far from thinking and feeling being at odds, the opposite can be true, as we shall see as we examine what Applied EI is, in the next chapter.

References

Damasio, A. R. (1994) *Descartes' Error: Emotion, Reason and the Human Brain*, Putnam Publishing Group.
Gallwey, W. T. (1986) The Inner Game of Tennis, Pan.
Gardner, H. (1983/1993) *Frames of Mind*, Fontana.
Goleman, D. (1995) *Emotional Intelligence: Why it can matter more than IQ*, Bantam Books.
Holmes, R. and Holmes, J. (1999) *The Good Mood Guide: How to Embrace your Pain and Face your Fears*, Orion.

3

What is Applied EI?

One of the confusing things for anyone exploring emotional intelligence is actually getting a handle on what it means and what it is. Not only are there various schools of thought on the actual subject, there are also various other personal development constructs that overlap with emotional intelligence, for example Neurolinguistic Programming (NLP) and Transactional Analysis (TA).

To help create some clarity, first let us define certain key words that are used in association with EI and are commonly used on development training programmes and in personal development books and resources.

What is emotion?

Emotion stems from the Latin word "movere", meaning "to move". This is revealing of the fact that emotions are at the root of our doing, our moving towards or away from. The words "motivate" and "motivation" come from a similar root.

In her book *Molecules of Emotion*, neuroscientist Candace Pert explores the brain–body communication systems, which suggest that emotions do not occur just in the brain as has been commonly believed until very recently. Emotions now appear to be based in biochemical reactions that occur throughout the body and have been found in the heart and in the immune system as well as throughout the central nervous system.

What are feelings?

It is important, therefore, to note that although there is a part of the brain which specialises in processing feeling, *feelings are bodily states* that:

- do not live in the mind/brain;
- are whole-body experiences (hence: "having cold feet" and "getting hot under the collar"), mediated largely by hormones as well as neurons;
- may have thoughts / ideas which go with them, may describe / define them and be used to express them, but these are not the feeling itself, which is a bodily state.

Feelings can usefully be divided into one of three categories:

- physiological feelings, e.g. hunger, thirst, nausea;
- emotional feelings, e.g. anger, anxiety, happiness;
- intuitive feelings, i.e. non-cognitive, gut feelings, inner knowing.

We need to understand our feelings, where they are coming from and what information they hold for us in order to be able to manage them effectively, and to integrate our feeling with our thinking.

What is an attitude?

This first part of this book is entitled "How Our Attitudes Underpin Our EI" and it is our emphasis on the importance of attitudes which most clearly distinguishes our approach to EI from that of others. So, we had better make clear what we mean by "an attitude". For us, an attitude is an evaluative position that we hold about a thing, a person, an idea or perhaps an organization (Figure 3.1). It is evaluative in that it is feelings-based and feelings tend to be evaluative – positive or negative rather than neutral, i.e. we see something or someone as good or bad, or in a positive or negative light, and will want to move towards or away from that object / person. Attitudes tend to be associated with relevant beliefs and the association of attitudes and beliefs is two-way. On the one hand, we hold our attitudes not towards what is really "out there" but towards how we perceive it, which may not be the same thing. On the other hand, if our evaluative attitude is strongly held,

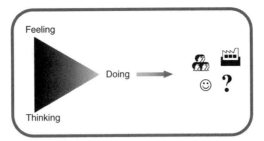

An evaluative position (based largely on feeling, with related
thinking / beliefs, and strongly influencing doing / action) towards
a person (including ourself), a group, an organisation, an idea, etc.

Figure 3.1 *What is an attitude?*

we will tend to align our beliefs with it. Thus, our perceptions will be altered
so as to reflect, support and justify our attitude. The feelings aspects of our
attitudes are of vital importance because it is our feelings that galvanise us
into action, to move, to choose what to do. So our feelings are highly significant in understanding our behaviours.

Who controls our feelings?

The old psychological paradigm used to be

$$S \rightarrow R$$

a stimulus leads automatically to a corresponding response. Pavlov rings the
bell and the dog salivates.

And then, about sixty years ago, academic psychologists got really sophisticated and realised that the full picture was:

$$S \rightarrow \boxed{O} \rightarrow R$$

a stimulus goes into an organism, which is effectively a black box and we don't
know what goes on inside it, and then a response comes out of the organism,
but it may not always be the same, even when the stimulus is the same.

So, we may give a number of people the same stimulus and they will have
different emotional responses, or the same person may have different emotional responses to the same stimulus on different occasions. This means
we can give someone a pretty strong invitation to feel something but they

are in charge of how they respond. For example, sometimes when he is training Tim invites a trainee to "make me angry". The response is usually one of embarrassed helplessness, but occasionally someone rises to the challenge and kicks Tim. This is often a pretty strong invitation to someone to feel angry. And Tim might feel angry. But then he might not. He might think "Oh, I thought this person and I were getting along pretty well; I thought we were going to be friends", so he might feel sad. Or he might think "Well, that didn't hurt much, but if they all start kicking me I shall take a real beating", and so he might feel afraid. Or he might just be amused by the trainee's pretty pathetic attempt to make him angry. So the same stimulus on the same occasion might elicit anger, sadness, fear or amusement. And the choice between these is down to the feeler, not the kicker. We are responsible for our own feelings.

We can raise our own conscious awareness of why and how we respond to a stimulus and we can learn to understand and be aware of the great variety of types of stimulus that we respond to. This will enable us to change our perceptions should we so choose.

Our definition of EI

The easiest way for us to explain our definition of emotional intelligence is by exploring the triangle in Figure 3.2. If you have had some counselling training this triangle may seem vaguely familiar to you. That is because it is derived from the "ABC" triangle of Affect (a pretentious medical name for feeling or emotion), Behaviour (a grander word for doing) and Cognition (a pretentious psychological name for thinking). We have

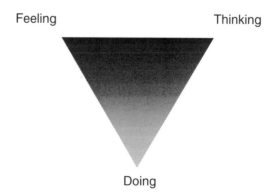

Figure 3.2 *A revised ABC triangle.*

made two changes. We have used common-or-garden English words instead of unnecessary technical terms and we have also turned the triangle on its head. The ABC triangle sits on one of its sides, with a point (Affect, for no good reason other than that A is the first letter of the alphabet) at the top. But the triangle is not symmetrical with reference to its three points: thinking and feeling are broadly inputs and doing generally an output. So, to emphasise that doing is the result of feeling and/or thinking, we put feeling and thinking together on a level, with a similar relation to doing.

All human beings have to feel, to think and to do things in order to survive and get on in the world. So we all do all three, but most of us have a favourite corner to the triangle, one where we tend to start. Thus, in a family we know, the husband is primarily and initially a thinker, though that does not mean that feelings are not important to him (they are) or that he does not also do things. The wife is primarily a feeler. That does not mean that she cannot think well (she can) or that she is not an effective doer or performer (she is), but her initial response is from her heart, whereas the husband's is from his head. And the husband's only brother is primarily a doer: he thinks and feels, of course, but he is always very busy and his initial response is to be active – to do something rather than indulge in thought or feeling.

Furthermore, there are some people who tend to favour two corners of the triangle but to ignore the third. For example, there are some people, often men, who fancy themselves as cost–benefit analysts and claim that they work out in their head what the best thing to do is and then they do it, ignoring feeling. Even to the extent of producing some pseudo-rational justification for buying a red Ferrari in terms of retained second-hand value and of performance figures, rather than acknowledging that the point really is that driving a red Ferrari helps them feel powerful and sexy. Similarly, there are some people (known to psychopathologists as hysterics or histrionics) who respond to a stimulus by having an immediate feeling and then jumping to action of some kind (perhaps laughing, crying or screaming) without engaging the thinking brain on the way.

These are emotionally unintelligent patterns because:

Emotional intelligence integrates feeling, thinking and doing.
It is the habitual practice of thinking about feeling and feeling about thinking when choosing what to do.

One comment on this definition. To be theoretically precise, EI should be defined as "the tendency to" rather than "the practice of". The reason why it is not so defined here is to point up the distinction between our definition of EI and the cognitive psychology kind of definition of EI, which sees it as a capacity or an intelligence. Although we all have the capacity to behave with emotional intelligence, most of the time most of us do not, because we have interferences (beliefs, attitudes and habits) which impede us from doing so. Also, this is a definition often presented to managers, and what they are interested in is not whether people have a capacity or tendency to do something, but whether they actually do it.

The feeling, thinking, doing and body pyramid

An important corollary of the bodily nature of feelings which we have noted is that the triangle which we have just looked at ought really to be represented as a pyramid: the feeling, thinking, doing and body pyramid, as shown in Figure 3.3.

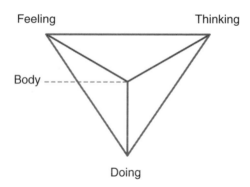

Figure 3.3 *The feeling, thinking, doing and body pyramid.*

Fully taking on board the bodily nature of emotions helps to make sense of what otherwise can seem an extreme and difficult finding, if an oft-quoted one: the work of Albert Mehrabian on responses to messages. In his experimental set-up Mehrabian arranged for the deliverer of an ambiguous message to vary (a) the content, (b) the way they said the words and (c) their body language on delivery. The resulting analysis of the variance in the recipients' responses to the delivery of the message showed that

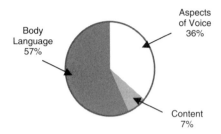

Figure 3.4 *What determines a recipient's response to a message.*

content accounted for only 7 %, the way it was said for 36 % and the deliverer's body language for the remaining 57 % (Figure 3.4). For a thinker it is difficult to comprehend that the content, the meaning, the words used only accounted for 7 %. What this experiment reveals, however, is that it is the underlying feeling that the message recipient is responding to (particularly when the words are ambiguous), and the underlying feeling is conveyed in the body language and in how the words are said, rather than in what the words are.

A process definition of emotional intelligence

The definition of EI on page 29 is fine as far as it goes, but it doesn't tell what you actually have to do, what process you have to go through, in order to act with emotional intelligence. Hence, the following process definition of applied emotional intelligence.

To act with emotional intelligence we need to:

- *notice feelings;*
- *pay attention to them;*
- *give them significance;*
- *think about them; and*
- *take them into account in choosing what to do.*

This applies both to our own feelings and those of others.

An intrapersonal example: if there is a funny feeling in the pit of my stomach, the first thing I need to do is to notice it, to be aware of it. Having done that I need not to ignore it, not to say, "Oh well, never mind, onwards and upwards", but rather, "That's a strange feeling. I wonder what it means."

That may allow me to recognise it, to say to myself, "I know that sensation. It is what goes on in my body when I am scared", so giving it significance. Then I need to think about it, "So – I am feeling scared about something. What can it be? I know – it must be about having to go and see the Bank Manager tomorrow to negotiate that loan." Then I can decide what to do about it. Knowing myself, I will know what would be the most effective form of self support: to prepare really well and to take a sheaf of supporting papers with me, to get some professional advice from my friend Fred who is an accountant, to talk it over with my partner, to get someone to come with me to the interview – whatever would work for me.

And an interpersonal example. Let us suppose that I am a departmental manager in a company which is undergoing financial pressure and is facing "restructuring". One morning I am talking to a member of my staff about future work allocations and he goes white as a sheet. Again, the first thing I need to do is to notice it, and having done that to pay attention to it rather than just to plough on regardless. Attending to his colour change, I might well say to myself, "He looks scared half to death", and then, "I wonder what that's about", and then the penny might drop: "Oh, I see. He is scared that his job is for the chop, which I know isn't the case." Then it is easy to decide what to do: I can reassure him about his job security, so that he can relax and discuss things with me without being distracted by his fear.

Same step-by-step process, but pointed in different directions.

A working definition of emotional intelligence

So far we've had two definitions, one in very general and abstract terms ("feeling", "thinking", and so on), and a process definition, which spells out sequentially the various steps you need to go through in order to act with emotional intelligence. But what does it all add up to in practice? Here is an alternative, working definition which sums it all up:

Emotional intelligence is the habitual practice of:

- *using emotional information from ourselves and other people;*
- *integrating this with our thinking;*
- *using these to inform our decision making to help us get what we want from the immediate situation and from life in general.*

The five crucial aspects of EI

Our understanding of EI and why it is important can be summed up in five key points.

1. EI is multifaceted
2. EI predicts performance
3. EI is measurable
4. EI is changeable and developable
5. EI is an aspect of the whole person.

1. EI is multifaceted

Emotional intelligence is not a thing; still less is it *one* thing. It is a handy label for a bundle of related, but separate, variables which together constitute what we conceive of as EI. Thus, whenever we use the term "emotional intelligence" or "EI", we are using shorthand for "*all those related, but separate, variables which together characterise the behaviour of those people who integrate their feeling and their thinking when choosing what to do, and therefore excel at self management and relationship management*", which is a bit of a mouthful. Similarly, whenever we say "it", we should strictly say "they" or "them". Hence, as we have seen, it is misleading nonsense to reduce somebody's emotional intelligence to a single figure and say, "Your EQ is X". People may be strong in one aspect of EI, yet relatively weak in another. We are all of us unique and have our own unique experiences and view of the world, and hence our own unique pattern of emotional intelligence.

2. EI predicts performance

This we have looked at already when examining False fact no. 3 about intelligence in the previous chapter. It is, of course, the key reason why interest in emotional intelligence and its application is not proving to be the flash in the pan that some people expected it would be. Whatever we do we are interested in performance improvement, and that means we should be interested in emotional intelligence.

3. EI is measurable

That is to say, all those variables which go to make up emotional intelligence are, in principle, measurable (although there are some difficulties about the process which we explain in Chapters 6 & 17). We can measure the current emotional intelligence of individuals, of teams and of organisations. The point of this is not to evaluate and judge but to find out where we are starting from: since everybody is different, and will have a different pattern of emotional intelligence, we need to measure all the various aspects of EI in each individual involved before we, or rather they, can embark on a change programme. And by doing a retest further down the line they can see how they have developed and what may remain to be tackled. Similarly for teams and organisations.

While, for the sake of clarity, we have broken down the crucial aspects of EI into five separate points, they are, of course, far more valuable in combination than they would be on their own. For example, having something which predicted performance would not be much practical use to us if we couldn't measure it. And having something which we could measure would be of only academic interest if it bore no relationship to performance. Even together, these two points wouldn't help much if it weren't for the next point as well.

4. EI is changeable and developable

As we have seen, our EI changes over time – with age. This is not automatic. How much we learn from our experience in the school of life depends, rather like ordinary school, on how much attention we pay: if we reflect on our experience and draw conclusions from it, then it will contribute to enhancing our emotional intelligence. If not, then not. (See our discussion of Reflective Learning in Chapter 13.) We can accelerate the process by taking action to develop aspects of our emotional intelligence. We have already seen that all aspects of EI are changeable, because they depend not so much on innate capacities as on the number and degree of the interferences, particularly the internal interferences, that prevent us from realising our potential in our actual performance. And that, therefore, enhancing our EI will consist largely in identifying our interferences and then learning either to dismantle them or at least to manage them.

The connection between EI being measurable and being changeable and developable is very intimate, as well as powerful. Measurement allows a person to decide where to concentrate their development effort and can be used to monitor the success of it. But also the fact that EI is changeable, rather than fixed, means that being measured is not such a scary process. Many people are reluctant to undergo intelligence or psychometric tests because they fear that the tests, and the testers, will tell them how they are and will always be. And if they score "low", as they may fear, that will be an eternal condemnation, and they will be able to do nothing about it. By making clear to people, both in advance of their completing the measure and in the process of exploring the results, that all the things being measured here they can change if they want to, we can go a long way towards reducing this fear and reluctance.

5. EI is an aspect of the whole person

Because we see emotional intelligence as being to do with attitudes and feelings, rather than to do with skills or with particular abilities, we see it as being intimately bound up with our very being. If aspects of our emotional intelligence change, we change – to that degree we become a different person. Whereas, when you acquire a new skill or develop a particular ability, you are the same except when you are using that skill or that ability. So this means that if we facilitate someone to develop their EI, it is not just that their job performance is likely to change between 9 and 5 on weekdays: they will be different in the evenings, at weekends and on holiday as well – at home, at work, at play.

The corollary is that emotional intelligence practitioners need to behave in a professional and ethical manner as they go about their work, in a way that they would not have to do if they were teaching someone cost-accounting or French. This is particularly true because feelings are part of their stock in trade, and a person's feelings are involved with their very sense of themselves.

Reference

Pert, C.B. (1997) *Molecules of Emotion*, Prentice-Hall.

4

The vital importance of attitude

As we have already seen when looking at the three-layered cake model (pages 10–12), in our view emotional intelligence is not an aspect of personality (which would put it in the bottom layer), nor is it just a set of behaviours and skills (which would confine it to the top layer). Also, we do not see it as an aspect of relatively fixed, perhaps inborn, intelligence, which would also place it in the bottom layer. Why, you may then ask, is it called "emotional intelligence"? A good question, and we wish it weren't, but since that was the title of Daniel Goleman's book, which popularised the concept, we are probably stuck with the term, at least in the world of commerce and of organisations. In the educational sector it is referred to as "emotional literacy", or EL, and this term has a lot to be said for it. It makes it clear that it is definitely not fixed but is something which can be learned, whereas – as we have already seen – the use of the word "intelligence" attracts to EI all the fallacies which tend to be attached in the popular mind to that concept. Even "emotional literacy" is not ideal because it suggests that what we are talking about is basically a set of skills, as the ordinary use of the word "literacy" suggests, and that would place it firmly in the top layer of our three-layered cake.

We, on the other hand, see EI (given its general acceptance, we shall continue to use the term despite its drawbacks) as residing in the middle layer of the cake and being composed primarily of beliefs, values and attitudes. All aspects of emotional intelligence are thus at the same time profound and changeable.

We believe that most people have the potential to behave with emotional intelligence but that so much of the time we do not because of our interferences – internal interferences mostly resulting from false beliefs and outdated feeling responses resulting in limiting attitudes and habits adopted often (for what were then good reasons) in childhood and retained, unwittingly, in adulthood. The process of enabling someone to develop their emotional intelligence therefore consists in helping them to identify and dismantle, or at least to learn to manage, these interferences.

So, for us, emotional intelligence is not a synonym for personality; it is about how we "manage" our personality.

Judgement – the enemy of understanding

Our four-part model of EI processes (Figure 2.1) makes it clear that awareness, of ourselves and of others, is the foundation of emotional intelligence. And the greatest block to awareness is the tendency to judge. As we sometimes put it, "judgement is the enemy of perception" or "judgement is the enemy of understanding". From this it follows that the chief prerequisite for behaving with emotional intelligence is an attitude towards self and towards others of unconditional acceptance.

If we accept – it doesn't necessarily mean liking but it does mean respecting – ourselves and others unconditionally, then there is nothing in the way of our seeing ourselves, or others, as we, or they, really are. But if our first step is to process our perceptions through a sieve of judgement, to categorise as being worthy of approval or of disapproval, this will get in the way of the open-eyed, open-minded, open-hearted stance that we need really to see another, or indeed ourselves – to feel what it is like to be them from the inside. What is more, our tendency to judge will leak out and the other (or indeed our inner self), fearful of our judgement, will conceal themselves from us, so that we cannot be aware of them and their feelings. Hence, the importance of life positions, which we explore below and which form the connecting thread of all the scales in the Individual Effectiveness questionnaire – our attitude-based EI profiling tool (☞ see Part II).

We are not saying here that it is necessary to accept everything everybody does – not their doing, just their being. See the exploration of the distinction between being and doing under False fact no. 3 in Chapter 2 and under Principle no. 4 later in this chapter.

Acceptance of self and others – I'm OK, You're OK

Transactional Analysis (see pages 48–53 below) is based on the idea that when babies arrive in the world they are confronted with three crucial questions:

1. Who am I?
2. Who are all these other people?
3. What am I supposed to be doing here?

The answers to the first two questions tend to be evaluative: I / other people are good, valuable, trustworthy, to be respected, safe (abbreviated to "OK") or else I / they are bad, worthless, unreliable, unworthy of respect and dangerous ("Not OK").

Putting these two evaluations of self and others together, we find that children tend to emerge into adulthood holding one of four "life positions", as in Table 4.1, known (from the Western movie The Gunfight at the OK Corral) as the "OK Corral".

Table 4.1 *The "OK Corral".*

	I'm Not OK	I'm OK
You're OK	I– U+ Submissive	I+ U+ Emotionally intelligent
You're Not OK	I– U– Stuck	I+ U– Critical

Of these life positions, "I'm OK, You're OK", known as the "healthy position", is the one most conducive to emotional intelligence. The more people move away from the "I'm OK, You're OK" position, the more difficult it is for them to have high emotional intelligence in all respects. In Part II of this book you will find that we have set out the relationship of each of the components of emotional intelligence that the *ie*™ (Individual Effectiveness questionnaire) measures to the life positions.

The tricky bit about applying the theory of life positions is that sometimes people who really hold one position claim to hold, and act as if they hold, another. For example, the "I'm OK, You're Not OK" position is always a cover up for an underlying feeling of "I'm Not OK". Think of bullies. They always have low self esteem underneath ("I'm Not OK") but the self-centred and aggressive way they behave suggests "I'm OK, You're Not OK".

Of course, these life positions are not fixed in stone; we may spend significant amounts of time in more than one. Amanda, for instance, emerged from childhood with an "I'm Not OK, You're OK" life position. "I now, I hope, spend most of my time in I+ U+, but if I get tired or stressed, or get a put down or criticism from someone, then I may slip into to I– U+."

The theory of life positions may seem very simplistic: put everyone into one of four boxes and that is supposed to explain something? Certainly we need to guard against oversimplistic use of it. Nonetheless, it is surprising how much of personal and interpersonal life may be in part explained by relating a number of variables to the life positions, as Table 4.2 shows.

Table 4.2 *Facets of the life positions of Transactional Analysis.*

	I'm Not OK	I'm OK	Key to descriptions
You're OK	**I'm Not OK, You're OK (I– U+)**	**I'm OK, You're OK (I+ U+)**	**Life position**
	Submissive	Emotionally intelligent	Attitude
	I lose, you win	*I win, you win*	*Negotiating position*
	Harmony	**Constructive discontent**	**Position in conflict**
	Passive	Assertive	Emotional control
	Get away from	*Get on with*	*Relationship position*
	Depressive	**Mental health**	**Psychiatric diagnosis**
	Suicide	Health	Ultimate pay-off
You're Not OK	**I'm Not OK, You're Not OK (I– U–)**	**I'm OK, You're Not OK (I+ U–)**	**Life position**
	Stuck	Critical	Attitude
	I lose, you lose	*I win, you lose*	*Negotiating position*
	Withdrawal	**Railroad**	**Position in conflict**
	Passive-aggressive	Aggressive	Emotional control
	Get nowhere with	*Get rid of*	*Relationship position*
	Schizoid	**Paranoid**	**Psychiatric diagnosis**
	Madness	Homicide	Ultimate pay-off

Take a look at the descriptors in each of the four boxes – which one particularly resonates with you and your own outlook and behaviours?

The eight principles of emotional intelligence
(the vital underlying beliefs and attitudes of EI)

We said earlier that to act with emotional intelligence you need a complex set of attitudes and skills. From what we have just said, it is obvious that unconditional acceptance of self and of others are the two primary requisite attitudes. What of the others? What are the other members of this complex set? We have reduced them to eight, which we call The Eight Principles of Emotional Intelligence. However, although we give them that name, we did not really invent them. They are no more, and no less, than a codification of the philosophical assumptions underlying humanistic psychology.

Before we look at them one by one, it is necessary to say a bit about their ontological status. We do not suggest that these principles describe what people believe, or can be deduced from how they act. On the contrary we believe that most people most of the time do not subscribe to these principles and that many of our prevailing cultural norms are in conflict with them. What we do say is that it is observably the case that to the extent that people subscribe to these principles they find it easy to act with emotional intelligence (and therefore to be personally effective in the world, good at self management and relationship management), and to the extent that they do not subscribe to these principles they find it difficult to act with emotional intelligence. Further, whenever anyone acts in an emotionally unintelligent way they will always be found, on examination, to have breached one or more of these principles in so doing.

We are not saying, "You have to believe this and act accordingly." People are entitled to believe whatever they want. We are just pointing out that if people want to increase their emotional intelligence (and thereby to enhance the effectiveness of their self management and their relationship management), they will find it helpful to align their beliefs with these eight principles. Whether they choose to do so or not is entirely up to them.

In short, the eight principles are neither descriptive nor prescriptive but they are diagnostic and predictive.

Principle no. 1

We are each of us in control of, and responsible for, our actions.

This one comes first because it is key: without it the whole house of cards comes tumbling down. But it is a tough one because it gives each of us individual responsibility – the buck stops here. No matter how awful the circumstances (think of Sophie's Choice) we still have choices over what we do and don't do, and are responsible for the ways we exercise those choices. No wonder people are reluctant to accept this principle and come up with endless ingenious cop-outs: "The woman gave me the apple and I did eat", "I couldn't help it – I was so angry", "It was the drink talking", "You made me", "I couldn't help myself."

Principle no. 2

No-one else can control our feelings.

This one originally read: "We are each of us in control of, and responsible for, our feelings", but people wouldn't buy that. In the long run we still believe that to be true, but in the short run we have to recognise that people have psychological buttons that other people can press. However, only if we let them. It is always us choosing what response to have.

Remember the old psychological paradigm from earlier, which used to be

$$S \rightarrow R$$

– a stimulus leads automatically to a corresponding response. That would suggest that one person could control another's feelings.

But we now know that:

$$S \rightarrow \boxed{O} \rightarrow R$$

– as we said earlier, a stimulus goes into an organism, which is effectively a black box and we don't know what goes on inside it, and then a response comes out of the organism, but this may not always be the same, even when the stimulus is the same.

So, we may give a number of people the same stimulus and they will have different emotional responses, or the same person may have different emotional responses to the same stimulus on different occasions. This means we can give someone a pretty strong invitation to feel something but they are in charge of how they respond.

Principle no. 3

People are different: they experience the world differently, they feel different things and they want different things.

This is what philosophers call *phenomenology*. We don't just react to the world differently from one another, we actually perceive it differently according to our genetic make-up, our personal history, our desires and our feeling states; effectively, we live in different worlds. This is well illustrated by a fascinating psychological experiment carried out in the US in the depression of the 1930s. Children were recruited from two sources: the rich suburbs and poor downtown slum neighbourhoods. They were told that they were participating in an experiment about the accuracy of size perception in children of differing ages. They were then shown various objects, which they had to match up with discs of an equivalent size. The objects were all coins – dimes, nickels, quarters, half dollars and dollars – and the results were clear. The children from the poor neighbourhood saw the coins, especially the more valuable ones, as being physically larger than the children from the rich neighbourhoods did. This makes perfect sense: a quarter was obviously psychologically more significant, "bigger", to a poor child than to a rich child. Nonetheless it is fascinating that their life circumstances affected not only their attitude towards the coins but their very physical perception of them. And yet we spend an awful lot of time assuming that everyone is the same, or that everyone is like us (which also means they are the same as one another). Think of all the generalisations about people we make. And we say things like, "You do, don't you?" and "We are all the same under the skin".

Principle no. 4

However you, and they, *are* is OK.
(Though this does not mean that whatever you and they *do* is necessarily OK.)

Here we meet the crucial distinction between being and doing. How people *are* is beyond judgement or reproach. It just is, and is to be accepted as such. If it is not the result of their genes, which they did not choose, it is the result of their history, and in particular their history as children, when they were primarily done-to rather than doers. What they *do*, on the other hand, as we have seen in Principle no. 1, they are in control of and they are responsible for. Their actions, therefore, may be judged, criticised and resisted. However awful their actions, however, their being still needs to be respected and unconditionally accepted, though this can sometimes be quite a test of emotional intelligence!

Principle no. 5

Feelings and behaviour are separate.
Being in touch with our feelings does not mean being out of control of ourselves and our behaviour.

This principle expresses the contrary to what most people in our culture seem to believe. It is generally held to be the case that if you feel a certain way you will be bound to behave in a corresponding way. Which is obviously not true (Principle no. 1). If you believe this implicitly, then the only way to avoid a particularly unwelcome piece of behaviour (like violence towards your nearest and dearest) would be to avoid feeling the related feelings (as if you could!). This attempt to batten down the hatches only results in an explosion when it doesn't succeed. It is the opposite strategy of being closely in touch with and expressing one's feelings before they build up to a dangerous level (letting off steam), which allows one to be in control of, and to choose, one's behaviour. The English language does not help here: to "get angry" can mean either to feel angry or to act aggressively, and that does not help attempts to establish that these two are not inevitably connected.

Principle no. 6

All feelings are self-justified, to be accepted, and important.

We are all different (Principle no. 3) and however we are, we are OK (Principle no. 4). One of the ways in which we differ is in the way we feel, and it follows therefore that all feelings are acceptable. They just are, largely as a result of our history, and are justified by merely being. They do not have to be justified in relation to some outside stimulus, as if there were a tariff which fixed certain feelings, and degrees of feeling, as appropriate responses to certain stimuli. Something may be appalling to me and fine to you, or vice versa, and it is not a question of who is right: we are both right. Because our feelings are intimately related to who we are, to our being, and our being is OK, all feelings are acceptable as well as self-justified even if what we then do about them may not be. And they are important because they are the best indicators of our likely behaviour and because they are bound up with our very idea of who we are.

Principle no. 7

Change is possible (including change of ourselves).

There are limits to this principle, though how many you think there are will depend on where you stand on the heredity vs. environment issue. Things which are purely hereditary are probably not changeable: if you were born an introvert you will probably remain introverted till the day you die. But that does not mean that you cannot learn to manage your introversion (or extraversion, as the case may be) and alter your behaviour. Born introverts, for example, for whom it can be quite stressful, can become excellent trainers if they set their minds on it. This is a principle which, like no. 1, people are reluctant to accept and generate many cop-outs to escape from. And for the same reason, if you deny this principle it gets you off the hook of responsibility – you just can't help it because you can't change. Hence: "You can't teach an old dog new tricks", "The leopard can't change his spots", "That's just the way I am", and so on.

Principle no. 8

All people have a natural tendency towards growth and health.

This is Aristotle's notion of physis (Greek for "inherent nature"), which he illustrated with a cabbage seed, pointing out that inside this tiny speck is a wonderful, big healthy cabbage trying to get out and that all we have to do is to provide the necessary conditions (sunlight, water, maybe a little earth, protection from injury) and the cabbage will emerge. While an identical looking speck, which is a cauliflower seed, will, given those same conditions, grow into a fine cauliflower. There are obvious limitations to this natural tendency: we all of us eventually grow old and die. And in individual cases the tendency may get diverted and overwhelmed: people who have damaging childhoods may have their growth stunted and behave in ways which are not conducive to their wellbeing. But underneath, the tendency is still there and, given the right conditions, can be resuscitated, just as a dying ember can be coaxed into flame by breathing on it.

The implication for EI practitioners, or any other development facilitators, is that we do not need to try to change people (which is a pretty self-defeating exercise), but just to provide the necessary conditions; the respondent's physis will do the rest.

The key determinants of performance: KASH

Our attitudes are one of four different kinds of factors which determine the quality of human performance in any given situation or context. These four factors form the KASH model:

> **K**nowledge
> **A**ttitudes
> **S**kills
> **H**abits.

Any performance improvement programme, in order to be effective and sustainable, needs to tackle all four of these. Yet when we ask people which of the four their organisation addresses, the almost universal response is "knowledge and skills", while attitudes and habits are ignored. This may explain why there is such a problem with the transfer of learning: people go on a training course, have a good time, return with enthusiasm for the new areas of knowledge and/or skill in which they have been trained, and yet a few weeks later are behaving at work as if they had never been on the training course in the first place. Why should this be? On the face of it, it seems daft that trainers and change agents should completely ignore 50% of what they should be attending to, in a manner which vitiates the effectiveness of their work. We believe there are a number of reasons for it.

1. An overly cognitive and mechanistic view of human nature.
2. Habit: this is what people have traditionally focused on.
3. Difficulties of measurement. Until recently people have not been able to identify the relevant attitudes or to measure them, but you can give someone an exam to quantify their knowledge or a test to evaluate their skills.
4. Ease of intervention. You can give someone a book or a manual to increase their knowledge, or a training course to develop their skills. But people don't know about, and feel awkward about, facilitating people to change their attitudes if they wish to do so, and they know that changing habits takes a long time. Furthermore, you can try to inject knowledge and skills into someone, but changing attitudes and habits can only be done by the person themselves. Skilled facilitation rather than straightforward instruction is therefore required.

Applying this model to the development of emotional intelligence gives rise to certain very significant conclusions.

1. Since EI is largely about attitudes, and since the interferences which will need identifying and dismantling probably have been there since childhood and express themselves as perhaps unconscious habits, it is fairly clear that the standard development programme which focuses on knowledge and skills and ignores attitudes and habits will be completely ineffective.
2. Since different people have different attitudes and different habits, any development programme needs to be individually designed and implemented. It must be learner-oriented rather than content-oriented.
3. Consequently, any EI development programme must start out with a measure of the current EI of the individual or team concerned, so as to be able to recognise the starting point and therefore the route to the goal.
4. Given that you can lead a horse to water but you can't make it drink, the EI practitioner involved will need to be a skilled facilitator rather than just an instructor or trainer.
5. Given the three foregoing points, it is highly likely that some individual one-to-one coaching will be required as an element of the development programme.

A word about Transactional Analysis (TA)

Transactional Analysis (hereinafter referred to as TA) is a model of human personality and interpersonal behaviour and a school of counselling and psychotherapy, founded by Dr Eric Berne (1910–1970). Dr Berne was a renegade psychoanalyst who understood that human beings are social animals and that their functioning needs to be considered not only intrapersonally but interpersonally too: hence "transactional" analysis. He was born in Canada but spent most of his professional life in the USA: TA grew up in San Francisco in the 1960s and 1970s. Although American in origin, it is probably now more widely used in Europe. For an introduction to TA we recommend *Born to Win – A TA primer with Gestalt experiments* by Muriel James and Dorothy L Jongeward (1996): simple, accessible and delightful, but American in origin (e.g. the title!) and a little dated. Or alternatively, for a very clear, more rigorous and up-to-date approach by British and American co-authors *TA Today* by Ian Stewart and Vann Joines (1987).

We must immediately make it clear that you do not have to have any prior knowledge of TA to understand and use this book effectively. But if you do, it may help you to know that particular reference is made to parts of TA theory at the following points;

Ego States	Chapter 4	pp49–53
(Coherent patterns of thinking, feeling	Chapter 8	p111
and doing)	Chapter 12	p164
Life Positions	Chapter 4	pp39–40
	Chapter 6	pp78–79
	Chapter 7	pp84–85
Strokes	Chapter 7	pp94–99
	Chapter 10	pp134–138
Drivers / Conditions of Worth	Chapter 8	pp106–110
Personality Adaptations	Chapter 8	pp110–111
Stuntz's 5 chair technique	Chapter 11	p151
Contracting	Chapter 18	pp292–293

Reasons for using TA

We have borrowed from TA in presenting our view of emotional intelligence for a number of reasons.

1. There is already a fair degree of familiarity with TA among British and European managers and it can be helpful to relate a new body of theory to one that is already familiar.
2. TA belongs to the humanistic (as opposed to the psychoanalytic or behavioural) approaches to human psychology. It is based on respect for the individual (including in this respect the "client" or "patient"). It does not see the client / patient as someone who has something wrong with them and who needs to be helped or put right by a practitioner who is an expert; its orientation, as is ours, is to empower.
3. As part of this approach, TA theory is, on the whole, expressed in simple and everyday language and is meant to be shared with the client and used by them, rather than retained as arcane knowledge. Unfortunately, there are exceptions to the general simplicity and accessibility of the language, most obviously in the label "transactional analysis" itself and most extremely in the theory of "ego states", about which see below.
4. TA takes into account feeling and thinking and doing, thus making it an emotionally intelligent model in terms of our FTD triangle (see Figure 3.2), whereas behaviourists, as the label makes clear, focus on behaviour to the exclusion of feeling and thinking (probably because the rats and pigeons on which the theory is based do not overtly do much feeling and thinking), while cognitive behavioural therapists include thinking but still ignore feeling, and the psychodynamic / psychoanalytic approach, although its subject matter may be assumed to be feeling, or at any rate non-cognitive, is an insight therapy which proceeds entirely cognitively, addressing only thinking.
5. The fundamental status of the "I'm OK / Not OK", "You're OK / Not OK" life positions in the TA model echoes our experience and belief that attitudes towards self and others are the primary determinants of overall levels of emotional intelligence, and hence largely of people's life outcomes.

Ego states / patterns

There is one aspect of the TA model which is so fundamental that we have not been able to avoid mentioning it at times, but which we have not else-where dealt with explicitly. As we have already recognised, the reason for this probably is that we are uncomfortable with the language: "ego states", a hangover from the psychoanalytic origins of TA. So here we remedy the omission and look at these concepts, which we prefer to refer to, admittedly more wordily, as "coherent patterns of feeling, thinking and doing". The TA model asserts that we have three categories of these: Parent, Adult and Child, represented as in Figure 4.1.

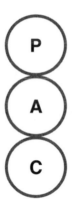

Figure 4.1 *The Parent, Adult and Child model.*

The Parent pattern derives from what, especially when we were children, we have incorporated or "swallowed whole" from influential others, such as parents, teachers, preachers, elder siblings, heroes (real or fictional), and so on. The Child pattern derives from our history; it is the sum total of our daily experiences to date. A child is born with an empty Parent pattern and a not yet functioning Adult pattern, so a good way to understand the essence of the Child pattern is to consider a new-born baby: wet, noisy, messy, full of feelings and needs and demanding instant satisfaction of them. Not much later, of course, we, while still children, learn to think and to become able to postpone gratification of our wants. The Adult, meanwhile, is engaged in responding appropriately and effectively to the here and now, without being overinfluenced by others (Parent) or by past experience (Child).

So what does this bit of TA have to do with EI? This becomes apparent when we consider the TA definition of a healthy person, and also what in TA terms may go wrong in the relationship between Parent, Adult and Child: "ego-state pathology". Let us consider a healthy TA person, who is represented thus as in Figure 4.2.

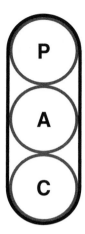

Figure 4.2 *Integrated Adult in the TA model.*

The defining feature here is the envelope surrounding the Parent, Adult and Child: we are dealing with someone who is integrated. The Adult is in charge but has full access to both Parent and Child. So the TA label for the healthy state is "Integrated Adult", and we see this as being exactly coterminous with "emotionally intelligent." When you are in Integrated Adult you are being emotionally intelligent and when you are being emotionally intelligent you are in Integrated Adult.

To understand this relationship further it is also helpful to look at what is amiss when things go wrong in these terms.

Excluded / excluding ego states

We have seen that to be emotionally intelligent your pattern needs to be integrated, with the Adult in charge. Sometimes people tend to look like the examples in Figure 4.3.

In (a) the Child is permanently in charge and the Parent and Adult patterns are excluded – immature and clearly not emotionally intelligent. In (b) the Parent is permanently in charge and the Adult and Child are excluded. This person will be full of judgements and "shoulds" and "shouldn'ts" and will tend to be critical and censorious of themselves and/or others – again, obviously not emotionally intelligent. In (c) and (d) the Adult may be in charge, but if so it has no access to the Parent where values tend to be held (in (c)) or to the Child, where feelings and wants

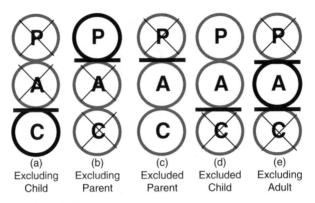

(a)   (b)   (c)   (d)   (e)
Excluding   Excluding   Excluded   Excluded   Excluding
Child   Parent   Parent   Child   Adult

Figure 4.3 *Excluded / excluding ego states.*

tend to emanate from (in (d)). Adult, perhaps, but not fully integrated and so not emotionally intelligent. Last, in (e), we have an excluding Adult who has access to neither Parent nor Child; in charge but completely unintegrated and so emotionally unintelligent. Such a person would be like a computer on legs: a good example is Mr Spock in Star Trek.

Contamination

In all the examples so far, the patterns have kept their own separate identities. The other main category of ego-state pathology is contamination, where they tend to overlap. There are three variations, as shown in Figure 4.4.

In (a) there is a "Child contamination of Adult", which means that sometimes the person is "in" and acting from Child but is unaware of it and believes themselves therefore to be acting from Adult: for example, someone who produces (to themselves as well as to others) a pseudo-Adult logical rationalisation of their own behaviour which is actually driven from Child needs. Correspondingly, in (b) we say there is a "Parent contamination of Adult", which means that sometimes the person is "in" and acting from Parent but is unaware of it and believes themselves to be acting from Adult: prejudice is a good example – if I genuinely believe that women, black

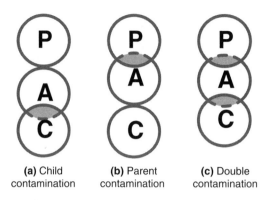

Figure 4.4 *Contaminated ego states.*

people or Muslims are per se worthless or dangerous, I am acting from Parent, even if I believe myself to be dealing with reality from Adult. Finally, as in (c), we may have both Parent and Child contaminations of Adult.

In (a) or (b) or (c) the Adult is not actually in charge, although we think it is, and so we are prevented from being emotionally intelligent. The recipe for those people who have contaminations of their Adult is pretty obvious: they need to increase their capacity for self diagnosis, for knowing which of their patterns they are "in", which is in charge, at any moment. This is part of the crucial importance of self awareness, which is emphasised throughout this book and particularly in Chapter 9.

References

James, M. and Jongeward, D. (1996) *Born to Win – Transactional Analysis with Gestalt Experiments*, Da Capo Press.
Stewart, I. and Joines, V. (1987) *TA Today: A new introduction to transactional analysis*, Lifespace Publishing.

5

Optimising personal performance

So far we have explored the theory behind applied emotional intelligence. In this chapter we start to look at what this actually means in practice by considering the impact our EI has on our personal performance, emotionally, physically and spiritually.

Remember Tim Gallwey's formula: Performance = potential − interference. Think of this in your own context. How are you performing currently, in any or all areas of your life? Are you maximising your potential as a human being or are you getting in your own way? Do you know the ways you undermine or limit yourself, for example by sabotaging your own attempts to self manage or by keeping a lid on your awareness through denial of a truth that's staring you in the face?

Remember also that the four key determinants of our performance are: our knowledge, our attitudes, our skills and our habits. Our potential is developed through gaining knowledge about whatever inspires us or is important to us, by honing our existing skills and learning new ones and through adopting healthier attitudes and habits. Again, these four determinants are liable to be undermined by our personal interferences.

But first, let's take a closer look at the links between our emotional intelligence and our body.

Body intelligence

Our human bodies are holistic systems, as represented by the feeling, thinking, doing and body pyramid in Figure 3.3.

These holistic systems are now studied through the subject of Psychoneuroimmunology, or PNI for short – yes, a big word, but also an important one. What it refers to is the study of the connections between the key systems in our bodies – how the brain, the heart, the nervous, the immune and the endocrine systems impact on each other and communicate with each other. Much of the early research into PNI was undertaken by the neuroscientist Candace Pert and is described in her book *The Molecules of Emotion*.

Dr Alex Concorde of the Concorde Initiative has been carrying out pioneering research in the UK into PNI and related subjects, in particular stress and the connections between all of the systems of the body, including the links between our psychology and our biology. Her understanding of how the brain functions has led her to identify that the limbic system is in fact the powerhouse and "chief executive" of the human-mind / human-body system.

Dr Concorde has described how the limbic system is the "house of our highest intents" – its overall purpose is to keep us healthy and safe. It is constantly determining whether or not we are under threat or safe, and whether or not we are well and in a state of well-being. It is active when we're asleep as well as when we're awake, monitoring our health and safety every millisecond, processing six *billion* bits of information per second. The limbic system takes all this incoming information and provides its best strategic response for managing the overall resources in our bodies, given the total demands. Accordingly, it transmits messages throughout our minds and bodies letting the whole system know "the state of play".

Going Limbic

We know that our feeling and thinking brains evolved separately, and they are separately located, the feeling brain in the midbrain and the cortex on the outside, particularly at the front and on the top, but that nonetheless they are well connected by neural circuitry. Our emotional and logical brains are completely intertwined. We cannot make a decision, or take action without engaging our emotional brain. And that's why our emotional intelligence is so important.

Dr Alex Concorde's study into the functioning of the brain has brought clarity to the interconnections between the limbic system and the cognitive mind (the cortex).

In contrast to the limbic system's ability to process 6 billion bits of information per second, the cognitive mind processes just 10-100 bits of information per second. Our cognitive mind is there to help process and organise information.

If the limbic system is working through its higher function of our meaning, it engages the cognitive mind to help devise a strategy with which to enable our meaning to be created through conscious thought and action.

This seems to describe the neuroscience behind the concepts of Self 1 and Self 2 that Tim Gallwey describes in his book "The Inner Game of Tennis". Self 2 powers the incredible human machine capable of achieving great intellectual and physical feats if it is left to get on with its automatic doing function. Self 1, which Tim Gallwey describes as the "thinking, ego-mind", "tells" Self 2 what to do, but more often than not ends up hindering the performance of Self 2 rather than helping it.

This also fits with the way the brain evolved, with the limbic system forming first, and the cognitive mind evolving as man became more sophisticated and needed to plan, organise and relate with other humans. The cognitive mind is a sophistication, but this does not mean it is – or should be – king, which is a bit of a challenge to many of us who value very highly our cognitive abilities. By not recognising the purpose of the limbic system and acknowledging its importance, we are under-utilising it, limiting our perceptions of what we can achieve, and not making use of our non-cognitive capabilities.

> *"Intuition is what your brain knows how to do when you leave it alone."*
> Dr. Paul MacLean, former Chief of Brain Evolution,
> US National Institute of Mental Health, 1988

A Self-Managing System

Dr Concorde's research is defining how the human body works as a self-managing system. The instructions that we give to our limbic systems define the level of safety and well-being at which they will manage our bodies' internal resources.

Besides ensuring your safety, the limbic system also checks all incoming information against its stores of data about your personal life experience, including all the data in your "brain banks" which is "tagged" with emotions. It then looks at all this information – current, past and future-oriented – in view of your highest intentions, your purpose in life, you as an individual, you as a being. And, having first secured your safety, it then determines how to use your overall resources in view of what it is that you seek to achieve – at the highest level.

So if we are coming from a position of purpose, intention and meaning, then our perspective broadens, and we can see more possibilities and opportunities that are in alignment with our aspirations. If however we allow our cognitive mind – which operates in a linear, reactive manner – to instruct our limbic system, the limbic system is stifled and we limit the effectiveness of our overall system. Anything that is negative, linear, to do with transacting (as opposed to really interacting) with another person, or small in its "outlook" and restricted is likely to be cognitive. Because the cortex works within a restrictive norm, it doesn't take much to go outside that norm – and when you do that puts stress on the system.

The limbic system is, however, expansive. It senses things and transforms minutely, second by second, updating your stores of information about what matters now and your personal experience. And so the limbic system codes information in a different way to the cognitive mind. To create transformational change the limbic system has to be involved. Transformational change (limbic) is change that fundamentally changes how you see things and how you do things as a consequence. Linear change (cognitive) tries to alter behaviours without really changing what drives them at a fundamental "this is who I am" and "this is what I am about" level.

This is why emotional intelligence is so important. Dr Concorde considers that the vast majority of coaching and consultancy is cognitive and linear. In her view, behavioural change that is not transformational simply adds stresses to the system because it further restricts the cognitive mind's already small outlook – "You can do this. You mustn't do that.", as opposed to "I really want to do this". Cognitive change is about providing more guidelines and rules – that is more restricting. Limbic change is about fundamentally changing the individual's intention by addressing any emotional intelligence that is not really in alignment with who they are *now*, their current purpose – and that creates more choices.

This matters in performance because any positive changes that happen at the limbic level enable an individual to do what is really going to make a difference with less effort. More performance for less stress! Isn't that what every individual and every business organisation wants? This is what Dr Alex Concorde calls "high performance, low stress systems". And because our emotions and feelings underpin our attitudes, by working with attitudes we have a means of starting to reach the limbic system.

So how does that work? The real question is: What is stress? Dr Concorde's formula for stress is

$$\frac{D > R}{T}$$

Stress arises when the demands on and within the human system exceed resources in any give timeframe. And so to reduce stress, the aim is clearly to ensure that demands are minimised and resources maximised. So if an individual *wants* to do something, well that makes it OK – fun, even! That adds resources even though they are working, so that is less stress. But if they are just doing something "cognitively" because that is what the rules are, then that requires effort which increases demands and reduces resources. So the same work can create less stress or more stress.

Dr Concorde emphasises that internal demands are therefore much more important than external demands – as we have just illustrated. And that is what we know from an emotional intelligence perspective also. In EI we know that demands and resources can be internal as well as external. The demands of a stressful job situation may appear to be external, but the individual's more unhelpful thoughts and feelings – which are internal and which are within an individual's reach – create internal stress that matters much more biologically than external pressures. This is because these thoughts and feelings generate stress that is internal, both by adding to the demands and by limiting the availability of resources.

Now if we come at this with a limbic approach by taking the highest possible perspective, we will enable an individual to have choices over a stressful situation, rather than viewing a limited range of options at a linear, cognitive level.

Heart rate variability

The Institute of HeartMath in the US has done pioneering work on the subject of Heart Rate Variability (HRV). Normally we measure heart rate as "so many beats per minute" as if the rhythm were even and each beat as far from its neighbour as the next. However, this does not adequately represent reality. In fact, how even the beat is, how equal the distance is between one beat and the next is itself a variable, and proves to be a very significant one. The book *The HeartMath Solution* describes what happens when someone is feeling angry or frustrated – a typical HRV pattern looks irregular and disordered. "The sympathetic and parasympathetic branches of the autonomic nervous system are out of synch with each other, battling for control over the heart rate – the sympathetic trying to speed it up and the parasympathetic trying to slow it down. It's as if you were trying to drive your car with one foot on the accelerator and the other foot simultaneously on the brake. Most of us value our cars too highly to treat them in this way – yet, without realising it, we treat ourselves in this way more than we know . . . The good news is that positive heart-based feelings create the opposite effect, generating smooth and harmonious HRV rhythms in a sine-wave pattern, considered to be indicators of cardiovascular efficiency and nervous system balance."

This further reinforces the need for the managing of internal demands and resources, the understanding and management of our emotions and ultimately non-judgement of ourselves and others – i.e. minimising our interferences.

Minimising your interferences and reducing stress

Our emotional intelligence depends upon:

- our current level of awareness;
- our skills and competencies;
- how we view the world and what we value in it, in particular the degree to which we value ourselves and also other people.

All of these will be limited by our acquired interferences. So how do we identify and start to manage and dismantle these interferences?

The simplest way to identify your interferences is to complete your *ie*™, which has been designed as a diagnostic tool to help you recognise the pattern of your relative strengths and weaknesses in the various components of emotional intelligence. This questionnaire is built upon the CAEI's four cornerstones of EI model discussed in Chapter 2. The profile it generates shows you the current impact, in terms of limitations of various aspects of your emotional intelligence, of your existing set of internal interferences. Since we can develop our EI at any time in our lives, you will find that as soon as you undertake any form of EI development your profile is likely to start to change as your attitudes and habits begin to shift.

The scales that inhabit the four cornerstones of EI are described in detail in Part II of this book, along with exercises on how to develop each scale.

There are, of course, other ways to identify and dismantle your interferences. Here are some ideas to get you started.

Considering your motivations

Maslow, the humanistic psychologist, suggested that we have a basic set of survival and growth needs, all of which need to be met if we are to achieve our potential (self actualisation). He represented these needs as a hierarchy with the basic physiological needs at the bottom, moving upwards towards self actualisation and self transcendence at the top (Table 5.1).

Table 5.1 *Maslow's set of survival and growth needs.*

Growth needs: areas where we experience and focus on the potential in our lives	Self transcendence	helping others self actualise, transegoic state
	Self actualisation	knowing who you are, where you are going, having a sense of wellbeing, being all that you can be
	Aesthetic	inner peace and peaceful surroundings
	Cognitive	knowledge and learning for learning's sake
Emotional needs: need to be satisfied but can become sources of worry and stress	Esteem	feeling of moving up in the world, recognition, few doubts about self
	Belonging	belonging to a group, close friends to confide in
Survival needs: need to be satisfied but can become sources of worry and stress	Safety	feeling free from immediate danger, security
	Physiological	food, water, shelter, sex

Whilst we are not here to add to the debate on Maslow's work, what we have noticed in our studies of emotional intelligence is that when we are acting in an emotionally unintelligent way, we are likely to be focusing on one or more of our lower needs. For example:

- Physiological issues may include worrying about putting food on the table or having somewhere to live.
- Safety concerns may include fear of attack on the streets, fear of financial insecurity.
- Belonging issues may include lack of friendships, many short-term relationships.
- Esteem issues may include a lack of self belief, worrying what others think.

Integrating feeling, thinking and doing

Applied emotional intelligence is about giving ourselves a choice in how we think, feel and act. To achieve this we need to be balanced in our thinking, our feeling and our doing. For most of us this can be quite a challenge because, as we saw before, each of us usually favours one of these three aspects of ourselves, rather than being able to switch naturally between them and to integrate all three. As we develop our EI we become unconsciously competent at integrating the three functions. Where do you think you sit in the triangle (see page 28)? Here are a few ways to develop each of the three capacities.

Giving significance to your thinking:

- Stop. Take a deep breath and count to 6. Allow your cognitive mind to connect with whatever your are feeling or doing
- Learn to think positively by seeking the positive aspects of a situation first before considering the negatives

Giving significance to your feeling:

- Take a moment to notice the feelings you are experiencing in your body
- Learn to recognise which of your feelings are emotional, which are physiological, and which are intuitive

Giving significance to your doing:

- Rather than asking "Why?", ask "What can I do to change this?"
- If you find yourself dwelling in thinking or feeling for a period of time, re-energise yourself by going for a brisk walk and getting some fresh air

You will find more ways to integrate your thinking, feeling and doing in the development exercises in Part II.

Checking your judgements or assumptions

The more you reflect on your thoughts, your feelings and what you do, the more likely you are to begin to notice patterns in your responses. Most feelings have an evaluative component but it is an entirely subjective one: we like something or we don't, we are attracted or repelled, we respond with sadness or with joy. Often, however, people move on from this subjective evaluation to a more cognitive pseudo-objective evaluation – to a judgement.

For example: "I like this cake" is an evaluative response coming from me. "That cake is nice" is a pseudo-objective statement, a statement of opinion dressed up as a fact. The cake may be nice to me, but my friend may not care for it. The key is to remember to always use "I" statements, to avoid pseudo-objectivity, and to own your views and opinions.

Beyond the variable of whether or not one moves from the subjective to the pseudo-objective, from emotional response to judgement, another variable is who or what the judgement is directed towards. One of the questions you can ask yourself is "Who am I judging here? Am I judging someone for what they've done or for how they are, or am I judging myself somewhere? Am I making assumptions about someone or something without checking the facts?"

For example: you may make a very generalised statement saying, "Peter is unreliable", when what you are actually saying to yourself is, "Peter should turn up five minutes early for any meeting like I do".

Having identified the nature of the judgement or assumption involved, if there is one, we can ask ourselves to what extent the judgement is justified or the assumption is accurate. Is there a different way to view the person or situation, thereby diffusing the emotional response and changing the possible outcome? Why is Peter always late for meetings? What could you do to help Peter be more self-managing?

Giving yourself choice

We can raise our own conscious awareness of why and how we respond to a stimulus, and we can learn to understand and be aware of the great variety of types of stimuli that we respond to. In doing this, we can intercept our automatic responses and start to give ourselves choice in all sorts of situations. Indeed, we sometimes use "choicefulness" as a synonym for emotional intelligence. For example, there may be a person who always manages to press one of your emotional buttons, causing you to respond in an emotional way every time you interact with each other. The first level of awareness is to notice this pattern of behaviour in yourself. As you become more aware of the pattern you may notice that it only happens when you're discussing certain things or when the other person speaks in a particular way. The second level of awareness is to then recognise what internal reactions are also triggered that can perpetuate the loop, making it difficult to step out of it without awareness.

Here are some examples of the different processes that can escalate an emotional discussion or keep us locked in the same response loop.

Over-generalisation

Over-generalisation is when we believe something to be true all of the time for all of the people. For example, "All men are unreliable", "I always drop the ball when someone asks me to catch one". A way to identify your own use of over-generalisation, or its use by other people, is to listen out for words such as "never", "always", "everyone", "no-one", "all", "nobody". To challenge your, or another's, over-generalisation, look for the exceptions: "Well, all men are unreliable except Jack, he's great. I guess there must be other men like him around!"

Judgement from Parent

We take on the values and attitudes of our parents when we are very small, for good or ill. When we respond to a situation or a person from our Parent ego state we are likely to use words like "you should", "she ought" and "we must". We can challenge these "rules" that we have long believed to be right, or challenge them in others who are coming from their Parent ego state. A way to move yourself to the Adult ego state is consciously to choose more helpful words, such as "I hope", and "I would like", again coming from the subjective "I" position rather than the pseudo-objective position.

Rigidity

Sometimes we believe so strongly that something is true that we resist or deny any information or evidence suggesting the contrary. Ultimately this can lead us to losing touch with the reality of the situation. This rigidity is fear-based and serves to protect our boundaries. The challenge with preserving our boundaries is that we can become imprisoned within them, shrinking into our comfort zones emotionally and physically and unable to act spontaneously in any way. Rigidity or inflexibility can be unlocked by remembering that everyone is different, that we all experience the world differently and we all want different things (EI Principle no. 3). So, apart from scientifically proven facts or knowledge, our beliefs are based on how we see the world (and indeed how we see the world may be distorted by our beliefs) whereas reality may well be different. Similarly, when it comes to actions, there are many ways to skin a cat and we don't always have to tackle something in the same old way.

Prejudice

Prejudice is an attitude towards a person or group of people that is not based on objective facts. This attitude is based on prejudgements often made without knowing the person or individuals within the group, i.e. it is a form of stereotyping – "All paedophiles are evil and should be locked up for good". To reconsider your prejudgements, consider again EI Principle no. 3 and become curious about other people rather than making assumptions. If you find their behaviour or attitudes challenging, ask yourself how they may have come to form their attitudes and behaviours. Also, become aware of any emotional experience you may have had with a similar person on which your prejudice has been built.

Trying to satisfy your conditions of worth

As we shall see in Chapter 8 most people in childhood acquire a belief that their OKness depends on fulfilling some specific criteria. In trying to avoid the unpleasant feeling of being "Not OK" we considerably limit our range of choice. For example, if we believe that we are only OK if we please other people, then we will tend to be conflict avoidant, which will mean that we will find it difficult to stand up for ourselves and get what we want.

Monitoring your emotional recovery rate

When any of us registers at a new gymnasium to get fit, we usually have to undertake an induction programme run by a trained instructor. This ensures that we know how to use the equipment safely and also provides us with a fitness assessment and a programme to follow. Part of this fitness assessment is to ascertain our "recovery rate" – the amount of time it takes our body to recover from a specific period of heightened physical activity – by monitoring our heart rate, which is also indicated by how out of breath we are. The aim is to reduce this recovery period as our bodies become fitter and more high performing.

We can do the same thing with our emotions – we can notice how long it takes to regain emotional stability after an emotional response – and identify our own emotional recovery rates.

Many of us hold on to our emotions for far longer than we need to or is in fact healthy for us. Emotions, as we know from the studies of PNI, are generated by rushes of hormones triggered by messages from our hypothalamus in the limbic system, the emotional centre of the brain. These chemicals course around our body communicating with the various systems in the body, formulating physiological responses to the original emotional stimulus. There are three ways in which we deal with our emotions:

1. We may suppress them, by ignoring them, so that we do not have to deal with them or suffer an outburst of any kind.
2. We may express them spontaneously, being "taken over" by our physiological response, and stay with the feeling until we're exhausted.
3. We may give ourselves choice in the moment, by acknowledging how we are feeling, then using the information to decide how we want to act or respond, and then releasing the feeling.

To suppress our emotions is potentially hazardous to our health. Unexpressed emotions stagnate in our bodies, the chemical responses that occur with emotions remain within the body and become absorbed in their original state into our cellular systems. When emotions are released, however, the chemical responses are neutralised and no residue remains to be absorbed into our cells. This process of suppressing our emotions results in feelings of stress in the body and, ultimately, if left unattended, leads to disease.

In *Destructive Emotions* Daniel Goleman observes how the Dalai Lama handles emotion. He seems to allow every emotion that is triggered within him momentarily to flicker across his face, and then it is gone. This demonstrates how we can be "free and in charge" of our emotions, not being ashamed of them and suppressing them and not being controlled by them. This is a demonstration of the emotionally intelligent way to handle our emotions.

There is a story of two pious Buddhist monks who were walking some distance to another monastery. Both had taken a vow of chastity and were not permitted to touch a woman. As they travelled along their way they came across a small river. On the near side was a woman sitting on a rock nursing an injured ankle. On the far side of the river was her horse. She had fallen from her horse, the horse had bolted and she had no way of getting to the other side to retrieve the animal. On hearing her plight, the first monk picked her up and carried her across the river to her horse, so that she was able to continue on her journey. The second monk was dumbfounded that his colleague should so easily break his vow of chastity. They continued along their own journey in silence. Some miles down the road, the second monk, beside himself with dismay, said to the first monk, "I cannot believe that you carried that woman across the river back there, breaking your vow of chastity!" The first monk replied, "My friend, I carried that woman for five minutes, you have carried her for 15 miles . . ."

We do not need to hold on to our emotions once we have understood what they are telling us. That is what they are for: to give us information and motivate us towards action. However, what tends to happen is that we get caught up in a perpetual loop of thinking and feeling without taking any action – the feeling inflaming our thoughts and our thoughts fanning the feeling. Becoming aware of this process within us is a crucial aspect of developing our emotional intelligence.

Maximising your potential

Developing our potential requires a positive attitude towards ourselves in the first place. We have to believe that there is some potential within us to develop. Here are some ways in which you can start to think about your own potential and, we hope, come to realise that your potential is unique and worthy of your utmost focus.

Recognise your strengths

Whenever we ask people to list their strengths and weaknesses, or to review what they did well during an experiential exercise, they can usually come up with a list as long as your arm about what's wrong with them. But to identify what their strengths and qualities are . . . well, that's a completely different matter.

Try it for yourself. Draw a table on a piece of paper with two columns, one headed "My Strengths" and the other headed "My Weaknesses". Now add as many items (qualities, abilities, etc.) as you can to each column. If you struggle with this, ask someone who knows you well to help you out. See if you can make the "Strengths" column longer than the "Weaknesses" one!

Be prepared to stretch that comfort zone!

Understanding comfort zones and how they work is a useful way to open up your self concept.

What is a comfort zone?

As the name suggests, a comfort zone is a place where you feel completely comfortable. There's no stress there, you do not feel inhibited or fearful. It is easy, comfortable and safe. And it's a great place to be . . . for a time. The problem with staying within our comfort zones is that, at some point, uneasiness will creep in. If you remember EI Principle no. 8, we all have a natural tendency for growth. If we do not permit ourselves this natural growth, our existing comfort zone will actually start to shrink as we feel the unease and try to compensate for it. A far healthier thing to do is to recognise that we are seeking some change and allow the process to start to unfold.

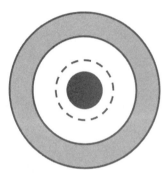

Figure 5.1 *Comfort zones.*

Figure 5.1 shows what a comfort zone looks like. The inner circle is our actual comfort zone. The next ring encircling this is what is called the "stretch zone". When we decide to grow or change, we have to step into the stretch zone, for example when we start a new job. This will feel uncomfortable initially (i.e. outside of our comfort zone) and irrational fears may start to bubble to the surface. What we need now is a safe place in which to retreat and to reflect on our experience in the stretch zone. This could be a physical place, like the comfort of your own front room, or a place within you where you can nurture and reassure yourself that all is well. The next time you step into the slightly uncomfortable space, e.g. your second day at your new job, you will find that it feels a bit more familiar, slightly less scary and something that you know you will be able to feel comfortable with eventually. What is happening here is that by stepping repeatedly into your stretch zone, the stretch becomes comfortable and your comfort zone expands. You have created a new comfort zone through your own personal growth. We see this with toddlers as they start to venture further out into their little worlds, taking a few steps forward then running back to Mummy or Daddy before taking a few steps more.

The outer ring is called the "panic zone" – this is when we take a step too far, physically or emotionally, and we trigger our fight or flight response, e.g. when we get stage fright and forget our words when we present to a large group of people. Obviously this is a zone that we want to avoid, and developing our emotional intelligence will enable us to become more aware of our emotional vulnerabilities, so that we can create coping mechanisms should they be triggered and eventually work towards dismantling our irrational fears.

Variable comfort zones

As we become more adept at recognising our comforts and discomforts in situations, we can start to see how we have variable comfort zones, i.e. we have a number of comfort zones operating at any one time (Figure 5.2). As we work with these we can start to hone in on the specific situations that cause us particular discomforts, so that we can look at these more closely as we develop our EI. We can then start to observe our emotional recovery rates in different situations too, again giving us more information on our emotional make-up, which in turn will give us more choice in how we respond to and handle the more challenging aspects of our lives.

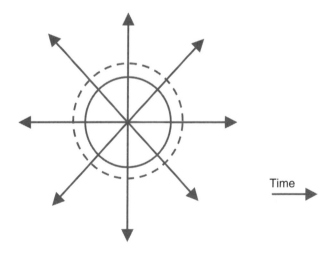

Time

Figure 5.2 *Variable comfort zones.*

So, how comfortable are you with change and uncertainty? How easy do you find it to learn new skills or to think differently about things?

Achieving our potential requires change. This takes courage – courage to embrace the unknown. The real challenge in our pursuit of growth as human beings is to create our own change rather than waiting for circumstances, or other people, to force change upon us.

"Sometimes you just have to take the leap, and build your wings on the way down"
Kobi Yamada

Align with your purpose

Maslow's concept of self actualisation means knowing who you are, where you are going, having a sense of wellbeing and being all that you can be. Self awareness, and self knowledge built upon it, is the key to achieving this. Without understanding who we are, and separating our values and beliefs from the ones we were taught as children, we cannot easily identify what is uniquely important to us. When we take time to reflect on what is truly important to us and find something in which we want to invest our energy, time and resources, we can speedily move towards being all that we can be.

Each of us, on our journey to writing this book, have followed our own personal meaning. For Tim, his passion is Truth and he wanted to get to the truth of EI. For Amanda, her meaning is found in Equality, that we all have as much right as the next person to be here and to experience a happy and successful life. By recognising the importance of our meanings, and by committing ourselves to these, we were then able to make choices that enabled us to live through our meaning.

The art of discovering your meaning lies in the higher function of the limbic brain. Dr Concorde's research is showing that by identifying our highest meaning and focusing on this, our limbic system marshals all of the resources in the body towards the achievement of this meaning. The biological messages sent from the hypothalamus in this instance are not reacting to any stress situation and therefore are positive in their structure, boosting our immune system and establishing a state of health and wellbeing.

Working on your self awareness and identifying your innate strengths and qualities will help you discover your meaning. Ask yourself these three questions:

1. Who am I?
2. Where am I going?
3. What matters to me?

Identifying your highest meaning will enable you to realise your potential. And living through your meaning, purpose or potential facilitates a state of wellbeing, of experiencing being fully alive.

Optimising your personal performance

So, to maximise our personal performance we need to do three things:

1. Recognise where we are now – our current performance.
2. Identify where we want to be and what we want to change, and believe that this is possible.
3. Take the brakes off by minimising our interferences.

By managing our interferences our performance becomes much closer to our real potential. Potential is achieved by dismantling internal interferences. This allows us to attain the interpersonal state of "presence" as described by Peter Senge in his book, *Presence: Exploring Profound Change in People, Organizations and Society* (2005). The intrapersonal counterpart to this is perhaps "flow", "a state of joy, creativity and total involvement, in which problems seem to disappear and there is an exhilarating feeling of transcendence", encapsulated in Mihaly Csikszentmihalyi's book *Flow* (1996).

Each of them require a high level of emotional intelligence. We explore how to develop our emotional intelligence in Part II.

References

Childre, D. and Martin, H. (1999) *The HeartMath Solution*, HarperCollins.
Csikszentmihali, M. (1996) *Flow: The Psychology of Optimal Experience*, HarperCollins.
Gallwey, W.T. (1986) *The Inner Game of Tennis*, Pan.
Goleman, D. (2004) *Destructive Emotions: A Dialogue with the Dalai Lama*, Bloomsbury.
Pert, C.B. (1997) *Molecules of Emotion*, Prentice-Hall.
Senge, P., Jaworski, J., Scharmer, C.O. and Flowers, B.S. (2005) *Presence: Exploring Profound Change in People, Organizations and Society*, Nicholas Brealey Publishing.

PART II

Developing Emotionally Intelligent Attitudes

6

Measuring our personal EI

In order to act with emotional intelligence you need, as we have seen, a complex set of attitudes and skills, and the good news is that the skills can be learned and the attitudes can be adopted, which is why emotional intelligence is changeable and developable.

To develop more emotionally intelligent attitudes and skills, we first need to understand how emotionally intelligent our current attitudes and skills are. As we have said before, we believe that most people have the potential to behave with emotional intelligence, but so much of the time we do not because of our interferences – internal interferences mostly resulting from false beliefs and limiting habits adopted (for what were then good reasons) in childhood and retained, unwittingly, in adulthood. The process of enabling someone to develop their emotional intelligence therefore consists in helping them to identify and dismantle these interferences.

For us, emotional intelligence is not a synonym for personality (something that is relatively fixed); it is about how we manage our personality and *that* we can change.

Self awareness is the key attribute underpinning our emotional intelligence, and is therefore crucial to measure. The more aware from moment to moment we are of what is going on inside us in emotional and hormonal terms, knowing what we need to do about that and then doing it, the more in control of our behaviours we can become. This directly impacts on our ability to self manage and on our awareness of others, our knowing what's going on for them, and therefore on our ability to manage ourselves in our relationships.

Our emotional intelligence model

We are repeating here an explanation of the CAEI model, as it is important to understand the underlying model on which the Individual Effectiveness questionnaire was built. Please do skip this section if you are comfortable with your understanding of the underpinning model.

Our model of emotional intelligence, you will remember, is derived from two of the nine ways (so far researched) in which we can be intelligent – known as our multiple intelligences and identified by the Harvard educational psychologist Howard Gardner and his team. These two intelligences are: our *intra*personal intelligence (how self aware we are and how well we manage ourselves) and our *inter*personal intelligence (how aware of others we are and how well we manage our relationships with them).

Intrapersonal intelligence

- Being intelligent in picking up what is going on inside us and doing what we need to do about it.
- Helps us make sense of the things we do, the thoughts we have, the feelings we feel – and the relationships between them all.
- With it you can learn how to stay in charge of yourself and your emotions.

The *self awareness* that underpins our intrapersonal intelligence helps us become *self-managing*: managing our moods, motivating ourselves, dealing with setbacks, using our intuition, managing our energy, dealing with stress and avoiding depressions and addictive behaviour.

Interpersonal intelligence

- Being intelligent in picking up what is going on in other people and between people and doing what we need to do about it.
- Helps us tune into other people, empathise with them, communicate clearly with them, inspire and motivate them and understand our relationships with them and the relationships between them.
- With it you can inspire other people, develop their trust in you very quickly, create a team that performs rather than storms and is effective and creative.

The *other awareness* that underpins our interpersonal intelligence helps us with our *relationship management*: motivating others, leading others, developing others, collaborating with others, confronting others and facilitating relationships between others.

Each of the two intelligences is composed first of an awareness and then a category of effective management (Figure 6.1). As you can see from the causal arrows, our self awareness is needed to be truly aware of others (rather than projecting our assumptions on to them, such as assuming that they are feeling what we would be feeling in a similar situation) and underpins our ability to be self managing. Awareness of others is clearly crucial for managing our relationships effectively, as is our responsibility for how we manage ourselves in our relationships.

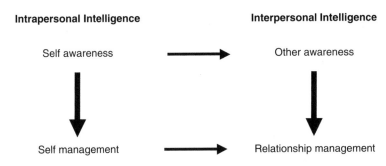

Figure 6.1 *Our basic EI model.*

Trace the causal arrows back and you will see how self awareness is a key element in our emotional intelligence, and is a fundamental and crucial part of what needs to be measured. The trouble is that with questionnaire-type tests, self awareness and self knowledge are being presumed and relied on in the process of measurement: we ask people to tell us what they are like, and if they do not know we cannot rely on the answers. This is a methodological dilemma, not only in principle but also in practice. For example, if you ask someone who is very unselfaware how well they know themselves, they may reply, quite truthfully as it seems to them, that they know themselves very well: they are unaware of their lack of self awareness. Conversely, someone who is very self aware compared with most may be exquisitely aware of the limitations on their self knowledge and may represent themselves as less self aware than they truly are. We have to remember that emotional intelligence is not a thing, merely an abstract concept; still less is it one thing. It is a collective shorthand for "*all those separate qualities and behavioural tendencies which tend to characterise those who integrate their thinking with their feeling when choosing what to do, and thus are effective at self management and relationship management"*. So every time we say "emotional intelligence" we mean, in effect, all that, and every time we say "it" we mean "they". These different components are separate in the sense that they can vary independently: you can be high in one aspect of EI and low in another. What significantly differentiates one individual from another is the pattern of their EI profile: their relative strengths and weaknesses in the various components. It is therefore pointless, and missing the point, to try to reduce this complexity to one individual figure, an "EQ score", as some EI measures do.

So, let's take a look at the way our measure helps us identify the interferences that impact our levels of emotional intelligence.

Our emotional intelligence diagnostic tool

The Individual Effectiveness Questionnaire

The $i\mathcal{e}$™ (IE – developed in collaboration with JCA (Occupational Psychologists) Ltd and marketed by them) measures 18 aspects of emotional intelligence, 17 directly and one as a derivative from Scales 1 and 2.

Life position

Scales:
Self Regard (1),
Regard for Others (2),
Derivative: Relative Regard (3)

In our model there are two aspects or scales, which, in combination, affect all the others. These are Self Regard and Regard for Others. These two initial scales correlate with the concept in TA of "I'm OK, You're OK". Our personal sense of "OKness" refers to the degree to which we value and accept ourselves as we are, warts and all. Similarly, the "OKness" we feel about others refers to the degree to which we value and accept others as they are, warts and all – even though they may be very different to us. The significance of "OKness" is that it relates to a person's "being" and not their "doing", and is highly correlated with EI Principles no. 3 and 4 (see Chapter 4).

If the person being profiled is low in either of these it is most improbable that they will be able to behave with truly high emotional intelligence in any of the other respects which may be measured. We spell out the relationship between scores on these two scales and scores on the other scales, and that – as well as in our view being an appropriate representation of reality – allows people to have a simple structure that holds all the scales together.

Awareness scales

Scales:
Self Awareness (4),
Awareness of Others (5),

Similarly, the scores in the scales which measure Self Awareness and Awareness of Others are likely to cause high and low scores in other scales – you need these awarenesses in order to be able to carry out the aspects of self management and relationship management measured by the other scales. Self awareness is about being in touch with our bodily and emotional state in the moment, and awareness of others is about being able to pick up on another's bodily and emotional state.

Self management scales

The effectiveness of our self management is demonstrated through the following aspects of EI:

Emotional Resilience (6)
– I bounce back from pressure and disappointment.
Personal Power (7)
– I am in control of my own destiny.
Goal Directedness (8)
– I know what I want and move towards that.
Flexibility (9)
– I willingly adapt my behaviour to different circumstances.
Personal Openness and Connectedness (10)
– I am open and share myself with others, consequently making good relationships with them.
Invitation to Trust (11)
– I am consistent, reliable and known and so can be trusted by others.

Relationship management scales

Our relationship management is demonstrated through these skills:

Trust (12)
– I am able to trust others while keeping myself safe.
Balanced Optimism (13)
– I am optimistic and, at the same time, realistic.
Emotional Expression and Control (14)
– I am free to express my emotions and in charge of when and how I do so.
Conflict Handling (15)
– I am assertive and handle conflict effectively.
Interdependence (16)
– I can choose when to be independent and when to be a team player.

Learning to know yourself scales

Scales:
Reflective Learning (17),
Self Knowledge (Accuracy of Self Assessment) (18)

The next scale, called Reflective Learning, is not so much an element of emotional intelligence itself (combining feeling and thinking when choosing what to do), as an essential prerequisite for it. One of the key practices of an emotionally intelligent person is reflecting on experience and thus learning from it, about oneself and about others. Reflective learning allows one to convert self awareness and awareness of others in the moment into self knowledge and understanding of others, which are longer term attributes. This is reflected in the extended version of our overall model of EI processes shown in Figure 6.2.

You will see from this figure that in order to self manage effectively we need both to be self aware in the moment and also to have self knowledge as a result of reflecting on and learning from our past experiences. Similarly, in order to manage our relationships effectively we need both to be aware of the other(s) in the moment and also to have some knowledge of how others work as a result of reflecting on and learning from our past experiences with them.

The last scale, Self Knowledge (Accuracy of self assessment) has a dual role. On their own the answers to the items in this scale give us a measure

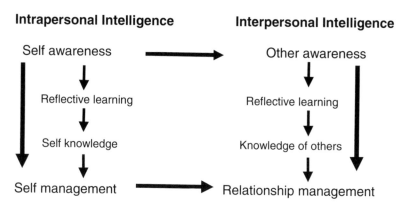

Figure 6.2 *An extended model of the processes involved in EI.*

of how the respondent sees themselves in terms of emotional intelligence, of their self-assessed EI. When used as a basis for comparison with how they actually scored on the various scales, and particularly when compared with 360° results, they allow us to measure the accuracy of someone's self assessment, or their degree of self knowledge.

Chapters 7, 9 and 11 to 13 explore these EI qualities one by one.

Reference

Maddocks, J. and Sparrow, T. (2000) The Individual and Team Effectiveness Questionnaires. Users Manual: JCA (Occupational Psychologists) Ltd, UK.

7

Kind regards

*"You can tell more about a person by what he says about others than
you can by what others say about him"*
Leo Aikman

This chapter discusses the scales of:

1 Self Regard
2 Regard for Others
3 Relative Regard.

Within each scale you will find:

• a definition;
• a more in-depth description;
• more information to help you understand the relevant EI theory;
• exercises to help you develop each scale.

1   Self Regard

Accepting and valuing yourself

Self regard is needed, to a greater or lesser extent, for all aspects of emotional intelligence. It is the prerequisite for health, happiness and success. Having high self regard enables you to have high regard for others, and so genuinely to understand and accept others, even when they are very different from you.

It also enables you to be accurately aware of your strengths and weaknesses and to welcome negative feedback from others rather than feeling threatened by it or defending against it. It is a direct measure of your self-perceived OKness.

2   Regard for Others

Accepting and valuing others

This is about accepting and valuing others as people, as distinct from liking or approving of what they may do. Regard for others is needed to create and maintain loving, healthy and productive relationships.

If you are low in regard for others you will tend to come across as judgemental, critical, blamey, rejecting, mistrustful and disregarding of others. This behaviour will make it difficult for you to be accurately aware of others and their feelings or to have good relationships with them.

Our regard for others is revealed by the quality of responses we give to others, by the pattern of our stroking of them. This scale is a direct measure of how you perceive the extent to which you hold others OK.

3   Relative Regard

Our life position

Emotional intelligence is as much about attitudes as it is about abilities. It is hard to behave consistently with emotional intelligence if you are not coming from an "I'm OK, You're OK" position. The particular difficulties encountered will depend on whether it is regard for self, regard for others, or both that is deficient.

The derived scale we call Relative Regard gives a measure of the amount and direction of the difference, if any, between how much in your view you accept and value yourself and how much you accept and value others. It is, therefore, as near as you can get to a measure of what in TA is called your "life position", the combination of your holding yourself and others OK or Not OK. If you value others significantly more than you value yourself, then you are likely to hold the "I'm Not OK, You're OK" life position. Contrariwise, if you value yourself significantly more than you value others, then you are likely to hold the "I'm OK, You're Not OK" life position. If there is a negligible difference between your valuing of yourself and of others, it is a little more complicated. If you value both highly, then you will be coming from an "I'm OK, You're OK" position, but if your valuing of yourself and of others is equally low, then you will be coming from an "I'm Not OK, You're Not OK" position.

The TA life positions are usually represented in a 2 × 2 grid known, after the Western movie, as "The OK Corral" (see Table 4.1).

The significance of life positions

So how important are these life positions? It is difficult not to be equivocal in answering this question. On the one hand, it is an incredibly crude characterisation: dividing the whole population into just four apparently discrete groups – it sounds worse than the things some people do with the eight letters of MBTI results (see page 261)! And of course it is true that not everybody has a single clear life position; indeed, we all move round and experience all the positions at times. And it is wise not to give too much significance to the identity of the preferred life positions if the scores on relative regard are middling (say Deciles 4 or 7), rather than extreme (say Deciles 1 to 3 for I– U+ and Deciles 8 to 10 for I+ U–).

On the other hand, the life position a person holds affects all other aspects of EI (as measured by the other scales) and does seem to be extraordinarily important in determining how they will think, feel and behave, and therefore what their life outcomes will be.

Moving towards the I+ U+ emotionally intelligent position

The one tricky thing about the OK Corral is that the I+ U– position is always a cover up for, and a defence against, an underlying feeling of "I'm Not OK". Consequently, whether your prevailing position is I+ U–, I– U+ or I– U–, the place to start is always with raising your own self esteem. You need to be sure that, if your self regard is apparently high, it is genuine (as part of "I'm OK, You're OK"), rather than a cover up – part of "I'm OK, You're Not OK" held as a defence against "I'm Not OK, You're OK".

There are two simple tests to check on this. If your self regard is genuinely high you will also genuinely understand and accept others, even when they are very different from you (Scale 2). Also, if your self regard is genuinely high you will be accurately aware of your strengths and weaknesses

(Scale 18); you will welcome negative feedback from others rather than feeling threatened by it or defending against it.

Self regard (or self esteem) is affected by the quality of responses you get from people (yourself and others) towards your being rather than your doing.

Raising self esteem / self regard

How people treat us has a direct result in how we feel about ourselves. And equally, how we treat others has a direct result in how they feel about themselves.

What is self esteem?

- The same as self regard.
- The feeling of personal security about who and what you are and your right to be here.
- "An evaluation, a feeling, a child's basic sense that who they are is OK".
- Not the belief you have about yourself but the feeling you have about these beliefs.
- Self worth – feeling valuable as a human being and liking ourselves.

The relationship between self confidence and self esteem

- Both are attitudes of mind.
- They can both be high or low; positive or negative.
- They are interactive: high self confidence and high self esteem, low self confidence and low self esteem are likely to go together.
- The distinction is:
  Self confidence is how we think and feel about what we are or are not able to **do**.
  Self esteem is how we think and feel about who we **are**.

Commonly not much distinction is made between self esteem and self confidence. We, however, find it helpful to make a clear distinction. They are obviously similar and related, but the fundamental difference is that self esteem is about being and self confidence is about doing. Although levels of self esteem and self confidence usually go together, this is not always the case.

You get people who appear very confident on the outside but are shivering jellies on the inside. (See Petruska Clarkson's book *The Achilles Syndrome*.)

Expectations and self confidence

Before moving on to look at self esteem in more detail, let's take a quick look at one of the most fundamental influences on self confidence development: expectations. The tricky thing about getting these right is that the appropriate level of expectation (requiring people to stretch themselves but allowing them frequent opportunities for a sense of achievement) changes all the time. If they are developing, what we should expect of them this month is more than we expected of them last month and less than we should expect of them next month. So it is continuous, quite tricky work to get your level of expectations right.

Note that there is a crucial distinction between having high expectations of someone in a framework of conditional evaluation: "I expect you to be able to do this well and if you don't you are not OK", so that the other believes "I have got to do well", and having high expectations of someone in a framework of unconditional acceptance: "I believe you are fine and that you can do this well", so that the other believes "I can do this well" and lives up to the inner belief. (This, you will realise, is very relevant to the question of what characterises a good leader.)

The three components of self esteem

Our self esteem (or self regard) has three aspects, which can vary separately. To have high overall self esteem, we need to be high in each one of these aspects.

- a sense of unique acceptable self;
- a sense of belonging;
- a sense of personal power.

A sense of self means having a good idea about who you are, knowing that who you are is "OK" – for example, knowing and being comfortable with your likes, dislikes, strengths, vulnerabilities, preferences, temperament, feelings and needs.

If you are supported by the inner knowledge of the connections you have, even when they are not around, you have a sense of belonging. In our society people are usually members of several groups, for instance family, work groups, church, sports team or a particular group of friends. Knowledge of our connections with others enables us to feel well supported and more secure in the world.

Personal power goes beyond just knowing you are good at certain tasks (which is self confidence). It is more concerned with knowing that you are in charge of your destiny and a person who can learn from, cope with and make changes to things you don't like or want. Psychologists sometimes refer to this as our perceived "locus of control", and another, rather psycho-babbly, way of referring to the sense of personal power is as our "sense of self efficacy". Our sense of self efficacy is largely determined by our experience of how effectively we act:

- how well we use our minds;
- how well we use our bodies;
- how adept we are socially;
- how well we handle our feelings.

The self esteem bank account

Our self esteem is like a bank account that is fluid – with currency flowing in and out every moment. We need to be sure that we are keeping it topped up, as much can flow out in response to the daily knocks of life. So how can we do this?

The currency that we need for our self esteem bank account is "units of recognition". Units of recognition are called "strokes", and they either build our esteem count or deplete it depending on their intrinsic value.

The notion of "strokes" is taken from TA (see page 53). The origins of stroke theory lie in immediate postwar Europe, when lots of orphan refugee babies were brought up in large makeshift hospital wards by a few over-worked and harassed nurses. They had time to make sure that the babies' physical needs were all satisfied (they were fed, changed, kept warm and pro-tected from physical harm), but they did not have time to interact with them, to cuddle them, play with them, sing to them, etc. As a result, many of the babies failed to thrive or to reach their physical developmental milestones on time, and in extreme cases developed marasmus, where the spinal cord shrivels up and you die. This was because just as to survive and thrive we need food, water and warmth, so too – because human beings are social animals – do we need recognition from other human beings (or at least other mammals – pets give us lots of strokes) to survive and thrive psychologically. For newborn babies, human contact is most fundamentally tactile: touch is the predominant sense, so units of recognition are literally "strokes". TA has generalised this usage, so that for adults, strokes may be visual (e.g. a wave, a disapproving frown, a smile), auditory (e.g. a greeting, something we say, a raspberry), tactile (e.g. a pat on the back, a handshake, a kick, a hug, a kiss) or combinations of these three. Of the various ways that strokes can be classified, the most important are positive versus negative and conditional (for doing) versus unconditional (for being). If we combine these two distinctions we get a 2 × 2 matrix, which we call the *Stroke Grid* (Table 7.1).

Table **7.1** *The Stroke Grid.*

	NEGATIVE	POSITIVE
UNCONDITIONAL For Being	Put downs **XXX**	Expressed value ✔✔✔
CONDITIONAL For Doing	Negative feedback ✔	Praise ✔✔

Starting with the top right-hand corner, positive unconditional strokes, expressions of our being valued by other humans, are what we need to survive and thrive. They, provided they are genuine and believed in, are an unalloyed good and we cannot have too many of them. The prevailing doctrine a generation or so ago that letting a child know too much that it was loved would "spoil" it was just so much pernicious nonsense. Positive unconditional strokes do not need to be dramatic ("You are the light of my life"): low-intensity ones might be just a smile, a handshake, a grin, a nod, or "Hi, Fred". We need some high-intensity ones, but mostly it is the frequency rather than the intensity that matters. Note that what is needed here is not just love (it is love we are talking about; we call it "value" because some people, especially some men, and particularly some businessmen, are allergic to the notion of "love" but feel at home with, and can cope with, "value"), but expressed love. It is no use loving people if you don't let them know it by what you say and what you do.

Put downs, unconditional negative strokes, on the other hand are toxic – harmful to all human beings – and are to be completely avoided: not to be given, and if one comes your way, not to be let in. Examples: "You stubborn cow", "I hate you", "You're useless", and all forms of violence. All negative attributions are putdowns and people live down to them. If you call a child "Butterfingers!" when it drops something, it is likely to grow up to be clumsy. "You bitch", "You idiot" and "You are a liar" are all put downs and should be converted to "I am really angry with you for doing that", to "That seems to me a stupid thing to have done" and to "I think you are lying".

Praise is nice too, but it isn't as nice as expressed love. So it only gets two ticks, not three, and they are of a different nature. Conditional and unconditional positive strokes are not convertible currencies: if you are short of love, getting lots of praise will not do the business. This takes us back to self confidence and self esteem not always being both high or both low. Consider, for example, business tycoons like Rupert Murdoch or Robert Maxwell. Both low in self esteem (Robert Maxwell committed suicide) and struggling hard to get lots more money and power, more admiration and praise, but it doesn't get them anywhere: Rupert Murdoch complained publicly in 2005 about not getting "the respect I deserve". He is over 70 and perhaps now could consider retiring and settling down with Wendy to relax and enjoy himself!

Negative feedback, rather surprisingly, also gets a tick. It consists of negative strokes and is usually uncomfortable to receive, yet it gets a tick. That is because negative feedback about our doing conveys useful information which we need to have and to let in. If what we do upsets someone else, we need to know. We can then choose what to do about it: to continue doing it in the knowledge that they don't like it or perhaps to find an alternative way of behaving. So, children need to know when what they do is dangerous, likely to have bad consequences, seen as ill-mannered or likely to upset someone else. (Not giving children negative feedback is what is likely to lead them to behave in a "spoilt" way.) But, because they are uncomfortable, negative strokes, even if conditional rather than unconditional, need to be rationed and to be outnumbered by positive strokes of both kinds.

How much and how often?

The difference in the values of the different kinds of strokes means that the numbers we need to give out (and hopefully that we receive) of the different kinds are very different. Table 7.2 shows the pattern to aim for in most cases.

Table 7.2 *The numbers of different strokes needed.*

	NEGATIVE	POSITIVE
UNCONDITIONAL For Being	Put downs 0	Expressed value 3
CONDITIONAL For Doing	Negative feedback 1	Praise 2

So, for every one piece of negative feedback we give, we need to give two pieces of praise and three strokes of expressed love or value. Quite a bit different to what generally occurs! But achievable if we put our minds to it and form new habits of recognising ourselves and others.

This is the desired pattern for most people. The exception is people who have until today received lots of negatives and few positives. Those who have had lots of negative unconditionals (put downs) will have very low self esteem and will not be able to digest this sort of diet of strokes; like people who are starving and cannot cope with rich food. They would not believe the offered positive strokes and would reject them. For very damaged people like this, you need to start by giving them plenty of negative conditional strokes (not put downs but negative feedback). They know where they are with negative strokes and will believe them, and because they are not getting put downs, their self esteem – such as it is – will not be further harmed. Then, having established your credibility, you can begin to slip in the odd bit of praise among the negative feedback, and then more and more, until you are giving them twice as much praise as negative feedback. Then they may be ready to accept that they are potentially lovable and to take some unconditional positive strokes. Eventually, you work your way to this pattern.

What has all this stuff about strokes got to do with self esteem or self regard? A person's **self esteem** is set by the ratio of positive to negative **unconditional** strokes:

- lots of expressed love value and few put downs leads to high self esteem;
- lots of put downs and little expressed love value leads to low self esteem.

Similarly, a person's **self confidence** is set by the ratio of positive to negative **conditional** strokes:

- lots of praise and limited negative feedback leads to high self confidence;
- lots of negative feedback and limited praise leads to low self confidence.

As this shows, the top row of the Stroke Grid shows where self esteem comes from and the bottom row shows where self confidence comes from. The word "set" used above is perhaps a bit strong. Adults have choices about what to do with the strokes that come their way and, as they grow older, so, too, do children. There is a famous TA story of a mother who used to say to her two sons, "You boys are crazy. You'll both end up in the asylum." Many years later, when she was dead, it turned out that she had been right. Both her sons were at the local lunatic asylum: one was a patient and the other was working there as the medical director.

There is one important aspect of stroke theory that the Stroke Grid does not encompass. Negative strokes may undermine our self confidence or self esteem but they are at least units of recognition from another person and as such they are better than no strokes at all. Being ignored or neglected is worst of all. This is illustrated by the outcome of a particularly gruesome psychological experiment carried out on white rats. When examining rats' intelligence and behaviour, a common experimental set-up is to give the rats a lever which they can press, this either leads to them being given a pellet of food (positive reinforcement) or an electric shock through the metal floor of the cage (negative reinforcement). Under normal circumstances rats will do whatever they can to avoid electric shocks. In this particular experiment, however, single rats were put in cages on their own in a small room and left alone for long periods. In each cage was a lever: pressing the lever did not produce a pellet of food but an electric shock. At first the rats' behaviour was as predicted: they explored their new surroundings and, in the process, pressed the lever and got an electric shock; thereafter they were careful not to press the lever again. But the rats were left alone in their cages for a long period of time, with the only stimulation that of being fed once a day. After a bit they got so bored, so understimulated, so neglected, that they began every now and then to press the lever voluntarily to give themselves an electric shock, because that was better than nothing at all.

This makes some sense of stroppy teenagers who seem deliberately to go out of their way to get punished. They are usually poor performers at school who come from homes where positive strokes are in short supply, so they have low self esteem. They don't know how to get positive strokes, so – because negative strokes are better than no strokes at all – they go out of their way to get some attention in the only way they know how, by being a pain in the butt to everyone else (particularly teachers and other adults).

How do strokes come packaged?

As well as being either positive or negative, and for someone's being or for their doing, strokes are transmitted either verbally or non-verbally by our bodies – think of a smile or a scowl. Nonverbal strokes can come on their own, but verbal strokes are always accompanied by nonverbal strokes (not just what we say but how we say it.) They can be given directly to someone, they can be overheard or they can be passed on indirectly – for example, through talking to a mutual friend who relays the stroke back. And they can be more or less intense – they can be impassioned or lightweight and everyday.

On the whole children have not much choice about the pattern of strokes which comes their way. But adults have lots of choices about what to do with strokes: they can be given, received, asked for, declined, filtered out and not received, and also distorted so that what is given is not what is received.

How to develop your self regard

Here is a quick checklist of the key ways to boost your self esteem bank account:

- self stroking: positive self-talk;
- letting in positive strokes and asking for them;
- avoiding and refusing unconditional negative strokes;
- recognising and declining unwarranted negative feedback.

Let us look at these one by one.

Positive self-talk

Who is the person we spend most time with?	Ourself.
Who is our biggest source of strokes?	Ourself.
Who is the only person whose behaviour we can control?	Ourself.

So, obviously the first place to start in improving the balance of positive and negative strokes we get is ourself. We can't control what has happened to us in the past, but the sad thing is that if we have had lots of negative strokes in the past we tend to perpetuate this by giving ourselves negative strokes in the present. That we *can* do something about. Even those who appear to have an "I'm OK, You're Not OK" life position, and are overtly critical of others, are in our experience often covertly just as critical of themselves, thus further undermining their actual, if un-acknowledged, low self regard.

The biggest problem with this is that we have probably been keeping up a stream of negative self-talk since the age of four. And unlearning well established old habits is a very difficult thing to do. So do not say, "I will stop criticising myself and running myself down", because if you do you will find that within a day or so you will do it anyway, and then you will start criticising yourself for criticising yourself: the last state will be worse than the first. The trick is to forget the criticism but to decide to treat yourself, and talk to yourself, as if you were a much-loved four- or five-year-old. Be loving, supportive, encouraging, delighted, patient and entirely accepting. Despite doing this, sooner or later you are bound to find yourself criticising yourself in the old way. When this happens, do not get cross with yourself. Forget the criticising bit and come to the aid of the criticised bit. "Oh! How horrid! What a nasty thing to have said to you. I am so sorry. I am sure you don't deserve it. How can I help you feel better after that?" And so on. If you keep up this loving, positive self-talk for three weeks or so, you will find that

1. From feeling artificial and strange, and needing conscious control, the positive self-talk will become something you do naturally, automatically and unconsciously.
2. The self criticism will fade away, because it is incompatible with this new way of being with yourself.
3. You will be feeling a lot better, because your self esteem will be much higher.

What kind of positive self-talk will you respond to? Jot down a few examples that will help you form this new habit.

Letting positive strokes in

Here we are beginning to look at the options people have about dealing with strokes. We can give people strokes, but that does not mean that they will receive them as sent, if at all. People may have a variety of ways, unconscious or conscious, of avoiding receiving positive strokes which come their way.

Receiving positive strokes, which are the essential psychological food we all need to thrive, should be the most natural thing in the world. They are, after all, nice gifts being offered us by someone else. However, by the time the grown-ups have done what they do to us in childhood, most of us find them difficult to let in. If we have low self esteem, they will create what psychologists call "cognitive dissonance": "I know I am bad, but this person is telling me I am good. That does not fit." Which is uncomfortable, so we deal with it by ingeniously finding ways not to let the positive strokes in. This generates a vicious circle: low self esteem leads to keeping positive strokes out, which leads to lower self esteem, and so on. There follows a set of guidelines about what we need to do to dismantle those ways of not letting the strokes in. Hopefully, we can then move to a virtuous circle: letting positive strokes in raises self esteem, which makes it easier to let more positive strokes in, which raises self esteem even further, and so on.

1. **Make sure you slow down.**
   Some people avoid letting positive strokes in by rushing on to another topic of conversation. The first thing we need to do when receiving a positive stroke is to stay with it, to slow down and give it time to go right in. A useful analogy to receiving a positive stroke is eating a delicious canapé at a cocktail party: we need not to gobble it, but to savour it at our leisure.

2. **Keep good contact (e.g. eye contact) with the other.**
   A stroke is a unit of recognition from another human being. In order for it to move from one human being to another, the two of them must be in contact, and the main way of achieving that is eye contact. Yet it is amazing how many people particularly here in the UK, when someone says something nice to them, look at their shoes or embarrassedly out of the window. Anywhere but at the person who is giving them the stroke.

3. **Keep breathing, slowly and deeply.**

   In the long run, if we stop breathing we are dead. In the short run, holding our breath creates a barrier between head and heart and stops us feeling. Again, it is surprising how many people stop breathing when someone says something nice to them.

4. **Don't discount it.**

   "Discounting" is artificially lowering the value of something. For example, if A says to B, "What a lovely blouse!" and B replies, "Oh, it's just something I picked up at the Oxfam shop for 50p", that is a discount. It is not a question of the facts but the attitude towards the facts – "just" is a dead give-away here. B could have replied, "I am glad you like it, and, do you know, I got it for only 50p at the Oxfam shop", thus inviting a further positive stroke for her clever shopping. The classic discounter was perhaps the nineteenth century English gent, who, having dived into a flooding river and rescued a young woman, replied to her heartfelt gratitude and thanks for risking his life and saving hers, "Oh, it was nothing."

5. **Don't bounce it back.**

   "Bouncing back" is distracting attention from the stroke given you by immediately giving a larger stroke to the stroke giver. It is as if you hold up a rubber shield between you and the stroke giver so that the stroke they try to give you bounces back into their face. Of course it is fine to give other people positive strokes, but not when that is an interruption to them giving you a stroke.

6. **Repeat it back.**

   When you have a very nice canapé, you take another one. Similarly, one way of prolonging the pleasure of a positive stroke is to repeat it back to the giver. "So you thought I gave the most brilliant speech of the evening! I am delighted to hear that."

7. **Let it right in till you feel warm inside.**

   Stick with Rules 1, 2 and 3; take your time, keep good contact, keep breathing slowly and deeply, and use your self awareness to monitor the effect on you, bodily and emotionally, of letting the stroke in.

8. **Ask for it to be repeated.**

   This is fairly postgraduate level stuff. As well as repeating it yourself, you can ask the stroke giver to repeat the stroke. "Oh, how wonderful. I loved hearing you say that. Do tell me again!"

9. Thank the other.

This is a piece of sheer manipulation. There is no requirement to thank people for giving you a positive stroke. Indeed there can be dangers in doing so. They are saying this nice thing to you because they want to and because they believe it to be true. To thank them might suggest that you believe that they are being condescending and saying something untrue to you just to be nice. But thanking is a form of giving a positive stroke, and "the stroked behaviour repeats". In other words, if you thank someone for giving you a positive stroke, they are more likely to give you more positive strokes in the future. Which will be nice for you and good for your self esteem.

One way of avoiding positive strokes that following these guidelines will not deal with is filtering them out, because that is an unconscious process. It is particularly common with people who have extremely low self esteem. For them, receiving a positive stroke would generate an intolerable level of cognitive dissonance, so they actually prevent themselves from hearing it. Of course, they do hear it really, because only by hearing it can they identify that it is intolerably positive for them, but having done that they then suppress it unconsciously before it reaches the level of consciousness, so that at a conscious level it is true that they actually don't hear it. If you do this, you will by definition be unaware of it. You will therefore need someone else to pick it up, to repeat the stroke and ensure that you hear it and let it in.

Once you have learned how to let positive strokes in, you can maximise the number that come your way by asking people to give them to you. Of course it is very unEnglish to ask for strokes. And people justify not doing it with lots of strange assertions like, "They wouldn't count" or "People would be forced to give me a positive stroke if I asked for one, whether they meant it or not." In fact, strokes is strokes is strokes, whether asked for or not. If someone asked you to give them a positive stroke, you wouldn't respond with the first lying thing that came into your head, but would look for a stroke which you potentially had for them but hadn't given them. Most of us are full of potential positive strokes for others, warm feelings, bits of appreciation or admiration which we haven't expressed. When we ask someone for a stroke, we are not asking people to invent something, but to let out something which is already there.

You can ask both for unconditional positive strokes (e.g. "I am feeling very depressed and lonely; will you tell me how you care about me?") and for conditional positive strokes (e.g. "I am worried about this presentation I have to do tomorrow; will you remind me of how well it went the last two times I gave one?").

Another strategy for maximising the number of positive strokes that come your way is to be very generous with the positive strokes that you give others. That way, people will unconsciously feel indebted to you and will even things up by giving you positive strokes too, and you will create a social and emotional climate where lots of positive strokes are given and received. Very important in teams (see Chapter 16).

Avoiding and refusing unconditional negative strokes

Just as we need to let positive strokes in, so also we need to keep many negative strokes (all unconditional negatives and all undeserved conditional negatives) out. Put downs, negative reactions from others towards our being rather than our doing ("You're a waste of space", "You stubborn cow", "You are so selfish", etc.) are toxic to our self regard and never justified. Sometimes, therefore, we need to decline strokes. This can be done either overtly or covertly. Overtly, when someone offers us a put down, we can say, "No, I am not useless and I do not want you to tell me that I am. I acknowledge that I made a mistake here, and I am sorry for it, but that does not make me a useless person." Or, if someone blames us for something which is not our fault, then we can say, "No, that's not down to me. It was not my responsibility and I am not taking the blame." Sometimes, of course, it is hard to do that: if the person offering us an unacceptable negative stroke is a quick-tempered boss or an important customer, or if this is in the middle of a public meeting. In such cases, we still need not to take the stroke in, even if we do not make it obvious to others that we are avoiding doing so. So we may remain silent, but say to ourselves, "That's not fair and I am not accepting it", or "That's just because he got out of the wrong side of bed this morning."

Avoiding unacceptable negatives is a question of either getting the people to change or changing the people. Getting the people to change means pointing out when they put you down, saying you don't like it and it isn't good for you and asking them to stop. (If you are low on assertiveness (Scale

15), you may need to shift on that first, and if your self regard is very low, you may first need to raise it a bit by other means before you feel able to do this.) They won't stop immediately, but keep objecting when they continue to put you down and they may start to shift eventually. If they don't, or won't (some people seem pretty stuck in I+ U– Critical Parent), then you need to change the people. Stop spending time with people who are bad for you and spend time instead with people who give you positive strokes.

Receiving negative feedback

Just as there are rules to help us receive positive strokes, so too are there guidelines on how to respond when someone offers us negative feedback.

1. **Do you want it? (Context?)**
   This is the other side of the coin of the feedback giver's duty to contract before they start delivering the feedback. If one person comes up to another at the watercooler and, a propos of nothing, says something like, "I thought you were a real pain in the meeting this morning", the other is perfectly entitled to say, "I didn't ask you what you thought and I am not interested." Or they may be open in principle to feedback from the other, but not when they are busy and stressed and not in public, and then they need to stop it right at the beginning until the conditions are right.
2. **If unconditional, reject the feedback. Either explicitly if you can, or, if not, internally.**
   All put downs, all negative unconditionals about our being, are toxic and not to be entertained. See above.
3. **If conditional, is it clear and specific? Is it personalised, i.e. subjective rather than pseudo-objective?**
   If you are offered non-specific and/or impersonal negative feedback, then the first step is to ask for it to be made specific and personal. If someone says, "The way you dress is very sloppy", then ask, "What in particular about the way I dress is it that seems to you to be sloppy?"
4. **Do you understand? (Remember people are different)**
   Because everybody is different, sometimes people will have a negative reaction to something we have done which we just don't understand, because it is so far from the way we would react. It is important to be

clear where they are coming from and to understand what it is they are objecting to, and it may take a bit of enquiry to arrive at this.

5. **Do you wish you hadn't done it?**

In giving you negative feedback the other is giving you useful information about them and their reactions, and you need to review your position in the light of this information. Maybe you had no idea that they would object to what you did. Now you know, do you wish you hadn't done it? Would you do it again or would you make some changes?

6. **If not, negotiate.**

If you decide that, despite their negative feedback, you are not sorry that you did what you did, then you and the other are in a potential conflict situation and need to have a negotiation about it.

7. **If yes, work out what, if anything, you wish to do about it: acknowledgement, apology, reparation for the past or undertaking for the future.**

If, after learning their reaction, you decide that you regret that you did what you did and would not have done it had you realised what effect it would have on them, then you need to decide what you want to do about it. The minimal level of response is perhaps a mere acknowledgement of the effect it had on them. The next step up is not merely to acknowledge but to apologise too – to say sorry. And then comes reparation, perhaps buying them a drink or buying a replacement for something you have broken. Or perhaps an undertaking for the future: "Now I know how much that upsets you I won't do it again." Or "I won't do it between nine at night and eight in the morning when you might be sleeping."

8. **Express this, and then negotiate if necessary.**

Having decided what you want to do, you express it to the other. If you are lucky, they will be happy with what you propose. If not, then again you need to have a negotiation.

9. **Make sure your self esteem is unaffected.**

At the end of all this, check that your self esteem is unaffected. That if you were offered a put down you effectively declined it, and that if you were offered proper negative feedback on your behaviour you did not convert any of it to a reflection on you and your being. If your self esteem has been undermined, go and get some positive unconditional strokes from someone who cares for you. One of the ways that people end up with damaged self esteem, even when they have been offered negative feedback in a skilled and emotionally intelligent way, is to distort the stroke. For example, there are potentially only two short false steps from receiving some negative feedback to feeling bad.

| Step 1. | She doesn't like what I did | SO: *I did wrong* |
| Step 2. | I did wrong | SO: *I am a bad person* |

There are two logical errors on top of one another here:

- Confusing someone else's response (which is a fact about them) with the value of what we do (which is to do with us). Just because A doesn't like something that we do, it doesn't follow that it was a wrong thing to do: B, C, D, E, F, G and H might think it was absolutely fine. A's disliking it is about A, not about us.
- Confusion of the levels of doing and being, of conditional and unconditional strokes. Had we made a mistake (doing), that would have nothing to do with whether or not we are a bad person (being).

Many texts on self development have a section urging their readers towards exercising forgiveness. We do not. As Alexander Pope put it: "To err is human, to forgive, divine". In TA terms it is something that belongs in the Parent ego-state, whereas emotional intelligence involves Integrated Adult. The reason for this is that forgiveness presupposes judgement, and judgement of a person (rather than an activity – see the preceding section) is not an emotionally intelligent process. If you find yourself judging others, look at the section below on "Stretch to Understand".

How to develop your regard for others

Distinguish between their being and their doing

We tend to confuse how people are and what they do, and to react similarly. We need to be careful about the distinction because the appropriate reactions are very different. What people do and say may be judged, challenged and resisted, but who they are and what they feel just are and need to be accepted. As the religious precept has it, "Hate the sin but love the sinner."

1. Practise the distinction by picking yourself up when you judge, reject or attack someone for who they are, rather than opposing what they do or say.
2. When you find yourself thinking, "I dislike X", reframe it as, "I dislike what X has done" or even, "I dislike what X often does."

Make a note of any significant observations you have made about whether and how you judge other people.

Stretch to understand

Judgement is the enemy of understanding.

1. When you respond to what someone does or says by rushing to judgement, stop for a moment.
2. Ask yourself, "Why have they done this? How do they see the situation that makes this, for them, the best thing to do?"
3. Attempt to put yourself in their shoes and understand things from their point of view, with their history, their limitations and their desires.

You may not like what they have done or said any better, but you will be better able to deal with it, and with them, if you understand where they are coming from and how it makes sense to them.

Describe any experiences you have had whilst undertaking this exercise of putting yourself in someone else's shoes and coming to understand how they see the world by understanding something about their personal history.

Learn to listen

Conversations too often consist of people taking it in turns to talk and then to plan what they will say next while the other speaks. That way we never get to understand the other.

1. Practise every day listening to someone else without paying attention to yourself.
2. Don't interpret what they say in your terms.
3. Don't think about its implications for you.
4. Don't judge.

5. Just listen.
6. Let them know what you have heard and understood.
7. Try to understand how they are feeling.

That's all: no response of your own, no advice, just being with them. It is remarkably difficult at first (because most of us don't do it much), but it gets easier the more you practise it.

Do you notice any shift in the balance of power between yourself and another whilst actively listening to them? If so, describe your experiences.

Attending and listening well to others is obviously also a prime route towards the Awareness of Others, and we shall look at that in Chapter 9.

Understand their values

A powerful way to get to know, appreciate and understand an individual is to understand their values. Values underlie people's behaviours and motivations; understanding these can lead to greater awareness and respect for them.

1. One way of identifying those values that are important to an individual is to ask questions:
   What's really important to you?
   What do you really value?
   What are your motivators?
2. Ask follow-up questions to get below the surface:
   For what reason do you think that?
   For what reason is that important to you?
3. Notice when their values clash with yours.
4. Who is right? Or can we both be?

List the different values that you are coming across whilst undertaking this exercise.

Reference

Clarkson, P. (1994) *The Achilles Syndrome: Overcoming the Secret Fear of Failure*, Element Books.

8

Facilitating EI development 1 – "Meeting"

"We come to love not by finding a perfect person, but by learning
to see an imperfect person perfectly"
Sam Keen

The development of emotional intelligence is most easily facilitated from within a warm, close, emotionally intelligent relationship, and in order to create such a relationship we need to meet the other where they are. Which means that the first thing we have to do is to *find out* where it is that they are; in other words, to do a bit of diagnosis. Of course, the *ie*™ results will help a lot with this, but there are other things we need to know which the *ie*™ will not tell us directly. In particular, we need to know more about the other's self esteem / self regard.

Conditional self regard

So far we have considered self regard in rather a simplistic way, as either "OK" or "Not OK". In fact, things are a bit more complicated than that.

If we are very lucky and choose an excellent family to be born into, we may emerge from childhood with a secure sense of our own value, and consequently will value others too. We will occupy the I+ U+ life position and will experience ourselves as unconditionally "OK". If, on the other hand, we have a childhood with little love and lots of put downs, violence perhaps or parents who just aren't interested in us and don't care about us, then, alas, we shall emerge from childhood convinced of our lack of value, our unworthiness. We shall experience ourselves as unconditionally "Not OK". Most of us, however, most of the time, will hover between these two extremes and will experience ourselves as being conditionally OK. That is to say, we are OK on the condition that we fulfil the rules of life as laid down by our parents and other significant adults in our childhood, sometimes explicitly and sometimes implicitly. As everyone is different, there is an almost infinite number of these rules and combinations of them that children take on as what you have to do to survive in the world. Nonetheless, there is a small number of such rules which seem to drive the behaviour of large sections of the population. When people are behaving in a certain way because it feels to them as if they have no choice, they *have* to do so, are *driven* to do so because that is what the rule enjoins, we say they are engaging in "driver behaviour". More colloquially, the rules themselves tend to get called "drivers". There are four and a half classic drivers; the "half" refers to one which tends not so much to occur on its own, but as a reinforcer of one of the other drivers.

Most people have a principal condition of worth (or "driver"), a main rule which they have to adhere to in order to feel OK, and many people have one or two others in support, which they also feel obliged to obey. The "obligation" comes from the consequences which flow from not obeying the rule. These rules are literally "conditions of worth": if we obey them and fulfil their requirements, then we feel more or less OK about ourselves. But if we disobey, if we don't fulfil the requirements – for example if our job is to keep everybody happy and we upset someone and they get cross with us, or if our job is to get everything perfectly right and we make a mistake – then our self regard, our sense of our own OKness, will plummet and we will "feel bad". Not a pleasant experience.

Understanding our conditions of worth

The point of identifying which conditions of worth are the ones we are most subject to, i.e. what some of our main interferences are, is, in part, that in themselves they have a considerable effect on what we do, and so if we want to change our behaviour, then we need to start by identifying our conditions of worth. So, first set about identifying your own by completing the questionnaire in Table 8.1.

Table 8.1 *Conditions of Worth Questionnaire.*

No.	Question	Yes	No	To some extent
1.	Do you set yourself high standards and then criticise yourself for failing to meet them?			
2.	Is it important to you to be right?			
3.	Do you feel discomforted (e.g. annoyed, irritated) by small messes or discrepanicies, such as a spot on a garment or the wallpaper, an ornament or a tool out of place, a disorderly presentation of work?			
4.	Do you hate to be interrupted?			
5.	Do you like to explain things in detail and precisely?			
	Total no. of ticks			
6.	Do you do things (especially for others) that you don't really want to?			
7.	Is it important to you to be *liked*?			
8.	Are you fairly easily persuaded?			
9.	Do you dislike being different?			
10.	Do you dislike conflict?			
	Total no. of ticks			
11.	Do you hate "giving up" or "giving in", always hoping that this time it will work?			
12.	Do you have a tendency to start things and not finish them?			
13.	Do you tend to compare yourself (or your performance) with others and feel inferior or superior accordingly?			
14.	Do you find yourself going round in circles with a problem, feeling stuck but unable to let go of it?			
15.	Do you have a tendency to be "the rebel" or "odd one out" in a group?			
	Total no. of ticks			
16.	Do you hide or control your feelings?			
17.	Are you reluctant to ask for help?			
18.	Do you tend to put (or find) yourself in the position of being depended upon?			
19.	Do you tend not to realise how tired or hungry or ill you are, but instead "keep going"?			
20.	Do you prefer to do things on your own?			
	Total no. of ticks			
21.	Do you have a tendency to do lots of things simultaneously?			
22.	Would you describe yourself as "quick" and find yourself getting impatient with others?			
23	Do you tend to talk at the same time as others, or finish their sentences for them?			
24.	Do you like to "get on with the job" rather than talk about it?			
25.	Do you set unrealistic time limits (especially too short)?			
	Total no. of ticks			

How to score the Conditions of Worth Questionnaire

1. Check that the total for each section = 5 ticks.
2. For each section, using Table 8.2:
   - Write down in the 2nd column the total number of "Yes" ticks.
   - Multiply this score by two and write this in the 3rd column (Yes × 2).
   - Write the total number of "To some extent" ticks in the 4th column.
   - Add up the 3rd and 4th columns (for the total of the previous two columns).

The result of this addition gives you the total score for that section, which will lie in the range 0 – 10.

Table 8.2 *Finding your conditions of worth.*

	No. of Yes ticks	Yes × 2	No. of 'To some extent'	Total of previous two columns
Section 1				
Section 2				
Section 3				
Section 4				
Section 5				

This score gives you a measure of the degree to which your behaviour is driven by the need to fulfil the particular condition of worth covered by that section. The conditions the various sections measure are as follows:

Section 1 (Q1 to 5):	**Be Perfect**
Section 2 (Q6 to 10):	**Please Others / Please Me**
Section 3 (Q11 to 15):	**Try Hard (. . . and don't succeed)**
Section 4 (Q16 to 20):	**Be Strong**
Section 5 (Q21 to 25):	**Hurry Up**

Releasers from the conditions:

Be Perfect	"Good enough is good enough."
Please Others / Please Me	"Please yourself."
Try Hard	Traditional: "Do it!"
(. . . and don't succeed)	Better: "You can do it for yourself if you want to."
Be Strong	"You can have needs."
Hurry Up	"You can take your time."

Just as we need to identify our own conditions of worth as part of getting to know our own interferences, so that we can be in a position to dismantle them, such is also the case with facilitating others to change their behaviour. So, here are some of the characteristic signs of the various conditions of worth.

Be Perfect

Language: parentheses and qualifiers: "as I said", "we might say", "possibly", "completely", and so on. Counting down lists "a", "b", "c" or "one", "two", "three", sometimes ticking them off on one's fingers.
Facial expression: speaker often looks up while pausing in speech, as if trying to read the perfect answer written on the ceiling.
Tone and posture: quite like Adult – well modulated and upright.

Please Others

Language: high-*but*-low sentence structure, e.g. "I've really enjoyed your teaching, but I don't know if I'll remember what you said." Interspersing querying words and phrases, e.g. "OK?", "hmmm?", "all right by you?", "kind of", "sort of" and very frequently "you know?" or "you know".
Tone: high voice, squeaky tone, typically rising at the end of each sentence.
Gestures: reaching out with the hands, usually palms up. Head nodding.
Posture: shoulders hunched up and forward. Leaning towards the other.
Facial expression: looking up with face turned slightly down, so needing to look up from under with eyebrows raised. Consequently horizontal lines in the brow. Often a tense smile.

Try Hard (. . . and don't succeed)

Language: extensive use of "try" (implication: will try but won't actually do it). Also: "difficult", "can't", "what?", "It's hard to . . .", and "huh?", "uh?".
Tone: sometimes muffled and strangled, with tense throat muscles.
Gestures: often one hand by eye or ear as if striving to see or hear. Fists may be clenched.
Posture: hunched up, straining forward.
Facial expression: crunched up brow so that two vertical lines appear above the nose. Sometimes eyes and whole face screwed up into tight wrinkles.

Be Strong (In other words:
Don't have feelings. Don't have needs. At the least, don't express any.)

Language: words that convey "my feelings and actions are not my responsibility but are caused by agents around me", e.g. "makes me angry", "forced me to". Also, distancers instead of "I", e.g. "one", "you", "people", "it", "that".

Tone: flat, monotonous, usually low.
Gestures: absence of.
Posture: frequently closed, immobile. Arms or legs crossed.
Facial expression: absence of, immobility.

Hurry Up (This is the auxiliary driver.)

Language: "hurry", "quick", "get going", "let's go", "no time to . . .".
Tone: staccato, machine-gun-like.
Gestures: finger tapping, foot tapping or wagging, shifting around in chair, repeated checking of watch.
Posture: agitated movement.
Facial expression: frequent, rapid changes of gaze.

For a more complete list, see Chapter 16 of *TA Today* by Ian Stewart and Vann Joines (1987).

As well as the various individual conditions of worth significantly motivating our behaviour, they also clump together to form particular patterns of dealing with the world that (following Paul Ware in his article in the *Transactional Analysis Journal*, 1983) are called "personality adaptations" (Table 8.3). The best introduction to personality adaptations is to be found in *Personality Adaptations* by Vann Joines and Ian Stewart (2002).

Table 8.3 *Personality adaptations and drivers.*

1a	Brilliant sceptic ("paranoid")	BS BP
1b	Responsible workaholic ("obsessive compulsive")	BP BS (TH PL)
2	Enthusiastic overreactor ("hysteric / histrionic")	PL TH / HU
3	Creative day-dreamer ("schizoid")	BS TH / PL
4a	Playful resister ("passive aggressive")	TH / BS
4b	Charming manipulator ("antisocial")	BS (PL)

BP: Be Perfect; BS: Be Strong; HU: Hurry Up; PL: Please others; TH: Try Hard.

You need to be cautious about putting people firmly in one personality adaptation box. Sometimes people have aspects of more than one adaptation. And sometimes they have very different adaptations in different ego states. For example, Tim has a Responsible Workaholic adaptation in his Parent ego state and a Playful Resister adaptation in his Child ego state.

In any case, there is no point in categorising people unless the category you put them in is going to affect what you do. Diagnosis is only useful for selecting treatment. But what personality adaptation people hold is very significant if you want to work with them effectively, particularly in a one-to-one relationship such as coaching. We have already seen the significance of the Feeling, Thinking, Doing triangle, and indeed how key this is to the whole concept of emotional intelligence. Knowing the other's personality adaptation helps you negotiate your way around the triangle with them, and to manage your relationship with them effectively, particularly if it is a change facilitation relationship. The relationships between the various personality adaptations and Feeling, Thinking and Doing are summarised in Table 8.4.

Table 8.4 *The doors to influence.*

	Open——▷	Target——▷	Trap
1 (a and b)	T	F	D
2	F	T	D
3	D	T	F
4 (a and b)	D	F	T

T: thinking; F: feeling; D: doing.

Always move from left to right, not from right to left
Based on: Paul Ware, Transitional Analysis Journal, 1983

You will see that while there are three processes of Feeling, Thinking and Doing, there are six basic personality adaptations, and that the "Target" door is either Feeling or Thinking but never Doing. This means that of the six adaptations, two pairs share their sequence of doors to influence: Responsible Workaholics and Brilliant Sceptics have the same sequence, and so do Playful Resisters and Charming Manipulators.

The significance of the sequence is this: the left-hand column, the "Open" or "Contact" door, represents the process through which a person is most open to contact when interacting with other people. It is, therefore, the place where you need to meet them initially. The middle column, the "Target" door, represents the process that wasn't properly valued or satisfied when they were children, and where deep down underneath they want to be met and what they want to be valued for. The right-hand column, the "Trap" door, represents the process that either they avoid or they use nonproductively and as an avoidance of the other two useful doors. So this is where you *don't* want to meet them, particularly at first. In fact, the general rule for effective relationship management and change facilitation is always to move from left to right across the sequence of doors, and never from right to left.

If you do go straight into the trap door, what will happen will depend on the person's personality adaptation, but it will always be unwelcome and unproductive. If you start by trying to change the behaviour of Responsible Workaholics or Brilliant Sceptics, they will tend to get frightened and/or angry. These people are motivated by fear and they are already doing the best they possibly can to survive, so if you suggest they do something different, they will either be frightened because that will mean that they are no longer doing what they need to do to allay their fear, or angry because they are already doing their best and they can't do any more. Similarly, if you start by trying to change the behaviour of Enthusiastic Overreactors, it won't work. Their doing will be chaotic and ineffective (thinking having been overlooked) and they will feel unmet and misunderstood by you because you do not respond to their surface feeling. The Creative Daydreamers, on the other hand, will respond well if you confront their withdrawal (a behavioural intervention), but will run a mile if you start by trying to relate to them on a feeling basis and to explore their feeling, because initially they are terrified of feeling: they have decided that the way to survive is not to feel and not to need. Playful Resisters and Charming Manipulators are again different: they will not run a mile if you meet them with thinking, in fact that is what they may offer you, but if you think with them, you (and they) will just go round and round in circles and get nowhere. The Playful Resisters have an investment in this (they need to try hard but not succeed) and the Charming Manipulators will, in a regretful and unblamey way, suggest that it is all your fault and they are not responsible. With both, you need to start by confronting their behaviour, the passive aggression of the Playful Resisters and the manipulation of the Charming Manipulators.

There are other little tricks that you can employ if you have diagnosed your coachee's personality adaptation. For example, using humour and teasing works very well with Playful Resisters, but is a recipe for disaster with Brilliant Sceptics. However, the main point of determining someone's personality adaptation is to help you decide in which order in the development of the relationship to relate to them in terms of Feeling, Thinking and

Doing. So crucial is this that as a rule of thumb you can take it that if the relationship is going nowhere and you (and your coachee) are stuck, that will be for one of two reasons: *either* you do not have a proper contract for change with your coachee *or* you are playing into their trap door.

Conversely, you can use the connection between trap doors and negative relationship outcomes in a diagnostic way: if you start a relationship with someone and it seems to be going all wrong or getting nowhere, that probably means that you are playing into their trap door, and that will help you in identifying their personality adaptation.

You will notice that all the personality adaptations except one (the Enthusiastic Overreactor) have Be Strong as one of their component conditions of worth (or "drivers"), and that in two cases (Creative Daydreamer and Charming Manipulator) it is the sole primary driver, and in one case (Brilliant Sceptic) one of two joint primary drivers. Given that "Be Strong" means "Don't have or express feelings or needs", this underlies how crucial feeling is to being a well-functioning, emotionally healthy human being, and how much feelings are not responded to properly in childhood. This is where a good chunk of the interferences which impede us from being emotionally intelligent in adulthood come from.

Interindividual differences

Individuals differ one from another in an infinite variety of ways apart from their level of self regard. The particular patterns of difference, which it will often be important to take into account in a change facilitation relationship, may be summarised under the following headings:

- TA
- MBTI
- NLP
- Gender.

TA

We have already looked at the most important variables derived from the TA theoretical framework: life position, conditions of worth ("drivers") and personality adaptation. It will also help in managing the relationship to recognise the other's ego states, their ego-gram (what proportion of the time they spend in each of the five functional ego states of Controlling Parent, Nurturing Parent, Adult, Free or Natural Child and Adapted Child) and their primary Adapted Child mode: Rebellious, Conforming or Procrastinating.

MBTI

If you are familiar with the Jungian typology used in the Myers Briggs Type Inventory and find that to be a useful indicator of how to respond to and relate to others, you may find it helpful to classify your coachee in MBTI terms. And of course this may be easy to do, since they may have previously completed the MBTI and be willing to share the outcome with you. A word of warning, though, about the differences between the Jungian MBTI approach and our EI approach, because they are fundamentally different. On the whole, the MBTI approach is non-evaluative and descriptive in nature: either end of the polarities is considered equal in value to the other. And, though there appears occasionally to be some equivocation on this point, the preferences indicated by the inventory are seen to be inborn and relatively fixed. Apart from the introversion–extraversion dimension (for which there is evidence that our position is indeed inborn – see the work of Hans Eysenck), we see some of the positions on other dimensions to be acquired and to be the result of interferences, and consequently an impediment to emotional intelligence. Someone who has a high preference for S, and therefore a low preference for N, we would see as probably someone who is low in bodily awareness and therefore not in touch with the information coming to them non-cognitively through their intuition. Someone who scores as either an extreme F or an extreme T is, by definition, not going to be able to integrate their thinking and their feeling and is therefore going to be to that extent less emotionally intelligent. And someone who prefers J rather than P we would see as in that respect likely to be lower in emotional intelligence, in that attitudinally they will be less likely to be able to respond to themselves and others with non-judgemental acceptance, which is likely to interfere with their Self Regard, their Regard for Others, their Self Awareness and their Awareness of Others, indirectly with a number of other scales and with their capacity for effective relationship management in general.

In the case of extraversion–introversion, we agree with the Jungian position that these are relatively fixed, and neither is better or worse than the other: emotional intelligence is demonstrated by how you manage being extravert or introvert, rather than by being one or the other. There is another polarity to some degree overlapping and correlated with extraversion–introversion, which you may find it helpful to situate your coachee on: Fear of Abandonment – Fear of Engulfment. To some degree one can argue that extraverts will fear abandonment and introverts will fear engulfment, and often this will be the case. But not always. And also, whereas one either is extravert or introvert, to whatever degree, in many people insofar as abandonment / engulfment is concerned, the fear of one often seems to overlay and protect against an even more profound fear of the other. (A possible indicator of where they stand on this dimension will be furnished by their score on Scale 16: those with a fear of abandonment are likely to be dependent and those with a fear of engulfment overindependent.)

Despite the theoretical differences between our EI approach and that of users of the MBTI, in practice they prove remarkably complementary. Many experienced MBTI users find the *ie*™ very useful, in that it suggests to them and to their clients what sort of thing can be done in practice about the preferences turned up by the MBTI. A study of the correlations between the two tools is given at the end of Chapter 17 (pages 271–274).

NLP

Neurolinguistic Programming is basically a bundle of techniques for relating to and influencing others, derived from minute observation of the practice of a number of highly skilled therapists. One of its main typologies is based on "sense modalities", in other words the primary sense with which we respond to the world, and through which we are most influenceable by others. There are three flavours:

Visual	(over 60% of the population)
Auditory	(over 30% of the population)
Kinaesthetic	(about 5% of the population).

The general rule is: for successful communication, use the other's primary mode and not your own if that is different.

So, with people who are predominantly visual, use pictures, graphs, charts, photographs, slides or anything that has a visual impact; invite them to imagine, to see in their mind's eye; use language such as, "Is this clear to you?" "Let me show you." "Does that look good to you?" (Their use of similar language can help you diagnose them as Visual). With people who are predominantly auditory, vary the pitch, tone and volume of your voice as you speak; talk to them on the telephone; use language such as, "Does that sound good to you?" "I'd like to amplify this point for you." "Are we in harmony on this?" (Their use of similar language can help you diagnose them as Auditory.) With people who are primarily kinaesthetic, get them moving physically, not just sat in a chair all the time; do whatever is necessary for them to get a feel for what you are talking about; let them trial any proposals before making a firm decision; make sure this person feels comfortable with you and is indeed sitting comfortably; use language like, "How will you get to grips with this?" "What needs to happen so that you'd feel more comfortable with the idea?" "I want to get a handle on your objectives." (Their use of similar language can help you diagnose them as Kinaesthetic.)

Gender

This section is not about helping you learn to diagnose whether your coachee is a man or a woman: we hope you will know the answer to that already! Rather, it is about the characteristic differences in values and in communication style between the two genders, and as such is bound to consist of very broad generalisations. First, an interindividual difference which correlates to a degree with gender, but with a significant number of exceptions: product-orientation versus process-orientation. Those people who are product-oriented (a greater proportion of men than of women) are primarily interested in the outcome, the end product, the *What*. Those people who are process-oriented (a greater proportion of women than of men) are primarily interested in how you get to the outcome, the process, the *How*. For both kinds, where their primary interest lies will affect how they tackle issues, and you can understand that there is room for a mutual misunderstandings, between one person who is product-oriented and another who is process-oriented.

The other common differences between male and female values and communication styles are perhaps best shown by Table 8.5.

Table 8.5 *The differences between male and female values.*

Women:		Men:
Intimacy	vs.	Independence
"We're close and the same"	vs.	"We're separate and different"
Connection	vs.	Status
Near / far	vs.	Up / down
Being	vs.	Doing
Feeling	vs.	Thinking and behaving

If you are working with someone of the same gender as yourself and you are both typical of your gender, you can probably ignore all this. But if you are working with someone of the opposite gender, you may need to make a conscious effort to meet them where they are coming from, rather than on your home ground, or at least to be aware of the difference in your frames of reference. (For more about gender differences in communication see Deborah Tannen's *You Just Don't Understand* (1992).)

The dangers of categorisation

The point about exploring these individual differences is to encourage you to respond more appropriately to the variety of individuals you will be working with. However, all generalisations are to some degree untrue (including this one), and the danger of providing diagnostic categories is that it will lead you to attach fixed labels to those you work with, rather than responding to their individual uniqueness in both a conscious and an intuitive way. Remember Principle no. 3: People are different. All diagnoses should be adopted only provisionally and should be revised as soon as they need to be.

References

Joines, V. and Stewart, I. (2002) *Personality Adaptations: A New Guide to Human Understanding in Psychotherapy and Counselling*, Lifespace Publishing.

Stewart, I. and Joines, V. (1987) *TA Today: A new introduction to transactional analysis*, Lifespace Publishing.

Tannen, D. (1992) *You Just Don't Understand: Women and Men in Conversation*. Virago Press Ltd.

Ware, P. (1983) "Personality Adaptations", *Transactional Analysis Journal*, **13**(1), 11–19.

9

Body awareness

"The intuitive mind is a sacred gift and the rational mind is a faithful servant. We have created a society that honours the servant and has forgotten the gift"
Albert Einstein

This chapter discusses the scales of:

4 Self Awareness
5 Awareness of Others.

Within each scale you will find:

- a definition;
- a more in-depth description;
- more information to help you understand the relevant EI theory;
- exercises to help you develop each scale.

Awareness is about having our minds open. When we can perceive things as they really are, we can deal with that reality rather than our not necessarily accurate perceptions of that reality or our assumptions about what it is.

There are two kinds of awareness essential for acting with emotional intelligence: our self awareness, which is about being in touch with how we feel and being open to the non-cognitive information at our disposal through our body; and our awareness of others, how able we are to understand where other people are at and what may be going on for them. Both require an absence of judgement.

4   Self Awareness

Being in touch with your feeling states

This scale measures the extent to which you are in touch with your body, your feelings and your intuition. Self awareness is key to acting with emotional intelligence. The more aware we are of what we want and what we feel about things, the more able we are to make those things happen or communicate how we feel with conviction.

Self awareness is highly dependent on self regard – if you are secure in your "OKness", you can afford to be aware of whatever you are feeling without your value being threatened. However, if your "OKness" is dependent on you being and feeling a certain way, and so you judge the acceptability of what you feel, you will soon impair your capacity to perceive it – judgement is the enemy of perception and understanding.

Feelings don't live in the brain – they are whole-body experiences (think of "getting hot under the collar", "having cold feet"). They can be fleeting or, if you let them, they can take you over. They can last for a few seconds or as a mood they can, if you let them, last for days. By learning to pay attention to, and to attune yourself to, what is going on in your body, you will increase your awareness of your feeling states and intuition.

Feelings have a logic and a pattern of their own. You will be able to manage yourself much more effectively if you know your patterns. Some people, for example, don't find it easy to acknowledge that they are frightened, but turn the fear instead into anger. They gain a lot more control when they begin to understand this process, to know when their apparent anger is, in fact, fear disguised, and to work out what they are afraid of.

Try using your intuition. Most people who think of themselves as unintuitive are, in fact, as intuitive as the next person; they just don't pay attention to their intuition.

Understanding your PNI

In Chapter 5 we introduced the concept of psychoneuroimmunology – or PNI for short. Our bodies are like barometers, giving us additional information on how we are thinking and feeling. By becoming more bodily aware, we can tune in to what our body is trying to tell us. This is important for identifying what we really want out of situations and our lives (see Goal Directedness in Chapter 11) and crucial for helping us manage our stress (see Emotional Resilience, also in Chapter 11) and stay healthy – "The body only screams when we don't listen to its whispers . . .".

Feelings can be physiological (such as hunger pangs), emotional (expressions of anger or anxiety for example) or intuitive (non-cognitive information that may be useful). The more observant we become about our different bodily states, the more we will have access to the additional information at our disposal through our physiology. These bodily states will often have thoughts or ideas which go with them, which may describe or define them and which can be used to express them.

One of our aims at the Centre for Applied Emotional Intelligence is to continue our exploration into PNI further, particularly through the work of Dr Alex Concorde, as this is so important for the raising of self awareness (see Chapter 5).

Developing your feeling awareness

To get you started though, here are some exercises to help you raise your own bodily awareness. Of course, it is quite difficult to become aware of things you are not aware of, particularly as you are by definition likely to be unaware that you are unaware of them! It is rather like trying to pull yourself up by your own bootstraps. The exercises here will help people developing their EI on their own, but one of the advantages of having a coaching relationship with a skilled EI practitioner and facilitator is that they will able to draw your attention to your body language and your feeling patterns that you may otherwise be unaware of. They will be able to help you develop your feelings awareness more directly in a feelings oriented way, rather than going at it somewhat indirectly by adopting certain patterns of behaviour.

Do regular body checks

One simple way to increase your awareness of what is going on for you and in you is to use the following technique:

- At regular intervals briefly switch off from your thoughts and activities and from the world around you.
- Close your eyes.

- Let yourself be aware of what is going on in the various bits of your body.
- Ask yourself, "What does this physical feeling signify in terms of my emotions?", "Why do I feel like this?" and "What, if anything, do I need to do about that?"

Describe the feelings that you experience in your body. Which ones seem to occur more regularly?

Learn your feeling patterns

As we have seen, feelings have a logic and a pattern of their own, and you will be able to manage yourself much more effectively if you know your patterns.

- Get in touch with a feeling.
- Reflect on where it came from and why.
- Identify how it is connected with your other feelings.

This way you will begin to learn just how your particular feeling economy works.

List the emotions that you experience whilst undertaking this exercise. Which ones seem to be more intense or regular, and what head-talk seems to go with each one?

Develop your intuition

Again, as we have seen, most people who think of themselves as unintuitive are, in fact, as intuitive as the next person; they just don't pay attention to their intuition.

To change this, when you have a decision to make:

- After you have worked out in your head what is logically the best thing to do and before you commit yourself, pause.
- Check out with your gut and the rest of your body whether it really seems the best thing to *all* of you.
- Do you want to do it? If different parts of you (brain vs. gut, Adult vs. Child) give different answers, conduct a debate between them until you arrive at a compromise solution that all bits of you can live with.

After undertaking this a few times, describe any additional useful information that your intuition has provided you with.

5 Awareness of Others

Being in touch with their feeling states

A healthy awareness of others (as opposed to a hyperacute awareness) stems from a high regard for others. Being able to value and accept others for who they are means you can see past the behaviour to what is really going on with them.

To have good relationships with others, to work well with them and even to fight them effectively, you need to know accurately what is going on for them in feeling terms. Tuning in to the information supplied by people's bodies, starting out with high respect for others, is the foundation for relationship management.

Developing your other awareness

Empathy is a particular, feelings-based form of other awareness. You can be aware of other people at a purely cognitive level, noticing in a thinky way what is going on for them. Empathy is a process whereby you "step into another person's shoes" and imaginatively experience the world as they do. Empathy's Greek derivation literally means "feeling inside". When you are being empathic you will find that you can recognise and share other people's fears, concerns and feelings. Use the checklist below to identify where your empathic skills are high and where you may be able to improve them. For each of the points below decide whether you: "are competent at this skill and use it often", "use this skill sometimes but are aware that you could improve it", or "seldom or never apply this skill".

How often do you . . . ? When was the last time you . . . ?

- noticed how someone else is feeling;
- enquired genuinely about how someone is feeling;
- acknowledged someone's feelings;
- addressed the issue of conflict or anger with someone;
- tolerated silence;
- noticed your own body language;

- invited someone to express their feelings;
- felt comfortable with closeness/affection;
- helped someone to express their feelings;
- noticed the body language of someone;
- felt comfortable when someone expressed strong feelings.

Which of these do you find particularly difficult? Why do you think that is?

Check out your assumptions

We spend a lot of time making assumptions about what other people are thinking and feeling on the basis of their behaviour and body language. Yet we seldom take the trouble to check out how true or false our assumptions are. And, even with people we know well, we are often wrong.

You can greatly enhance the accuracy of your deductions about what people are feeling by checking out with them. "When you frown like that, I imagine that you are angry with me. How right am I?" The job of the other – and you need to ask them explicitly to do this – is not to contradict your guess flatly (there will usually be some basis for your assumption) but to hunt for the grain of truth. "I'm not angry, but I am preoccupied. I'm worried about X" or "Yes, I am feeling angry, but not with you".

Pay attention to others' feelings

If it is not something you normally do, focus consciously when interacting with other people or observing them on what you think they are feeling. See if you can learn the particular feeling patterns of some other people you know well.

Real listening

Effective listening helps us to understand other people. Without this skill we may find that we irritate other people, miss out on vital information, fail to understand the other person's point of view, negotiate poorly and damage relationships.

Rate the statements in Table 9.1 below from 1 (rarely) to 5 (very often), to assess how effective your listening skills are and to identify any unhelpful listening behaviours that you may wish to overcome.

Table 9.1 *How effective are your listening skills?*

When listening to others I:	Frequency (1–5)
1. Stop listening because I am planning what to say next	
2. Label the other person based on what they are saying	
3. Listen only through the filter of my existing knowledge of the person	
4. Interrupt the other person	
5. Stop the other person from following his or her own train of thought	
6. Allow myself to become distracted by thoughts or external events	
7. Diagnose situations quickly, providing what I think the right answer is	
8. Dismiss their concerns as silly or irrelevant	
9. Trivialise the matter, telling the other person that it is not worth getting upset about	
10. Turn the conversation around so that it is about me and not the other person	

Which of the ten behaviours do you sometimes, or even often adopt? Why do you think that is?

As an exercise with a partner, one of you talk about something you really care about and the other person *pretend to listen*, although you are actually thinking about something else. Swap roles. *What does it feel like?*

Another, even more uncomfortable, version of this exercise is for the person who is supposed to be listening to demonstrate, rather than attempt to hide, their distraction and lack of connection: don't make eye contact, look away, fidget, scratch, don't acknowledge the other. Again, do this both ways round. *What was that like?*

Listen with your eyes as well as your ears

Practise, when in conversation with someone else or observing others, consciously paying attention to the information which is coming to you from people's bodies rather than concentrating solely, as we often do, on the words they use.

A handy exercise to help you check how well you are doing with this is to watch a piece of television (start with a soap opera – the hammy overacting makes it easier!) with the sound turned down, and just from the body language work out what is going on. Then replay it with the sound audible and see how accurate your assessment is.

List the different aspects of body language you are noticing and the different messages they are giving you.

For more about effective listening see the following chapter, which looks at the topic of active empathic listening in the context of the development facilitation relationship.

10

Facilitating EI development 2 – "Being with"

"You cannot teach a man anything; you can only help him find it within himself"
Galileo

In the development facilitation relationship that lies at the heart of emotional intelligence development, you need to be with the other in a manner which

- promotes a warm, open, cooperative relationship;
- helps the other self explore and increase their self knowledge;
- attends to the other and allows you to gather more information;
- promotes the other's self regard; and
- models emotional intelligence.

Quite a list! Luckily the criteria for doing any one of these are pretty much the same as for doing any of the others, so it is not as daunting as it seems at first sight. There are three basic elements:

- active listening;
- the right attitude: respectful and empathic;
- giving strokes in an emotionally intelligent way.

Combining empathy and real listening

Active empathic listening

It is, in a way, unfortunate that real, effective listening has come to be known as "active listening". One can understand why: in contrast to more common-or-garden listening, which is limited to passively paying attention to what someone else is saying, it is certainly more active and acknowledges the two-way and multi-stage nature of interpersonal communication.

Communication is two-way and has four stages:

1. A expresses.
2. B hears and has a response.
3. B tells A that/what s/he has heard.
4. B tells A what his/her response is.

N.B. stage 4 is optional and can be delayed, or may constitute the beginning of another round.

This model is an improvement on the one-way single-stage model implicit in everyday English usage, where having a conversation with George is referred to as "talking to George", but actually it is still an over-simplification. It is impossible to carry out stage 3 without implicitly doing some of stage 4; even if we merely repeat back A's words verbatim, our manner of speaking and our tone of voice will give away the crucial attitudinal elements of our response.

The trouble with calling it "active listening" is that it suggests that the essence of it is an activity, something that you do to someone, whereas really it is more than that – it is a way of being with someone. This underlines how important the attitudinal elements are, as opposed merely to the skills involved (training in "active listening" is often called "listening skills training"). We attempt to acknowledge this distinction by referring to "active empathic listening" rather than just "active listening".

Elements (1A to 2B) and outcomes (2C to 5) of active empathic listening

1A. You hear how other feels, thinks and wishes about this issue
1B. Other knows you have heard their feelings, thoughts and wishes
2A. You accept other and their feelings, thoughts and wishes
2B. Other knows you accept them and their feelings, thoughts and wishes, so . . .
2C. Other accepts self and own feelings, thoughts and wishes, so . . .
3.   Other explores own feelings, thoughts and wishes further, and
4.   Other's relationship with you and with self is deepened, and
5.   Other's self esteem is raised.

It will be apparent from the above list that active empathic listening does much more than give us information about the other and their feeling state. It has a significant effect on the other's self esteem / self regard and therefore is an important weapon in our armoury if we are working as a change facilitator with someone whose self esteem is low. It also has a profound effect on the quality of the relationship between us and them and therefore is a significant element in effective relationship management.

Active listening skills

Despite the importance of attitudes in allowing us to be close to another using active empathic listening, there are certainly important skills involved, which we may consider under the four headings:

- reflective listening;
- active talking;
- validating;
- empathic listening.

Reflective listening

Mirroring

This refers not so much to the listening process itself, but to the necessary preliminaries of setting the scene for it and the physical accompaniment to it, to the process of "creating rapport". If we match the other's body postures, energy levels, voice pitch and voice tone, we are conveying the unconscious message, "I have noticed where you are at and I am joining you". This is experienced as respectful; it invites the other to be more wherever they are, and at the very least it does not provide a distraction by introducing an alien element derived from us rather than from them.

Verbatim reflection

The key element of active listening is that not only do we hear what the other says, but we let them know that we have done so, and the simplest and most direct way to do that is to repeat their words back to them. It is surprising how much you can do this without the other being irritated or distracted by your parroting or becoming suspicious of it as a "technique".

Paraphrasing

Eventually, however, verbatim reflection does get too much and some variation is needed. So, an alternative is to repeat back the meaning in different words – to paraphrase. This also has a particular advantage over verbatim repetition in that it provides a check on whether you have picked up the meaning of what the other is saying correctly. If you repeat something back verbatim, you may have interpreted the words in quite a different way from what was intended, but neither of you will ever know. But if you give a paraphrase of your interpretation, then it will become apparent if the meaning of that is different from the meaning the speaker attached to what they originally said.

Reflecting feelings

Here we begin to enter the realms of empathy. This is about reflecting back not what is said, but what is not explicitly said but is key. A lot of this we will pick up through the process of empathy by attending to the nonverbal aspects of the other's contributions: not just what they say but how they say it, the way they use their voice, their gestures and posture. Reflecting this back in words, and not just by mirroring, may bring to the other's con- sciousness aspects of what is going on for them, in particular their feeling responses to what they are talking about, of which they were not previously aware. But you need to be careful: getting it wrong can be a severe inter- ruption to the process, so you need to offer your reflection of what you expe- rience as their underlying feeling tentatively and not definitively.

Active talking

At various points – later rather than earlier – in the process of active empathic listening we may need to do more to facilitate the other in their exploration than just repeat back to them. When we or they are not clear about some aspect, or are vague, then some gentle questions (from within their frame of reference) are in order. And towards the end, or every now and then in a long session, it is helpful to summarise all of what has gone before.

Questioning / focusing

There are two kinds of questions you may need to use. When you are not clear exactly what the other is meaning you can use a clarifying question, such as, "When you say they couldn't care less, who are you thinking of?" And when you suspect that the other is not clear either, then you need focusing questions, such as, "I can hear that it seems hard to you. What about it is particularly hard? . . . In what way is it hard for you?"

Summarising

One of the benefits for the other of experiencing active empathic listening is that it allows and encourages them to put together into a coherent whole all the different responses they have on a particular issue. You can help them do this by summarising what they have said, and the key here is not to leave out any aspect when doing so. Often they will have a variety of conflicting responses, and they all need to be fully acknowledged rather than being smoothed away in an all-inclusive compromise. The key here is to use ". . . both . . . , and . . .", and not "either . . . or . . .", nor ". . . , but . . .".

Validating

Hearing

Just letting the other know, without comment or evaluation, that you have heard what they have said is, in itself, experienced by the other as validating of them and their feelings.

Accepting

The trick here is to be accepting without being evaluative. Not "that was a perfectly proper response", but "I can understand you responding in that way". (Even to say "Right" as an acknowledgement at the end of the other's paragraphs is dangerous: it implies that you are listening in a judging frame of mind, and although on this occasion the judgement was favourable, on another it might not be.) Mostly what is involved here is an absence of non-accepting responses: no frowns, no surprised "Did you really?", no judgement, let alone disapproval.

Respecting

This is about behaving respectfully towards the other, as well as being accepting of what they are telling you. So you are validating them with what they are telling you.

Active empathic listening

There are five requirements for empathic listening, for being with the other in such a way that you enter their frame of reference, understand their experience from the inside and feel what they are feeling:

- empty yourself: be with the other;
- attention;
- acceptance;
- no judgement or comparison;
- stay with the feeling.

Empty yourself: be with the other

You will not be able to attend to the other properly, let alone "get inside" them, if you are busy with your own concerns. "Empty yourself" sounds a tall order, but it can be learned with practice. You need to reassure the part of you that is busy with your own concerns that you are not uninterested and permanently abandoning it and them, that you will return and deal with what needs to be dealt with when this empathic listening session is over. And then you psychologically put your own concerns up on a shelf, out of sight, to be picked up later.

Attention

Having distanced yourself from your own concerns, you are in a position to attend to the other. Your aim is to understand what it is like being them, with their frame of reference, their needs and their feelings. To do this you need to attend to what they are telling you with their words, and the way they say them, and with their body language.

Acceptance

We have just looked at acceptance in terms of its effect on the other, as part of validating them and their feelings. Here, the focus is on the effect on us. If we do not accept the other, then we will not be able to see them as they are, let alone to join them there.

No judgement or comparison

One of the main requirements of acceptance is an absence of judgement or comparison. Judgement is the enemy of perception. And of course it would have a deleterious effect on the other and their response to us, as well as on our capacity to empathise.

Stay with the feeling

We have already seen that empathy means "feeling from within". The core of being empathic is therefore about joining the other in their feeling. And one of the virtues of being empathically listened to is that it encourages us to explore and go deeper into our feelings. So, if you find emotion, your own or other people's, difficult to be around, this is something you will have to address in order to be an empathic listener. Sometimes people are afraid that if they stay with a feeling it will last forever, but that is not the case. Feelings have their own time-limited life; it is only semi-suppressed feelings that drag on and on. Children can grizzle for hours and hours, but if they let themselves, and are allowed to, have a good cry, then it is over in a matter of minutes.

As Table 10.1 shows, active empathic listening has many advantages over questioning, both as an information-gathering technique and in terms of the effect it has on the relationship. Its one disadvantage is that it does take longer, but in the long run the time is far from wasted.

Still, there comes a time in any relationship when you have questions which you want to ask, and in any development relationship there comes a

Table 10.1 *The advantages and disadvantages of active empathic listening and questioning.*

Active empathic listening	Questioning
• Takes longer	• Speedy
• Open-ended, exploratory	• Focused, closed
• Elicits facts *and* feelings, values, motivation	• Elicits facts and thinking
• Elicits respondent's frame of reference	• Imposes questioner's frame of reference
• Experienced as respectful	• Can be experienced as controlling
• Heightens sense of your being "on my side"	• Can be experienced as exploitative
• Brings parties warmly together	• Establishes parties as being separate, apart

time when you want to pin the other down to something specific. So the question arises: how do you combine the virtues of active empathic listening and focused questioning? It is all a question of timing:

advanced empathic listening comes first;
focused questioning and closure-oriented negotiation comes second.

Giving strokes

In Chapter 7 we looked at how to receive strokes, both positive and negative, in a way that protected and enhanced our level of self regard. Here we are looking at the other side of the coin: at how to give strokes, rather than how to receive them, in a manner which protects and enhances the other's self regard. Giving strokes effectively is one of the marks of effective relationship management, and you therefore need to model that for all those you work with. Also, since most of those you work with, whether their life position is I+ U–, I– U+ or I– U–, will have a problem to some degree with low self regard, your pattern of stroking will potentially have a powerful effect on helping them deal with this problem.

Here are some guidelines.

Giving praise / appreciation

1. Work out what they want to hear.
   Of course, sometimes you feel impelled to respond to a person with a particular positive stroke in the moment. But if you want to help build a particular person's self regard or self confidence, then you will need to

work out what kind of stroke will be especially powerful for that person. For example, it used to be said that pretty girls liked to be told that they were clever and clever girls liked to be told that they were pretty. Certainly, positive strokes will be more powerful when they address those aspects of us that we are least confident about.

2. Public or private?

The general rule is to give praise and appreciation in public, but as always it is a question of individual judgement as to what is most appropriate on each occasion. Some very shy people would be mortified to be publicly praised, and for them, obviously, you do it in private. Also, some kinds of loving appreciation are quite intimate and perhaps best done in private.

3. Behaviour / doing *and/or* person / being.

Conditional or unconditional? Doing or being? Or both? Sometimes the combination of the two together is particularly powerful.

4. Specific *and* general.

The combination of specific and general is usually more effective than either on its own. Just the specific on its own can be very limited and can be dismissed as a flash in the pan. Just the general on its own can be very woolly and can be dismissed for vagueness. So say something like, "I think you are a wonderful speaker, and in particular I really enjoyed the way you touched people's feelings when talking at the school dinner last night."

5. Make and keep good contact.

Particularly eye contact. This may – if they break contact by looking away – involve asking them directly, "Hey! What I am saying to you is important and I'd like you to look at me while I am saying it to you."

6. Take your time.

Remember the first rule for receiving positive strokes: make sure you slow down.

7. Personalise.

Expressions of feeling that start with the word "I" are much more powerful and touching positive strokes than are impersonal judgements beginning "You" or "That".

8. Thinking *and* feeling.

Some people respond most easily to the world with feelings and some with thoughts. The way to be sure that you hit the target, and to double your firepower, is to express your positive strokes in both feeling and thinking terms. "I am absolutely delighted that you won the prize and I think you entirely deserved it."

9. Verbal *and* nonverbal.

Another way of doubling the impact. "Well done!" on its own is fine. A pat on the back on its own is also fine. But "Well done!" accompanied by a pat on the back has more effect than the sum of the two separately.

10. Repeat.

Either word for word or in a paraphrase.

11. Make sure they have taken it in.

Because people, especially people with low self esteem, have a tendency to filter out and to distort positive strokes which are given them, we need to check that they have received what we have given.

Giving negative feedback

1. Avoid shaming – usually in private.

The general rule is: positives in public and negatives in private. But this is not absolute and you need to make a conscious decision each time. Examples of occasions when you might want to give negative feedback in public include:

- When you want to enlist the support of those around in enforcing the behaviour you require rather than the one the person has used.
- When the feedback is directed not only at the person addressed but also (indirectly) at other people within earshot.
- When (and this is, in a sense, a subdivision of the previous category) issues of safety are involved.

2. Contract.

One of the most common ways to give negative feedback hamfistedly is to have an emotional reaction to something that someone else has done and then, without any preliminary or agreement, to go and dump your feelings on them. With an adult you should always contract, "I have some negative feedback for you about X. Is now a good time?" It is important to remember that the point of the exercise is the other's response, not your feeling better for letting off steam. (In terms of a distinction introduced under Emotional Expression and Control (see

Chapter 12), this needs to be *instrumental* behaviour rather than *expressive* behaviour.)

3. Behaviour – doing *not* being.

Negative strokes should always be conditional about doing, i.e. negative feedback, rather than unconditional about being, i.e. put downs.

4. Specific and succinct.

Negative feedback should be as specific as possible, with precise examples when a general point is being made. Overgeneral feedback about doing verges on the unconditional: "This is how you are", and may be experienced as a put down. "Specific" needn't mean a long rigmarole: keep it short and sweet too. Just tell, don't justify.

5. As soon as possible after the event.

Negative feedback should be given as soon as possible after the event, so that the recipient can do something about it and the giver avoids nursing their grievance over an extended period of time.

6. Ask for change / reparation.

To those who are conflict avoidant it may seem a bit over the top not only to give someone negative feedback when you don't like what they do, but then to ask for change or reparation. But actually, it makes it much easier for the other person to take and enables the relationship to be repaired in the process of dealing with the issue. If you just say to someone, "I didn't like it when you did that", they have two options. Either, from the "I'm OK, You're Not OK" position, they can say, "So?" implying that they are in the right and you are in the wrong; that they matter and you don't. Or, from the "I'm Not OK, You're OK" position, they can say, "Oh dear! I'm terribly sorry" implying that they are in the wrong and you are in the right; that they don't matter and that you do. Either way, the two parties in the relationship do not end up warm and close and on a level. But if you ask for them to do it differently, to apologise or to make it up to you, and after negotiation they agree to do something which satisfies you, then both parties can end up OK and can be warm, on a level and close again.

7. Personalise.

We often tend to give negative feedback impersonally, perhaps because it seems safer or it sounds more portentous, but this is always a concealment for the fact that we are telling them something about us, about a personal negative reaction we have had. When we say, "That was a horrible thing to do" we are being God-like, or at least Parent-like; what we really mean is, "I didn't like that; I experienced it as horrible." Everybody is different and other people might have had quite different reactions. And even if they didn't, what is important is that this is how *we* felt. To give an impersonal judgement is to come from "I'm OK, You're Not OK", from a one-up position, whereas to give a personal reaction is coming from "I'm OK, You're OK". We are not being judgemental, but giving information to the other about our feeling state.

8. The + − + sandwich.

The idea of this sandwich is that it makes it more difficult for the recipient of specific negative feedback to overgeneralise it and to convert it into a put down. The danger is that it may be done mechanically and in a way that leads the recipient to see through the stratagem. Lots of business managers have been introduced to the sandwich, but because they have not at the same time been trained to alter the overall balance of their strokes so that they give many more positives than negatives, it ends up that they only give positive strokes when sandwiching a negative one. Their employees recognise this pattern and when their boss comes and says something nice to them they immediately respond inwardly with, "Uh-oh, here comes the shit sandwich." So it is important not to overdo this one, nor to do it too mechanically. It is, nonetheless, useful for people with very low self esteem, who have a tendency to convert negative feedback into a put down. It is harder for them to do this if the specific negative feedback is sandwiched between generalised expressions of love and acceptance.

9. Avoid battles to be right.

People are different; they will like and dislike different things and think that different things are or are not OK. This is not about who is going to lay down the law, it is about telling one another where you stand and how you react and working out a way to coexist happily together despite your differences. So, when someone responds to a piece of negative feedback with some explanation and justification of what they did, what you need to do is to avoid an argument about who is right, but to acknowledge the differences. (See next point.)

10. Acknowledge the other first (before replying).

So, in response to the explanation / justification, you do not immediately leap into, "But I told you it upset me" or "That doesn't hold water because . . ."). What you do is acknowledge them first and then repeat where you are coming from. "I understand that your intentions were good and you thought you would save me trouble, but I have asked you before always to tell me when someone comes to the door; I am cross that you didn't and I want you to undertake always to tell me in future. Are you willing to do that?"

11. Summarise the discussion and any agreements made.

    At the end of the conversation, you need to summarise what has happened, what each person has told the other and what has been agreed. This makes it much more likely that such agreements will be kept. This review will also allow you to check that they have received your negative feedback as sent – from I+ U+ and addressed to their behaviour not their being. People with low self esteem are particularly prone to distorting legitimate negative feedback about what they have done into a put down of themselves as a person.

11

Managing oneself

"No man is free who is not master of himself"
Epictetus

This chapter discusses the scales of:

6   Emotional Resilience
7   Personal Power
8   Goal Directedness
9   Flexibility
10   Personal Openness and Connectedness
11   Invitation to Trust.

Within each scale you will find:

- a definition;
- a more in-depth description;
- more information to help you understand the relevant EI theory;
- exercises to help you develop each scale.

Our self management skills are underpinned by our Self Regard and our Self Awareness. The following aspects of self management are listed in decreasing order of their correlation with levels of Self Regard.

6   Emotional Resilience

The ease with which you pick yourself up and bounce back when things go badly for you indicates your emotional resilience. To hold on to our worth and ability in the face of disappointment or rejection we definitely need to believe "I'm OK", and to remain hopeful in a world filled with other people we need to believe "You're OK" too.

Some people are much better than others at supporting themselves and moving on in the face of disappointment, failure, rejection or under stress. This is related to a number of other aspects of emotional intelligence: Self Regard, Personal Power, Goal Directedness, Flexibility and – because when we are down we need support from others – Personal Openness and Connectedness. Emotional Resilience is also related to optimism. Above all, since both our stress response and depression are physiological phenomena, we need to be good at managing ourselves both physically and emotionally, and for that our Self Awareness needs to be high.

Developing emotional resilience

Developing any of the components of emotional intelligence discussed above, if they are low, will have a knock-on effect on your emotional resilience.

Support yourself physically

When we are stressed, depressed or just feeling unmotivated or a bit "down", this has a significant physical component and we need to look after ourselves bodily to rise above it. To do this, first we need to be aware of what is going on in our body (Scale 4), and then we need to know our patterns which tell us what we need to do about it (for example, extraverts tend to need stimulation and company when they are tired, whereas introverts need quiet and solitude). We can learn our patterns by tuning into our bodies and noticing what has an effect on us. Everybody, whatever their specific pattern, will be more resilient if they eat, drink, exercise and rest regularly and well, and if they have some fun and relaxation as well as endless work.

Get support from others

When we are in difficulty we need help from others. Not necessarily practical help but emotional help. We need to know that we are not alone, that other people care about us and what we are going through, and are on our side. For many people it is easier to talk to others about good things and successes rather than problems and failures. But it is just as important, if not more so, to talk to others when the going gets tough. If this doesn't come easily to you, make sure you start with someone you know well and trust to care about you, someone who knows how to listen and to empathise, someone who will not immediately come forward with advice about what to do (unless you ask them to). Eventually, the more people you have on your team the better.

Learn from your history of resilience

Even if we are not strong on emotional resilience, almost everybody has some kind of experience of picking themselves up and bouncing back successfully after a setback. By reviewing this experience we can learn what is supportive for us when the going gets tough and make sure that we get it for ourselves in the future. Different things work best for different people and we need to identify what works best for us.

7 Personal Power

This scale measures the extent to which you believe that you are in charge of, and take responsibility for, your outcomes in life, rather than seeing yourself as the victim of circumstances and/or of other people.

To fully own our personal power, we need to hold the "I'm OK, You're OK" position. Obviously, if we don't value ourselves we won't think of ourselves as in charge of our destiny. But also, if we think of other people as bad, we may fear their effect on us, so we need to hold them OK too.

As in so many areas of human behaviour, there is a self-fulfilling prophecy here: if we believe that we are in charge of our destiny, then, lo and behold!, we are: we are powerful and effective. If, however, we see ourselves as passive victims of others or of circumstances, then that comes about too: we do become powerless victims. Personal power is therefore highly correlated with effective performance.

Developing personal power

Your sense of personal power is intimately connected with your level of self regard, so if that is low you will need to raise it.

Get recognition for your achievements

If you underestimate your personal power, you need to register those occasions when you display it. So, at the end of every day run over in your mind the ways in which during the day you have been effective physically (manual dexterity, sport), mentally, socially, personally (handling your feelings and managing yourself) and organisationally. In the process you will probably learn how to be even more effective, but that is not the point. The point is to register how effective you already are. Also, get recognition from others. Ask for praise and acknowledgement of your achievements, your impact and effectiveness.

Calibrate your expectations of yourself

If you tend to set your sights low, to expect too little of yourself, you will seldom be stretched and have the experience of achievement against the odds, which would reinforce your sense of personal power. If you tend to set your sights too high, to expect too much of yourself, you will be setting yourself up to fail, and regular failure will undermine your sense of personal power. So you need to ensure that your goals are high enough to stretch you, not too easy to achieve, and yet low enough (below perfection!) to ensure that you more or less succeed most of the time.

Exploit the power you have

Sometimes it is true that we have little power: we are constrained by regulations, by circumstances, by authority or by other powerful people. But there are always corners, however small, where we are free to exercise our power. So, when you are feeling powerless, make sure that you identify the power you do have in the situation, exercise that and pay full attention to your impact when you do so. Even when you are forced to do something, you can usually choose when and how to do it, and you can always choose how to feel about it.

8   Goal Directedness

This scale measures the degree to which you direct your behaviour towards your own long-term goals. In order to set goals for yourself and to align your behaviour towards them whatever the temptations or distractions, you need to believe that you, and what you want, matter. Goal directedness is therefore dependent on feeling you are OK.

If you are going to realise your life goals, you need first to be aware of what they are – to know where you want to go. And then to keep those goals in mind so that what you do moves you towards them rather than away from them.

Developing goal directedness

What you most need to do to develop your goal directedness depends on what it is that currently interferes with your behaviour being directed toward the achievement of your goals.

Know what you want

If you are not a person who has realistic, clear, explicit and time-related goals, then your behaviour cannot be goal-directed. If this is the case, you need to set yourself goals on a number of time scales: where do you want to be in five years' time, in a year, six months, three months, one month, one week, tomorrow? If you find it difficult to do this because you do not know what you really want, you may find it useful to identify what you don't want and work backwards. And/or to concentrate on identifying what it is in your life which gives you pleasure and satisfaction, and then work out how to maximise the amount of that in your life. If you are not good at taking pleasure and satisfaction in things – and some people aren't – then you will need to develop that before you are able to work out what you want.

Avoid distractions

If you do have goals but your behaviour often does not move you towards the achievement of them, that may be because you are being distracted, either by yourself or by other people. If you tend to be distracted by yourself, then get into the habit of asking yourself at regular intervals, "Will this help me towards where I want to go?" "Will I be glad later that I have spent time and energy doing this now?" And adapt your behaviour according to the answer. If you tend to be distracted by attending to others and their needs, you need to realise that it is OK to please yourself rather than having to please others. See How to develop your self regard in Chapter 7.

Develop impulse control

People often don't move towards their long-term goals because they give into impulses which offer short-term satisfactions. This may be eating chocolate bars when you have a long-term goal to lose weight, or it may be losing your temper and being rude to someone whose cooperation you need. In either case, it can sometimes seem that you do this automatically and have no choice about it. But you do. The first thing to do is to reflect on and understand the pattern of these emotional hijacks after they have happened. As you begin to understand the process you will move from no-sight through hindsight to mid-sight and eventually foresight, so that you have a choice about what you want to do. The short-term tactic to increase your choicefulness is to count to ten before you react, and use that time to reflect on your choices and their long-term consequences.

9   Flexibility

This scale measures the degree to which you feel free to adapt your thinking and your behaviour to match the changing situations of life.

People who are very low on flexibility ("rigid") tend to be clinging to what they know and believe, and to their habitual patterns, from fear. To be flexible, to dare to experiment and risk failure, you need to value yourself, to feel OK about yourself. You also need to believe that the world is a relatively safe place not inhabited by dangerous people; in other words, that others are OK too. The most rigid people are sometimes those holding the "I'm OK, You're Not OK" position as a defence against "I'm Not OK, You're OK" and who do not want this façade to be undermined.

We live in a society which is changing faster than any society has changed before, and the rate of change seems to be increasing. Even if we have successfully solved life problems, repeating those solutions in the future is unlikely to work. So the premium on being flexible, on being ready, able and willing to react to changing circumstances in a different way, whether in terms of thinking, feeling or behaviour, is greater than ever. People sometimes think that flexibility is something you can have too much, as well as too little, of, but that is based on defining it as the *tendency* to bend and change, rather than as the *willingness* to do so when required, as we do.

Developing flexibility

Be aware of your automatic responses

If we are to learn to act flexibly, we need first to identify when we tend to react in a fixed, inflexible pattern. The easiest way to do this is to get feedback from others. Ask someone who knows you well to let you know when they think you are reacting in a standard, rigid way. Additionally, when you do something in an old familiar way, or when you resist someone's suggestion to do something in a different way, check whether you are exercising a free choice or whether you feel compelled to do it your own particular way. (You may need to raise your level of self awareness in order to identify the bodily tension that reveals the feeling of constraint and the fear of change and difference.) If you do identify a feeling of compulsion to do something a particular way, begin to think consciously about what would be frightening to you about an alternative.

Explore alternatives

Notice when people do things differently or react differently from the way you do. Observe the result. Find out from them why they behave the way they do and what that is like for them. If you want, you can use creative visualisation to explore what it would be like to behave or react differently from your usual way. Preliminary thought experiments may be less scary for you than plunging straight into doing it differently.

Remind yourself that change is possible

Move your watch from the wrist you normally keep it on to the other. Then, every time you need to know the time and search for your watch on one wrist and find it on the other, remind yourself that change is possible. When you get used to looking for it on the other wrist, move it back to the original one to keep yourself always on your toes!

10   Personal Openness and Connectedness

This scale measures the extent to which you make, and the ease with which you make, significant connections with other people by opening up yourself and your feelings to them.

The "I'm OK, You're OK" position is required for making good connections with others. People respond to being valued and respected, so "You're OK" is obviously required. But also, there is a risk involved in opening up to others, and in order to take that risk we need to be sure of our own value no matter what, so "I'm OK" is required too.

Our capacity for making connections with others is related to the quality of our work performance: it enables us to network effectively, to build alliances and to give and receive support in times of trouble. It also affects our whole life experience, since it will largely determine the quality of our relationships with other people. In order to connect with others effectively we need to open up ourselves and our feelings to them, to be high in Regard for Others (Scale 2), knowing how to listen acceptingly and nonjudgementally, and also high in Awareness of Others (Scale 5). We also need to be able to express our own feelings in ways that we choose as being appropriate (Scale 14) and we need to be the kind of person others are ready to trust (Scale 11).

Developing personal openness and connectedness

Take the risk of being open

We connect with others not just by sharing thoughts and ideas, beliefs and values, aims and objectives and by spending time together, but above all by sharing our feelings and our vulnerabilities. This may be difficult for you – there certainly is a risk involved; we need to choose the right person to share them with. If so, experiment. Pick people you are already close to and trust to be understanding and supportive, and who you would like to be closer to. Try telling them a bit more than you normally would about what you feel, what you want, what you fear, what you find difficult, what you think you are not very good at. Notice the effect on the quality of the relationship between you and them.

Be interested, curious and supportive

Relationships are two-way streets. To make a deep bond, you need to talk about the tender things in you, and the other needs to respond appropriately. And vice versa. So encourage others to talk to you about what is important to them by being interested and curious. And when they do, respond with understanding, empathy and support, not with judgement and not – unless they ask for it – with advice.

Devote time and energy to relationships

"A man, Sir, should keep his friendships in constant repair", opined Dr Johnson. Nowadays, the pressures on our time are greater than they were in the eighteenth century, but it remains true that in order to maintain good relationships we need to devote some time and energy to them. So, occasionally give someone a call or have a chat with them, not because you want something but just for the sake of it, so you and they can be closer to one another. It needn't take long; quality counts more than quantity. But if two people are never in touch, they can't really be said to have a relationship at all.

11   Invitation to Trust

This scale measures the extent to which you invite the trust of others by being principled, reliable, consistent and knowable.

Obviously to be worthy of others' trust, we need to hold them OK, so that we do not deceive or exploit them. But we also need to hold the "I'm OK" position too: people in "I'm Not OK, You're OK" will, for example, sometimes say things that they don't mean but the other wants to hear, to please them.

Trustworthy people walk their talk, they keep their promises, they behave the same when on their own as when observed by others, they are predictable in the sense that their behaviour can be relied upon. People who are reliable in this sense have largely resolved their internal conflicts, so that there are not different bits of them which believe and do different things. They have integrity ("wholeness"). And as well as all that, they are known to be so because they are open (see previous scale) and knowable. You will find it difficult to be trustworthy if you do not accept and value others. So, if necessary, you will have to raise your regard for others.

Developing your invitation to trust

Keep your promises

If others are to trust you, they need to know they can rely on what you say. First recognise whether your pattern is sometimes not to do what you have said you will, or sometimes to do what you have said you won't. In either case, you need to make sure that you don't give the undertaking in the first place unless you are committed to it. Always check before making an agreement that you really want to do it (or not do it), and are not just "agreeing" out of guilt or duty or a desire to please. Better to say No in the first place than to say Yes and then let the other down.

If you are agreeing to do something, make a habit of, at the same time, planning when and how you are going to do it, and what you will do if prevented from doing so. If you are agreeing not to do something, make sure you identify what the temptations will be and how you will deal with them, and plan in advance what action you will take if you do do what you are promising not to do.

Identify and resolve your inner conflicts

People will not be able to rely on you if there are different bits of you which feel, want and believe different things and which consequently cause you to behave in different ways, and if there is no way of knowing which bit is going to be in charge at any one time. So if this applies to you, by self reflection learn to identify the different conflicting bits of you and work out how you want to resolve the conflicts. You may find talking it through with someone else helpful to this process.

If you are familiar with the TA concept of ego states (see pages 49–53), here is a technique (Stuntz's five-chair technique) you can use to explore the different feelings, reactions and values of different parts of you. You can do it on your own, or preferably with someone to guide you through the process. Set out five chairs, or cushions, as the locations for your five functional ego states, and if you have a guide one for them, as shown in Figure 11.1.

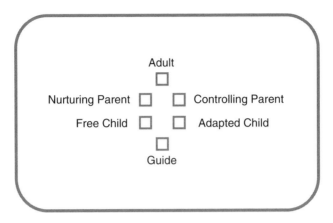

Figure 11.1 *Stuntz's five-chair technique.*

Start in the Adult position (unless on approaching the subject you experience yourself as firmly in another ego state, in which case go there) and
explore the issue from there until your guide suggests you should switch – if
you're on your own, until you want to find out what is going on in one of
your other ego states, or you feel yourself slide out of Adult into another ego
state. And so on. The main difference in doing it on your own is that you
will need to return, however briefly, to Adult after visiting each other ego
state. In either case, alone or guided, you will eventually end up, probably
having visited all the other ego states at least once, in Adult, and hopefully
from there will not only have a better understanding of the content of your
other ego states but will be able, after a bit of negotiation, to resolve any
conflicts between them.

Let yourself be known

We do not trust people whom we do not know and understand, who are a
mystery to us. So, to be trusted you need not only to be trustworthy but also
to be perceived as trustworthy. If you are a person who tends to keep yourself to yourself, experiment with letting people know a bit more about you.
Each day make sure you tell at least one other person at least one thing – a
fact, an insecurity, an excitement that you would normally keep to yourself.

12

The art of relationship management

"Coming together is a beginning, staying together is progress, and working together is success."
Henry Ford

This chapter discusses the scales of:

12   Trust
13   Balanced Outlook
14   Emotional Expression and Control
15   Conflict Handling (Assertiveness)
16   Interdependence.

Within each scale you will find:

- a definition;
- a more in-depth description;
- more information to help you understand the relevant EI theory;
- exercises to help you develop each scale.

Our relationship management skills are underpinned by our regard for others and our awareness of others (which includes being in touch with their feeling states).

We would not get very far without interacting with others. We form all sorts of relationships in our lives to help us achieve our goals and to fulfil our needs. Managing each of those relationships takes continued effort, and of course some are easier to manage than others. By developing our emotional intelligence we can make this much easier – by understanding what we want from our relationships and what others want from them too. Fostering emotional intelligence and making good relationships involves:

- acting with emotional intelligence yourself ("modelling");
- honouring feelings, paying attention to feelings, expressing feelings;
- using "I . . ." sentences, not "You . . ." sentences;
- checking out your assumptions.

You are 50% of every relationship you are in, so you have a lot of power to determine what each one will be like.

12   Trust

This scale measures your tendency to trust others. The scale ranges from being suspicious and mistrustful of other people (often from an "I'm OK, You're Not OK" position) to being very ready to trust other people, perhaps even to the extent of not looking after your own interests or keeping yourself safe (often from "I'm Not OK, You're OK"). A healthy balance between these two positions is: disposed to trust others but careful to take care of yourself in relation to others, from an "I'm OK, You're OK" position.

To work effectively and to exist comfortably in the world, we need to trust others. On the other hand, we can be too trusting, naïve and gullible: the consequence will be that we fail to protect ourselves and our interests as we need to. Again, there is a balance to be struck: we need to incline towards trusting others but at the same time to be wary for evidence that we should or shouldn't trust a particular person about a particular thing.

Developing a reasoned level of willingness to trust

If you find it difficult to trust others

- Develop your Regard for Others, your Awareness of Others and your Personal Openness.
- Build your trust in others by letting yourself know when and why you don't trust them. That way your distrust will become limited and specific rather than undefined and wide-ranging.
- When appropriate, and respectfully and tactfully, let *them* know how you don't trust them; that way either they can explain their behaviour so that it no longer leaves you mistrustful, or they have an opportunity to do it

differently in future. Check out with them the validity of your assumptions about them.

If you trust others too easily

- Develop your Self Regard, your Self Awareness – particularly your intuition – and your Goal Directedness.
- When you meet someone new, or someone invites you to trust them over something, check what your intuitive feeling is and pay attention to it.
- Pay attention to keeping yourself safe and protecting your interests. When you incline to trust someone, review the evidence for, and against, their being trustworthy.

13   Balanced Outlook

This scale measures how well you manage to balance optimism and realism. We may range from tending towards the pessimistic and focusing more on what may go wrong rather than the possibility of success, to being over-optimistic and expecting good outcomes when such hopes are not justified in reality. A healthy balance between these two positions is: you tend towards optimism but are sure to check out your hopes against reality.

If you tend to be "I'm Not OK, You're Not OK", you may take the view that "It's all hopeless and there's nothing anybody can do about it". If you tend to be "I'm OK, You're Not OK", you may say, "I know it's going to be fine no matter what anyone else says."

In one of life's self-fulfilling prophecies, if we are pessimistic and failure-oriented then things tend to go wrong and we fail. On the other hand, if our vision of the world is determined by our desires and we are un-realistically optimistic, we are prevented from dealing effectively with the world as it is. We need to balance optimism and realism, from an "I'm OK, You're OK" position.

Developing a balance between realism and optimism

If you are pessimistic and failure-oriented

- Be practical. When you catch yourself using sweeping phrases like, "That'll never work" or "I couldn't possibly do that", realise that this is merely the expression of a negative attitude and not a realistic assessment, and reframe your reservations in limited and specific terms.

• Stop catastrophising. Probably you're right: things will not go perfectly. That is not the end of the world, nor of you. Start planning what you will do to recover.

• Learn to be optimistic. Practise positive reframes. Develop your Self Regard and your sense of Personal Power.

If you are overoptimistic and unrealistic

• Consult other people and external authorities. Recognise that your initial response is likely to be biased. Demand evidence of yourself for your optimistic predictions and check out what other people think.

• Be detailed. Work out how things are going to happen rather than just assuming that they will.

• Learn from past mistakes. Reflect on the times you have been overoptimistic. What did you not take into account? What do you need to do differently next time to get it right?

14   Emotional Expression and Control

This scale measures how emotionally controlled you are. You may tend towards being emotionally undercontrolled, so that your feelings are in charge of you, rather than you of them, and you do not choose when or how to express them. Or, alternatively, towards being emotionally overcontrolled, so that you have some difficulty in being in touch with your feelings and expressing them freely. A healthy balance between these two positions is: you are free to express your feelings but are in control of whether and how and when to do so.

If coming from "I'm OK, You're Not OK", you may take the attitude, "My feelings are coming out whether you like it or not". If coming from "I'm Not OK, You're OK", you may believe, "My feelings don't matter and should be sat on in the presence of other people". The "I'm OK, You're OK" position is that my feelings are important but I will take you into account in deciding about expressing them.

The relationship between us and our feelings is a delicate one. In order to be fully alive, natural and spontaneous, we need to have easy access to our feelings; and in order to manage ourselves and our relationships we need to be free to express our feelings. On the other hand, we need to be in charge of our feelings rather than them in charge of us, so that we can choose if and how and when to express them; if not, we may find ourselves in trouble. There is a tension here between overcontrol, which means we do not have easy access to our feelings or freedom to express them, and undercontrol, which means that they are in charge and burst out whether we like it or not, stopping us from choosing our actions.

Developing a balance between emotional expression and control

If it is hard for you to be in control of expressing your feelings

- Develop impulse control (see under Goal Directedness in Chapter 11).
- Slow down. When you feel compelled to express a feeling, pause for six seconds and allow time before you do anything or say anything to think about your feelings, your possible reactions and their possible consequences. Remind yourself that you are OK and that they too are OK.
- Distinguish between expressive behaviour, which is an end in itself and sometimes makes us feel better, and instrumental behaviour, which is a means to an end and is intended to move us towards our goals. Understand that some expressive behaviour is counterproductive in instrumental terms, in that it actually moves us away from, rather than towards, our goals. This doesn't mean that we should abandon purely expressive behaviour – we have a need to express ourselves – but learn to express yourself in a way that is not counterproductive.

If it is hard for you to express your feelings

- Learn which feelings you censor the most. (In childhood girls are often brought up not to show anger, and boys not to show fear. Most families have an unconscious taboo on showing one particular feeling.)
- Observe other people expressing their feelings, in control and respectfully. Notice how you feel in response (probably closer to them because they come across as non-judgemental).
- Experiment, gently and little by little, with expressing your feelings (easiest ones first) more than you are used to. Notice the effect on you getting what you want and on your relationships.

15   Conflict Handling (Assertiveness)

This scale measures how well you handle conflict, how assertive you are. Here we can veer towards being passive, avoiding conflict even at the cost of putting up with things that are not right for us. Or we can tend towards being aggressive, going into conflict to defend our interests at the expense of others. A healthy balance between these two positions is: you are assertive, standing up for your wants and needs, but staying calm and respecting the other while doing so, from an "I'm OK, You're OK" position.

Those in the "I'm Not OK, You're OK" position will believe that what the other wants is much more important than what they want, or that there's no way they can effectively stand up to the other. Those coming from "I'm OK, You're Not OK" will act on the basis of "I matter; you don't".

People are different. They want different things, and often these things are incompatible. So, conflict between people is inevitable. There is nothing wrong with it, but it needs to be managed effectively. That means not avoiding or denying conflict, but meeting it head on if that is what it takes to stand up for what you want. On the other hand, it also means not attacking or undermining the other in the process of standing up for what you want, but treating them respectfully and, insofar as is possible, helping them to get what they want while you get what you want.

Developing effective conflict handling

If you are too passive in conflict situations

- Develop your Self Regard, your Self Awareness so that you know at the time when something isn't right for you, your Goal Directedness and your capacity for Emotional Expression.
- Rather than automatically going along with other people, practise paying attention to when you are unhappy and why. If it is too scary for you to speak out, at least work out what you would say and do if you were ready to. Then later, when you are ready, begin to practise standing up for yourself, starting with people and situations that are least scary for you.

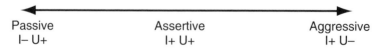

| Passive | Assertive | Aggressive |
| I– U+ | I+ U+ | I+ U– |

Figure 12.1 *The life positions and conflict handling.*

- If you don't know how to confront someone else in order to get what you want, start by developing your Self Regard and Self Awareness. Then get some assertiveness training and learn techniques to help you develop the behavioural skills to confront others effectively.

If you are too aggressive in conflict situations

- Develop your Regard for Others, your Goal Directedness, your Flexibility, your Personal Openness and your Emotional Expression and Control.
- To start changing your behaviour immediately, develop your impulse control (see under Goal Directedness in Chapter 11) and your Emotional Expression and Control.
- If you don't know how to confront someone else effectively in order to get what you want, instead of attacking them aggressively and therefore undermining your relationship with them rather than enhancing it, again start by working on your Regard for Others (which may mean bolstering your Self Regard first). Once this is under way, then get some assertiveness training and learn techniques to help you develop the behavioural skills to confront others respectfully but effectively.

Giving negative feedback

The first step in assertive conflict handling is giving effective negative feedback. Those who are passive will tend to avoid giving negative feedback at all, and those who are aggressive will probably deliver put downs instead. So here are some guidelines to doing it right.

Too often when giving someone negative feedback we point out the obvious, which only serves to undermine the other's self esteem and give them the experience of feeling judged before we start. The other doesn't need to hear (because they know it already):

- Who they are   ("You are only a junior.")
- How they are   ("You are being stubborn.")
- What they are   ("You are inefficient.")
- What they have done   ("You were late.")
- What they are doing   ("You are letting the team down.")

What they *do* need to hear (because they can't know it until you tell them) is what is going on for you, so use "I" sentences rather than "You" sentences.

The emotionally intelligent process to follow is set out in Chapter 10.

More about conflict handling

Here are some additional techniques that you may find useful when handling conflict.

In order for you to get what you want, it goes without saying that you will first have to identify what that is and – perhaps surprisingly – that is not always as easy as it might be. Here are some suggestions to help you in the process of identifying what you want.

1. Allow yourself to explore without judgement.
2. Focus on your body and your feelings.
3. Experiment, in practice and in thought.
4. Identify what you don't like, or are missing, and work out what would make a difference.
5. If you were a child, what would you want?
6. Check with all your ego states.

Having concentrated on yourself, on your wants, you then need to balance this by taking the other into account, because the key to resolving conflict is to move from the "*you against me*" position to a position of "*us against the problem*".

Take the other perspective

If you have difficulty staying in I+ U+ when in a conflict situation, and therefore find it difficult to be assertive and to negotiate properly, here is a useful exercise.

A1. Place two chairs so that they are facing each other and sit in one of them.
A2. Think about a situation where you are having difficulty with someone, specifically a situation where you have had difficulties in the past and are likely to have them again.

A3. Think of your own perspective imagining that the other person is sat in the chair facing you. Imagine or talk out loud what is going on for you.

A4. What do you see? How do you feel? What are you saying? How are they reacting to you?

B1. Now stand up and clear your mind by counting backwards from 20.

B2. Move to the other chair and sit down, taking on the body language of the other person as you do so. Try to become the other person.

B3. Looking at yourself in the chair opposite:
- What do you see?
- How do you feel?
- What are you saying?
- How are they reacting to you?

B4. What are your thoughts, feelings and beliefs about the situation?

C1. Empty your head again by walking around the room and counting backwards from 20.

C2. Stand back from the two chairs and picture the scene as a neutral observer might see it.

C3. Looking at the scene in a non-judgemental yet helpful way, how does the observer's perspective differ from that of the other two people?

C4. How would they suggest that Person 1 (you) should act to improve the situation?

Notice how much easier it is after having gone through this procedure to stay in I+ U+ in a conflict situation, which will make a mutually satisfactory resolution much easier to attain. "Us against the problem" is the emotionally intelligent approach to handling and resolving conflict.

Conflict handling and the OK Corral

Your behavioural tendency in conflict situations will be strongly influenced by your life position. In Chapter 4 we saw that the different life positions went with different styles in conflict situations:

"I'm OK, You're OK" (the emotionally intelligent position). People coming from this life position will adopt an attitude of *constructive discontent* in conflict situations. That is: "My discontent with what is going on in this situation is giving me useful information that something is Not OK for me. How can I use that information constructively to make sure that I do get what I want (or at least something I can live with) while treating the other respectfully and helping them to get what they want (or at least something they can live with)?" This attitude naturally leads into an "us against the problem" position, rather than a "me against you" position.

"I'm Not OK, You're OK" (the submissive position). People coming from this life position will go for *harmony* in conflict situations. In order to get that, they will give in to the other, so betraying themselves and their own needs.

"I'm OK, You're Not OK" (the critical position). People coming from this position will attempt to *railroad* the other into allowing them to get what they want, without any regard for the other's wishes. Their attitude will be: "This is a fight and I'm going to win and get what I want. Devil take the hindmost."

"I'm Not OK, You're Not OK" (the hopeless position). People coming from this position will tend to *withdraw* from a conflict situation. What is the point of going through the unpleasantness of it when nothing can be resolved and nothing can be done?

The Harvard Negotiation Model and the OK Corral

The TA life positions map very neatly onto the Harvard Negotiation Model, as we also saw in Chapter 4:

"I'm OK, You're OK"
(the emotionally intelligent position)   corresponds to **WIN WIN**

"I'm Not OK, You're OK"
(the submissive position)   corresponds to **LOSE WIN**

"I'm OK, You're Not OK"
(the critical position)   corresponds to **WIN LOSE**

"I'm Not OK, You're Not OK"
(the stuck position)   corresponds to **LOSE LOSE**

Emotionally intelligent conflict handling

By developing your self awareness, your awareness of others, your self management skills and your relationship management skills, you will be able to handle and resolve conflict from an emotionally intelligent position, creating win–win outcomes and minimising bad feeling.

Self regard in conflict handling

Recognise the importance of your self regard when handling conflict. When you find yourself in a conflict situation, remember to say to yourself: *"I'm OK; my needs are important."*

Regard for others in conflict handling

Recognise the importance of regard for others when handling conflict. When you find yourself in a conflict situation, remember to say to yourself: *"You're OK; your needs are important too."*

Self awareness in conflict handling

Recognise the importance of emotional self awareness when handling conflict. When you find yourself in a conflict situation, remember to ask yourself:

"How am I feeling at this moment?"
"What is my body trying to tell me?"
"Am I falling into my usual behaviour, which I would like to do differently?"

Awareness of others in conflict handling

Recognise the importance of emotional awareness of others when handling conflict. When you find yourself in a conflict situation, remember to:

- Notice the other's body language.
- Work out what are they trying to tell you.
- Check that your assumptions are right with the other person.

Self management skills in conflict handling

There are three self management competencies that are particularly important when handling conflict.

Goal directedness

This is about how your behaviour relates to your long-term goals. To be goal directed you need to believe that you, and what you want, matter – coming from the position of I'm OK. To realise your life goals you need to know what they are and where you want to go – and then keep these in mind so that everything you do moves you towards these goals rather than away from them. In a conflict situation you need to be sure of where you want to get to in the long term – is this conflict going to impact on you achieving your long-term goals and do you need this person's cooperation in the future?

Flexibility

This is about feeling free to adapt your thinking and your behaviour to match the changing situations in your life. It is about you being ready, able and willing to react to changing circumstances in a different way, whether in terms of thinking, feeling or behaving.

If you have low flexibility in EI terms it is likely to mean that you tend to cling to what you know and believe, and to your habitual patterns, through fear. To be flexible, you need to dare to experiment and risk failure, you need to value yourself (I'm OK) and you need to believe that the world is a relatively safe place (that others are OK too).

Flexibility is important in conflict handling – ask yourself where you are reacting in a rigid way. Is there an alternative way of doing things?

Personal openness and connectedness

This relates to how easy you find it to open up to others about yourself, and therefore to the ease with which you make significant connections in your life and to the number of them you have. People respond to being valued and respected (You're OK). To open up to others requires taking a risk, so you need to be sure of your own value no matter what (I'm OK too). To connect with others requires other EI-related skills, as shown in Table 12.1.

Table 12.1 *Skills needed for connecting with others.*

Regard for Others	Knowing how to listen acceptingly and non-judgementally
Awareness of Others	Understanding how they are feeling and empathising with them
Emotional Expression and Control	Being able to express your own feelings in ways you choose as being appropriate
Invitation to Trust	Being the kind of person others are ready to trust

In a conflict situation develop your Personal Openness by risking talking about your feelings, perhaps your fears, in the moment. Be supportive and build rapport with this person during your discussions.

Relationship management skills in conflict handling

There is one further EI skill which is needed to handle conflict well, and which falls under the banner of relationship management. This is Emotional Expression and Control – being free to express your feelings whilst being in control of whether, and how and when, to do so. If we are free and in control, rather than under- or over-controlled, we will be able to combine expressive and instrumental behaviour: expressing our feelings in a manner which helps us resolve the conflict.

Emotional Expression and Control is often the most obvious indicator of conflict. When you find yourself in a conflict situation, identify how you are feeling. Are you suppressing your feelings or do you feel like you are going to explode?

Combining your self management and relationship management skills

In order to handle conflict effectively we need to maximise both our self management skills and our relationship management skills (as well as our Self Awareness and Other Awareness). To summarise, these are the areas that you need to develop to handle conflict in an emotionally intelligent way:

1. Self Regard
   - Become aware of your internal dialogue and develop positive self-talk.
   - Refuse "unconditional negative strokes" and encourage positive ones!

2. Self Awareness
   - Begin to recognise your feeling states.
   - Learn to name your feelings and understand where they are coming from.
3. Regard for Others
   - Differentiate between others' being and their doing.
   - Understand the other perspective and learn to listen actively and empathically.
4. Awareness of Others
   - Recognise the feeling states of others and develop empathy.
   - Practise listening effectively and check out your assumptions.
5. Self Management
   - Know your long-term goals and move towards them.
   - Be aware of when you are rigid and inflexible.
   - Open up to others, take a risk.
6. Relationship Management
   - Know your feelings and practise expressing them.
   - Develop your impulse control, learn to take criticism and remove judgement.

Aim for that Win–Win mindset: "Us against the problem".

16   Interdependence

This scale measures how well you manage to balance taking yourself and taking others into account. You may swing towards being dependent on other people. Or you may tend to be very independent and prefer not to have to let others into the picture. A healthy balance between these two positions is: being confident in your own abilities but also willing to take others into account, from an "I'm OK, You're OK" position.

If you tend to be "I'm Not OK, You're OK", you will tend to believe, "I'm not all right on my own, I need the help of others". If, however, you tend to be "I'm OK, You're Not OK", you'll tend to think, "I'm fine on my own and everybody else is useless or tiresome".

Human beings are social animals and to maximise our effectiveness we need to be able to work alongside others. Yet to maximise our personal performance we need to be confident in our own abilities and capable of working alone where necessary. There is a balance to be struck between

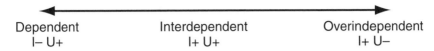

| Dependent | Interdependent | Overindependent |
| I– U+ | I+ U+ | I+ U– |

Figure 12.2 *The life positions and interdependence.*

being overdependent on other people and reluctant to stand on our own two feet, on the one hand, and on the other being so independent as to find everyone else an intrusive obstacle. The healthy position midway is called "interdependence", wherein people are able to act on their own when appropriate (being confident about their abilities and judgements), and also to be effective leaders, followers, or colleagues.

Developing your interdependence

If you are overdependent on others

- Develop your Self Regard and sense of Personal Power.
- Before you consult anyone else about anything, first work out what you think and what you would do if you were left to your own devices.
- Notice, take pleasure in and congratulate yourself for those occasions when you do things successfully on your own. And get others to acknowledge them too.

If you are too independent

- Develop your Regard for Others, your Personal Openness and your Trust.
- Notice how everyone is different and everyone has something unique to contribute, and that in team working the whole is greater than the sum of the parts.
- Before you take any action, stop for a minute to consider how it will affect other people; factor that into your decision making. Often you will go ahead and do the same thing anyway, but you will be forewarned of any adverse reactions. Sometimes you may decide to change your plans to take the other into account.

Giving positive strokes

One of the characteristics of a good team player, which is what interdependence is all about, and particularly of a good team leader, is to be a plentiful source of positive strokes for others. But of course giving others positive strokes is just as important in one-to-one relationships as it is in one-to-many situations.

People are often inhibited about giving positive strokes, as well as about receiving them. They may think, "Who am I to evaluate others and tell them my judgement?", in which case they will need to raise their Self Regard in order to feel comfortable giving positive strokes. Or they may feel uncomfortable about themselves and expressing their feeling and thinking, in which case they will also have to raise their level of Personal Openness and Connectedness (Scale 10) and Emotional Expression (Scale 14). Or they may not have the skills; they may not know how to do it right. For that case, see the guidelines set out in Chapter 10.

13

Knowing oneself

"By three methods we may learn wisdom: First, by reflection which is the noblest;
second, by imitation which is the easiest;
and third, by experience, which is the bitterest"
Confucius

This chapter discusses the scales of:

17 Reflective Learning
18 Self Knowledge (Accuracy of self assessment)

Within each scale you will find:

- a definition;
- a more in-depth description;
- more information to help you understand the relevant EI theory;
- exercises to help you develop each scale.

17   Reflective Learning

Reflective Learning is the prime mechanism for improving our self knowledge, but it is also a general mechanism for developing all aspects of our emotional intelligence, and indeed other kinds of intelligence: the habit of *reflective learning*. To what extent do you enhance your emotional intelligence by reflecting on what you and others feel, think and do, noticing the outcomes these produce and altering your patterns as necessary?

As so often, being non-judgemental is crucial here. To enable us to observe and appreciate dispassionately our own feelings, thoughts and behaviour, we need to hold ourselves absolutely, unconditionally OK, and to enable us to observe and appreciate dispassionately other people's behaviour, we need to hold them absolutely, unconditionally OK.

We know that on the whole levels of emotional intelligence increase with age and experience of life, but this does not happen automatically. It only happens if we learn from our experience, either intuitively or through conscious reflection.

Developing reflective learning

If you do not currently have the habit of learning by regular reflection on your experience, here are some ways of getting into the habit. Some of these focus specifically on converting a series of awarenesses of feeling states in the moment into long term self knowledge or, as the case may be, knowledge of another or of others in general. Others of these exercises look more generally at learning from the pattern of connections between what we do, our attempts at self management and relationship management, and the outcomes they generate for us.

Keep a journal or a learning log

One of the most effective ways of promoting the practice of reflective learning is to formalise it by reducing the process, or at least its outcome, to writing. So get into the habit of recording in a special book (or a special folder in your computer) your learnings about how you and other people work.

Review your experience, and the potential learnings in it, daily

As with all habit changes, to begin with this will feel artificial and constrained, but after three weeks or so it will become automatic and natural. Once a day, perhaps just before you go to sleep (but if so, you will have to make some arrangement for recording your learnings), review your experience of the previous twenty-four hours: what worked well, what didn't and why, what did you enjoy and what did you not enjoy and why, and what are your conclusions from all this about you and others?

Review your performance regularly

Adopt the habit of reviewing your performance after you have done anything significant: a presentation, a meeting (maybe at work, maybe with family or friends), perhaps a party. Use these questions to help you draw out the learning available:

- What worked and went well, and why?
- What didn't go so well, and why not?
- What will I do differently another time?
- What have I learned from this experience and from reflecting upon it?

Keep an emotional reactions diary

Keeping a record of your emotional responses can help to identify your emotional reactions, providing a first step to managing them. To do this, each time you notice your mood change ask yourself, "What is going on for me right now?" and as soon as possible record your thoughts and feelings. Possible headings are:

- Date/time
- First thoughts
- Emotions
- Response
- Outcomes.

Following the event you can also consider the following questions:

- What evidence is there of my first thoughts being true?
- Are there any alternative explanations?
- What was the pattern of my feeling reactions?
- What would have been the best outcome and the worst outcome?
- What was, or what would have been, the effect(s) of believing my automatic thoughts?
- What could be the effect of changing my thinking?

Create your time line

These next two exercises aim to identify previous life experiences that may still be affecting your behaviour.

1. Begin by drawing your life story in terms of pictures or metaphors along a continuum.
2. Think back to your earliest memories, the big events and the significant people in your life, right through to the present day.

3. Identify recurring patterns of behaviour or circumstances.
4. List the qualities you have developed through your life experiences.
5. Identify any unfulfilled wishes or regrets.
6. When you have done this, present it to someone you trust and who will listen but not judge you.

Make a note here of any significant observations you make during this exercise.

Identify your lost history

1. Reflect on experiences from earlier on in your life that had a big emotional impact on you.
2. Consider how these experiences may still be affecting your feelings, and/or your behaviour, today.
3. Write your thoughts down under the two headings "Experience" and "Continuing effects".
4. Again, when you have done this, present it to someone you trust and who will listen but not judge you.
5. A powerful technique that can be applied here is to visualise the scene but change the picture to something more pleasant.

Make a note here of old limiting beliefs that still seem to be inhibiting you now.

18   Self Knowledge (Accuracy of self assessment)

On its own this scale measures your self-assessed EI, but when compared preferably with raters' scores on the 360°, or in the absence of that with how you actually scored on the corresponding scales, it gives an indication of how well you know yourself, how accurately you assess your strengths and weaknesses in the various aspects of emotional intelligence.

People who believe "I'm Not OK" will often underestimate their emotional intelligence competencies. People who hold the "I'm OK, You're Not OK" position, usually covering up for "I'm Not OK, You're OK", will tend to overestimate the level of their EI competencies. And people in the "I'm OK, You're OK" position will have the security to be able to see themselves as they truly are, to acknowledge their relative weaknesses as well as their relative strengths. Their accuracy of self assessment will tend to be high.

If we have a false view of ourselves, we are unlikely to be able to manage ourselves effectively, or indeed to act effectively in the world. Self Knowledge (Accuracy of self assessment) is therefore highly correlated with effective performance.

Developing self knowledge (Accuracy of self assessment)

As well as being dependent on Self Regard, as noted above, Self Knowledge is also closely related to Self Awareness. Self Knowledge is the long-term correlate of Self Awareness in the moment. If necessary, you will need to raise your self awareness in order to raise your self knowledge.

The main route to self knowledge is through reflective learning from experience – see the previous scale. Meanwhile, here are three more specific suggestions.

Evaluate yourself dispassionately

Make a habit of reflecting regularly on specific items of your performance and behaviour, and learn from that what your strengths and weaknesses are. Challenge yourself about the conclusions you come to: what evidence do you have for them; are they things you are disposed to believe or are they borne out by reality?

Seek and listen to feedback from others

However self aware and however dispassionate we are, it is hard to assess ourselves. We need to temper our view of ourselves with the views of others. So consult people who know you well, have an opportunity to observe how you function and whom you trust, and ask them to give you straight feedback about how they see you doing. When you receive that feedback, be open to it. The more it differs from your own view, the more potentially valuable it is. If in doubt, talk it through with the other. And get more information by consulting more people.

Abandon perfectionism

We are all of us different, and better at some things than others. What matters here is not being superb at everything, an impossible perfectionism, but knowing what we are relatively good, and not so good, at. This will both help us to decide where to focus our personal development and how to manage ourselves, warts and all. Believing we ought to be good at everything gets in the way of learning the pattern of our strengths and weaknesses, so if part of you thinks that that is how you ought to be, do yourself a favour: give it up now.

The Overall Picture

So far we have looked at the significance of what is measured by the *iȝ*™ scales individually. However, they can often be even more revealing when taken together. The point is to get a coherent overall picture rather than just a series of unconnected measurements. Sometimes taking two or three scales together will suggest a particular pattern. For example, Goal Directedness is supposed to measure how directed we are towards the fulfillment of our own personal goals. Sometimes we see people who score high on this scale and yet low on Self Awareness, and such people often prove not to be going after their own goals but someone else's; their organisation's, their spouse's, their parent's, in a rather driven manner.

Sometimes looking at several scales together raises useful questions rather than providing answers. For example, the main prerequisites for high Emotional Resilience are high Self Regard and high Self Awareness. If someone has these but low Emotional Resilience, the question arises what is going on – what is undermining their capacity for high Emotional Resilience?

Managing interferences

As we said at the beginning of Chapter 4, we believe that most people have the potential to behave with emotional intelligence. For much of the time we do not because of our interferences – internal interferences mostly resulting from false beliefs and limiting habits adopted (for what were then good reasons) in childhood and retained, unwittingly, in adulthood. The process of enabling someone to develop their emotional intelligence therefore consists in helping them to identify and dismantle these interferences.

That is the ideal. But what about those interferences which are difficult to dismantle, for example those which arise from very early unconscious learning? It is certainly true that some of these cannot be disposed of overnight, and some of them may be very difficult to dispose of at all. In a sense, they form part of us – part of our personality. It is strange to think of, but there is a sense in which all of personality consists of interferences, of psychopathology. You can argue that if we didn't have our interferences, if we all behaved with maximal emotional intelligence (whatever that is) all the time, then – apart from some genetic differences – we would all be the same. To a degree, it is our interferences that give us our personality, that make us who we are.

That brings us back to the question of what the relationship is between emotional intelligence and personality. As we have said before, we do not believe that EI is part of, or coterminous with, our personality. We believe it is about managing our personality, and that means managing our interferences. We are always going to have some personal quirks and limitations; the question is how to manage them in a way that nonetheless allows us to behave most of the time in a reasonably emotionally intelligent way.

The first step towards managing our interferences is happily the same as it is towards dismantling them: to learn to recognise and acknowledge them. We cannot manage our interferences unless we know what they are and how they interfere with our being emotionally intelligent. So self knowledge, which involves knowing our interferences, is key to managing our interferences. Hence, the importance of reflective learning, which allows us to convert self awareness in the moment into self knowledge over time.

With self knowledge, with an understanding of how we tend to work, we can increase our choicefulness – an interesting synonym, or at least prerequisite, for emotional intelligence. The process will not be instantaneous and will take working at. The process will usually involve four stages: no sight, hindsight, midsight and foresight. We start at no sight: we do what we do and cope with the consequences, without knowing why we do it. When in a particular respect we are still at the hindsight stage, we will only recognise our interferences, and how they prevent us from acting in an emotionally intelligent way, after the event, after the damage is done. If we go through the reflective learning process, we are likely to begin to move into midsight, where, owing to our interferences, we still start to behave in an automatic, driven, choiceless emotionally unintelligent way but then recognise what we are doing as we do it and are able to recover. Then, finally, if we continue our reflective learning, we will arrive at a degree of self knowledge where we can anticipate when our interferences are likely to operate and can take the necessary avoiding action and retain our choicefulness. We will have arrived at foresight.

There is one essential prerequisite for the process we have described of learning how to manage our interferences and that is: self acceptance. Our sense of our OKness needs to be unconditional, so that we accept ourselves, interferences and all. If we think we ought to be interference free, or are bad or inferior for having interferences, then that will interfere with our recognising, exploring and managing them. Judgement is the enemy of perception.

21 Day commitment – changing a habit

One of the quickest ways to start your EI development is to undertake a 21 day change commitment. What this enables you to do is to initiate a new habit of behaviour in place of an old one, to move from conscious incompetence through conscious competence to unconscious competence. Our outline of the procedure below has been developed from the work of Esther Orioli of QMetrics, who use this with their instrument the EQMap.

There is nothing magical about the figure of 21 days. It is by way of a compromise. It is just about long enough to allow effective change in a behavioural habit, and it is not so long that people get put off and disheartened.

The first step is to pick a very specific place to start your programme of change. Think about your *is*™ profile and select one aspect that you want to change most immediately. Now follow the steps below to create a 21-day commitment to change.

Guidelines for creating your 21-day commitment to change

- Pick a scale that you are not wonderful at or terrible at – where there is room for improvement but you have something to build on.
- Select a behaviour not related to food, weight, smoking, drinking, gambling or other dependency issues.
- Identify the behaviour or situation you wish to change.

- Describe your current behaviour. (What do you do now? How do you currently respond?)
- Describe your desired new behaviour.
- Write all this down.

Do's and Don'ts for your commitment to change

- Select only one behaviour – just one at a time.
- Make it specific and clear, yet succinct.
- Express it in positive, not negative, form.
- Make it measurable.
- Make it something you can practise every day.
- Not more than ten minutes, if any, extra per day in total.
- You must want to do it for you.
- It must be a behaviour over which you have full control and for which you can take full responsibility.

Declaring your statement of commitment

Write down, and read out to an audience, your commitment:

"Every day, for 21 days, I will . . . . . ."

Buddy system – schedule of contacts

To help you stick with your 21-day commitment, ask someone to whom you give a copy of your commitment to help you by checking in with you regularly to see how you are doing. As a fail-safe, arrange to contact them at a particular time, and then for them to contact you if you don't. We recommend the levels of contact outlined in Figure 13.1.

Once you've got to Day 21, celebrate your success. Then you have options:

1. Start a new commitment tackling a different behaviour relating to the same scale.
2. Start a new commitment tackling a behaviour relating to another scale.

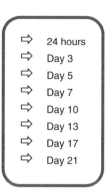

Figure 13.1 *Schedule of contact for the 21-day commitment.*

3. Take a holiday and return to self development later.
4. Decide you are as perfect as you want to be and don't want to dismantle any more interferences.

This is the start of your EI development journey – enjoy the process!

Part III

Applying Emotionally Intelligent Attitudes

14

The emotionally intelligent organisation

Meeting business needs

The uses of emotional intelligence

As we have seen so far in this book, the development of emotional intelligence of the individual is dependent upon the dismantling of their internal interferences, which affect their ability to be self managing and to enjoy healthy relationships at home and at work.

At the individual level within an organisation, emotional intelligence is essential for:

- self management;
- management of our relationships with others;
- facilitating relationships between others;
- developing others.

But individuals' propensity to act with emotional intelligence is affected not only by their internal interferences, which are personal and unique to them, but also by external interferences. If I work for a manager who clearly doesn't value me, isn't open to change and is very intolerant of anything – however good an idea potentially – which isn't proven to work, then it is unlikely that I am going to give expression to my creativity or my initiative in the work situation. Similarly, if I work in a team which is internally highly competitive and where the prevailing norm is to be self-oriented rather than team-oriented, to claim the credit and avoid the blame, then I am unlikely to share my concerns and my vulnerabilities with colleagues. And the same process applies at the level of the organisation as a whole. If I work for an organisation which does not respect the members of its staff but is exploitative of them, it is unlikely that I am going to be able to convey genuine respect to the organisation's customers that I interact with.

The same formula that we use for developing individuals is also highly effective at the macro level. We can consider a team, a department or even an organisation's performance by reviewing the potential of the group and their cumulative interferences.

In Chapter 16 we take a look at the Team Effectiveness questionnaire $i\mathbf{3}^{™}$, a sister profiling tool to the Individual Effectiveness questionnaire $i\mathbf{3}^{™}$. At the time of going to press, a third tool is under development – the Organisational Effectiveness $\mathbf{\omega}$ tool – which will assess an organisation's emotional health. This will look at two aspects. What it does and the attitudes that engenders towards the organisation in its staff, its customers, its suppliers and the community of which it forms a part. All this may be quite different from the way the organisation seeks to project itself. Putting "people are our greatest asset" in each annual report does not make an organisation emotionally intelligent. Handsome is as handsome does, so we shall need to do an audit of the organisation's policies and practices as well as the impact they have. Is the organisation really tolerant and appreciative of people's differences? Does it put a value on the personal development of all its staff? Are its appraisal procedures emotionally intelligent, in principle and in practice (see below for what this may involve)? Does it have flexible and family-friendly employment policies? And so on. And how do employees respond? Do they feel respected? Supported? Listened to? Valued? How does all this affect their contribution?

EI business applications

There are a variety of ways in which EI can be applied within an organisation. Here are the key areas:

- review of appraisal and performance management process;
- recruitment / selection;

- identifying and meeting development needs;
- individual / team / organisation diagnosis and development.
- profiling star performers;
- designing training;
- measuring training outcomes;
- review of competency frameworks;

For an organisation to incorporate EI into its business applications effectively, the organisation needs to either build the EI knowledge, skills and attitudes of key employees and managers involved in these processes, or to recruit EI consultancy to facilitate this.

Culture

Tackling these business applications is one aspect of developing the emotionally intelligent organisation. More fundamentally, the organisation needs to consider the underlying culture that has been created by management and staff alike.

Organisational culture has been described as "The way we do things round here …". We would like to suggest a slight extension to this definition – organisational culture is "The way we think, feel and do things around here …".

An organisation has its own form of EI. Whilst an organisation itself cannot have its own attitudes (because attitudes are based on feelings and to have feelings an entity has to be a sentient being with a body), the attitudes of any dominant minority of members, usually the CEO and senior executives, are critical. If you know that your organisation needs to develop a healthier culture – look at the top team first. Consider their attitudes towards staff, customers, each other and ultimately themselves. To what extent do they subscribe to the 8 principles of EI (see Chapter 4)?

What is the nature of your organisation's customer relationships?

Are customers and potential customers seen as adversaries or colleagues? What is the life position of your organisation? Does it relate with its customers in an emotionally intelligent, "We're OK, You're OK" kind of way, or does it slip into one of the other three attitudinal positions shown in Table 14.1?

Table 14.1 *What is the life position of your organization?*

	We're Not OK	We're OK
You're OK	I– U+ Overly helpful	I+ U+ Healthy
You're Not OK	I– U– Apathetic	I+ U– Inflexible

If your staff are overstretched and you're cutting profit margins to keep customers, consider where, at an attitudinal level, the organisation is undermining itself.

Equally, where staff are inflexible towards customers and customers are held in low regard, consider where, at an attitudinal level, the organisation is missing out on potential customer loyalty.

Where there is a sense of apathy within an organisation, staff morale will be very low and customer satisfaction poor – sure signs that business will be affected adversely.

Do your employees reflect the values of your brand?

A company can spend a fortune on devising a brand image, creating a set of organisational values and cascading these down through the echelons. But so often this becomes a wasted exercise. Why is this?

If the culture within the organisation is based on a "We're OK, You're OK" attitude, then employees are likely to buy into the prescribed values, indeed they are likely to be involved in the design process. More often than not, however, in an attempt to revamp the organisation's image, this time and money is lost because the underlying attitudes of the role models, the senior management team, have not fundamentally changed. They may well change their behaviours at a superficial level, but at the first signs of stress their true attitudes will shine through like a beacon and any goodwill amongst employees will have been lost – the management team will have been perceived as paying lip service to the espoused values.

Creating a set of core attitudes

Another pitfall of this kind of exercise is to associate a long list of behaviours with the desired organisational values. Employees at all levels are then measured against these desired behaviours. The problem again is that the underlying attitudes have not been looked at. People are expected instead to automatically change their behaviours, and sustain these changes, if they want to get on in the organisation.

The thing with behaviours is that there are so many of them. Our behaviours are an outward expresssion of our personal values and attitudes. Most training doesn't create long-term behavioural change because it doesn't address the underlying attitudes and habits that drive the behaviours that need to be changed. And why's that? Because it's hard for a conventional trainer to do and very few organisations really understand the difference.

What needs to happen is that the organisation identifies the core attitudes for employees to adopt, which would then be expressed in the desired behaviours. For example, a desired behaviour might be:

Flexible and adapts to change – The manager will be flexible in his/her approach to work. Seeking out and being open to better ways of doing things is one of his/her key qualities. He/she will embrace and lead change where appropriate, adopting a positive and willing approach.

Of course this all makes sense and is definitely a requirement for a successful business. But can we really expect people to suddenly become flexible, open and all-embracing? This can be pretty hard for a control freak, which many executives and managers can be!

All sorts of issues are wrapped up in this and the other behaviours identified, but they can all be distilled down to a core set of attitudes. An attitude is an evaluative, feelings-based position that you take towards something or someone – either positive or negative, moving you towards or away from it or them.

The organisation must work out the core set of attitudes that employees need to adopt to be able to build the desired new behaviours – e.g. an attitude could be "shares the values of the organization". It's not a behaviour, it's deeper than that – kind of a heart and mind thing.

If an individual adopts this attitude they will find it a lot easier to display the more surface behaviours, such as "being able to undertake agreed actions wholeheartedly, even if these are at odds with his/her own priorities or beliefs" or "remaining engaged in decision making, even when personally not affected", for example.

These core attitudes would fall out of the brand values that the organisation has identified and would define the organisation's culture – i.e. how do we want our employees to think, feel and act around here? In order for employees of an organisation to accept and adopt the values of the organisation's brand, they need time to absorb them and align them with their own beliefs and feelings, rather than being expected immediately to adapt their behaviours.

The challenge is that the difference between underlying attitudes and observable behaviour is subtle but profound. This distinction explains why employees of most organisations regard their organisation's "7 core values" as deserving only lip service – because they haven't bought into them, and because usually top management don't model them ("Don't do as I do, do as I say"). So it just won't work. What is important for an organisation is how their customers feel about the service they receive, or how their employees feel about the organisation, which determines their behaviours at a root level.

To make such an attitudinal change to the customer and employee relationship an organisation has to:

- identify the human experience in customer relationship management (CRM);
- ask why the human experience matters internally and externally;
- recognise the role of emotional intelligence in understanding the human experience;
- work out how it can integrate emotional intelligence into its CRM strategy.

And none of this will have the desired effect if it is undertaken with exploitive, manipulative intent, rather than coming from an "I'm OK, You're OK" position of truly valuing and respecting employees and customers alike.

EI and change

As we saw in Chapter 5 when we explored comfort zones, change requires us to step into our stretch zone. Where an organisation as a whole is changing every individual will be experiencing the discomfort of moving towards something new. The challenge for the organisation and for the individuals within it is to understand the emotional processes that are taking place, so that these can be acknowledged, accepted and released. This will take individuals different lengths of time depending upon the size of their comfort zones (the wider the healthier) and their emotional recovery rates which are defined by their emotional resilience or bounce-back-ability.

Richard Beckhard's formula for change incorporates our perceptions and the emotional processes that we go through when facing change. He defines change as an event that may be viewed as a gain. The transition is a process, and it is this that may be experienced as loss. Often it is the transition that we fight either because we're reluctant to lose what we have or because we are scared of the unknown that might replace it, not necessarily the change itself. His formula for change is

$$(V, D, S) > R$$

For change to take place our vision of the future (**V**) plus our dissatisfaction with the present (**D**) plus our knowing the first steps to take (**S**) must be greater than the cost of the transition and our inertial resistance to change (**R**).

As long as we have a picture of what the future will look like and we're dissatisfied enough with the present situation, plus we know the first steps we need to take towards the future, then emotionally we can take those steps into uncertainty – because the uncertainty is less uncomfortable than staying put. One of the real difficulties for a leader in today's uncertain climate is to understand and support people through the emotional stages of the change process which will be different for each person, and which will have different timescales.

EI in competencies and appraisals

Most organisations have a competency or performance measurement programme in some shape or form. These provide useful benefits such as:

- a common measure for assessment of contribution;
- increased objectivity in the recruitment and selection of staff;
- objective indicators for assessment of potential and succession planning;
- a solid base for career paths and options.

- a focus for relevant, structured development of skills, knowledge and behaviours;

The problem tends to be that many competency frameworks are a messy mixture of values, attitudes and skills. The first step towards generating a competency framework which encourages the development of emotional intelligence in an organisation is to separate these out so that they can be measured effectively.

The competency framework will usually give a structure to the staff appraisal process, the aims of which may include:

- determining future contributions to super-ordinate goals;
- providing feedback on good and bad performance to encourage learning and personal development;
- allocating rewards or creating disincentives;
- counselling to identify staff values and expectations or barriers to performance;
- identifying suitable development opportunities;
- determining capability and potential for promotion;
- keeping staff informed and establishing rapport.

The emotionally intelligent appraisal process

"Staff appraisal is the number one American management problem. It takes the average employee (manager or non-manager) six months to recover from it."
Tom Peters 1988

Is it really as bad as Tom Peters suggested nearly twenty years ago? Have things improved since then? Is it any better in the UK? Are there ways that we can make the process more effective? What does emotional intelligence have to offer?

According to the various responses we hear from people in organizations, appraisal interviews can be viewed with anything from horror to derision to enjoyment. Few of the people we speak to about them are neutral in their remarks and think little either way about them. Their responses seem to be based on the emotional experience they have had either conducting an appraisal or receiving one. There seems to be something about the process of appraisal that makes people particularly emotionally sensitive to the way it is conducted, and on which the ultimate benefit they derive from it depends.

Why emotional intelligence is necessary to make appraisal systems work well

Being emotionally intelligent means that the feedback and communication between the two people takes place in a sensitive and positive way. Given that appraisals are another way of saying "evaluations" and evaluations are another way of saying "judgements", it is not surprising that people are sensitive to the process. Not many people enjoy the experience of being judged, although they may feel very differently about being the one to do the judging! Of course many appraisal systems are designed to get away from purely subjective judgements: they are based around competencies and behavioural indicators, so that some degree of objectivity is built into the system.

Self regard: our personal protection or our Achilles heel?

Any system that attempts to evaluate someone, either in comparison to benchmarks set for the task or against their own previous performance record, contains the potential to be difficult for the appraisee to take in. That is human nature. We place a great deal of importance on our ability to perform, and for many people it is a measure of their self esteem ("I must be a good, worthy person if I can work this hard / get that kind of rating / earn that much money"). We rely on our skills and abilities at tasks and the knowledge we hold to get us work and bring us money to live on. These are survival issues for us. Given all that, the potential for people to feel quite devastated if their appraisal session is clumsily managed is high. They are likely to enter the session with some anxiety, just because it is an exposing process where their gaps will be explored. Add to that the underlying survival issue mentioned above as an extra force in their unconscious, and there is a bad emotional experience just waiting to happen. Douglas McGregor wrote in his famous book *The Human Side of Enterprise* that "the conventional approach (to the appraisal process), unless handled with consummate skill and delicacy, constitutes something close to a violation of the personality". Forceful and frightening words but understandable in the light of the issues being raised above.

Four reasons why appraisals have such a mixed response

Given that there is a mixed response to appraisals, what seems to be important is to work out how and why the ones that do work are successful and why the others are not. There seem to be four main reasons why appraisals have such a mixed reaction.

1. Lack of clarity about the aim of the interview.
2. Lack of clarity about who the interview is for.
3. Timing.
4. Lack of emotional competence on the part of both manager and appraisee.

1. Lack of clarity about the aim of the interview

The general purpose of an appraisal system is to ensure that individuals are performing to the best of their abilities towards improving the efficiency and effectiveness of the organization, and to identify their future development needs. An appraisal interview may therefore consist of one or more of the following:

- performance review of achievements in the preceding period;
- potential review to determine development needs and plan career;
- reward review to determine a salary increase or bonus;
- planning of activities and focus for next period;
- review of the individual's progress with their personal / emotional competence development programme.

Of course many appraisal sessions contain all of these. Not only that, within an organisation different people will use different appraisal processes and have different aims. It is not surprising therefore that the manager and appraisee may find themselves in emotional hot water as they attempt to make something workable out of all that. Each process is hard enough on its own and combining them without being specific about any of them is going to compound the difficulty. From our experience it is asking a great deal of people to take in and use all the potential information encapsulated in these aims in one go, especially when they are nervous. Emotional intelligence research has shown us the neurophysiology behind "emotional hijacks" and the difficulty there can be in connecting with our so-called "thinking brain" when we are flooded with fight or flight biochemicals. And remember that if the interview includes a link to a pay review, the interviewee will at some level be aware of the fact that this interview may affect their basic survival needs and so they will be primed physiologically for fight or flight.

Making a contract

We have found that helping manager and appraisee establish clarity about the aims of the session they are about to have has increased the success rate of these interviews. That initial contracting and specifying of what is happening, how they are going to go about it and what they want out of it, helps to establish a modus operandi that is safer for the appraisee. It is also helpful for the manager, since it gives them something to keep coming back to, providing a route through the discussion. Contracting like this is a skill and one that can be taught quite easily. This skill alone makes a big difference to the emotions experienced by both parties. If the session is supposed to cover all three aspects, the time can be apportioned for each section. Or at the end of a part of the discussion, the aspects covered can be referred to under one or more of these headings. We look at contracting in more depth in Chapter 18.

2. Lack of clarity about who the interview is for

There are a number of stakeholders in the appraisal process and this seems to add to the general confusion about what is happening and why, which dilutes the potential power of an effective human performance management process. We have identified the following as the main potential "beneficiaries" of this process:

- appraisee;
- appraiser;
- second appraiser;
- HR system / requirements.

The appraisal process is usually undertaken as part of the HR system within the organisation. The extent to which it is identified as a process that is mainly for another department's benefit will take some force and power out of the process. We hear a lot of lip service being given to the benefits of appraisal systems from managers in other functions, but when this is not supported by good training, which builds their confidence in their capacity to use the system well, and by being the recipient of emotionally intelligent appraisal themselves, there is a clear reluctance to commit to the process and embrace the benefits.

Obviously, the most desirable state of affairs is that both the appraisee and the direct manager (appraiser) are clearly the main beneficiaries. However, the presence of the second appraiser also needs to be recognised. This manager is responsible for the appraising manager and also the appraisee, who is an indirect report of theirs. This senior manager needs to have a process for formalising his regular performance reviews too. This individual in fact has a double interest – they are responsible for the effective performance of their direct reports as well as that of their indirect reports. They cannot sit in on the process, as that would greatly distort it, but they do need to have a monitoring system that allows them to see how well the appraiser is managing the performance of the team below, and at the same time allows them to keep up to date with the developing potential of the indirect reports. So that, for example, a regional manager would know, if an area manager role became vacant, which of the team would be a strong candidate to take over.

3. Timing

It seems to us that the net result of this combination of shortcomings leads to one of the basic problems with appraisal systems, which is that at least some aspects of the interviews are not integrated into the day-to-day conversations that take place between colleagues and managers during the course of the working day.

In approaching these shortcomings we are reminded of two of the principles we put over when we are training people to give and receive feedback in an emotionally intelligent manner and discussed in Chapter 10.

Negative feedback should be delivered as soon as possible after the event.

For example, in the iterative cycle of Plan → Do → Evaluate → Plan, etc., the evaluation needs to follow as soon as possible after the doing.

Negative feedback should always be accompanied by a request for change or reparation.

What this means in terms of the cycle above is that the evaluation and the planning need to be integrated. For example, if you just tell someone that you are displeased about their behaviour, without asking for anything, they have two options: one is to accept what you say and agree with it. This is often accompanied by the inner thought "I'm bad for doing that wrong." The second option is to overtly or covertly reject what you say and accompany this with the inner thought that "You are bad." Neither of these options is good for future performance, nor for the relationship between the two of you. However, by moving on in the evaluation to what can be different in the future, the atmosphere is transformed from negative to positive; both people feel respected and accepted and the relationship is strengthened, not weakened.

Going back to the objectives of an appraisal system listed earlier, it seems to us that some of the aims need to operate on a different scale compared with some of the others. This is shown below:

Performance review of achievements in the preceding period	1 / month
Potential review to determine development needs and plan career	1 / year
Reward review to determine a salary increase or bonus	1 / year
Planning of activities and focus for next period	1 / quarter
Review of the individual's progress with their personal / emotional competence development programme	1 / month

Managers who are using appraisal systems may find it helpful to think about their aims and try to tackle different aspects at different times and so make progress clearer for both themselves and their appraisees.

4. Lack of emotional competence on the part of both manager and appraisee

The last, but by no means least, reason we have found to be the cause of such mixed responses to human performance improvement is the amount of emotional competence held by both the manager and appraisee. A manager needs to have the right skills, attitudes and, perhaps, value system to conduct an effective appraisal interview. What to do about the appraisers (and indeed appraisees) who do not have sufficient emotional competence? Training in carrying out appraisals is not laid on often enough or well enough. There seems to be an (entirely false) assumption that if you have got to a man-agement, let alone a senior management, position, then you must know how to appraise effectively. One organisation we know ran a very creative and successful training scheme in this respect. They knew that among their man-agers they had some excellent appraisers and some rotten ones, and realised that formal training in appraisal techniques probably wouldn't convert the rotten into the excellent, that something more experiential and more prac-tical was needed. So they arranged that those managers who thought they needed help with their appraisal capabilities could, with the appraisee's consent, sit in on an appraisal carried out by an excellent appraiser in another division of the company, to see what sort of thing goes on when the process is well handled. This led to a welcome spread of healthy attitudes and of good appraisal practice.

What emotional intelligence competences are important?

This can best be answered in terms of our overall model of the processes of emotional intelligence, repeated here in Figure 14.1.

If we look at the basic model that outlines the key areas and levels of emotional intelligence, we can see that both the capacity to be aware and the ability to manage emotional states in oneself and in other people are important. When we assess a manager's emotional intelligence, the scales that are most useful for conducting good appraisals are: Self Regard, Regard for Others, Awareness of Others, Goal Directedness, Invitation to Trust, Trust and Conflict Handling.

Self regard helps because it helps a manager distance themselves from the criticisms that an appraisee may take the opportunity to voice. With high

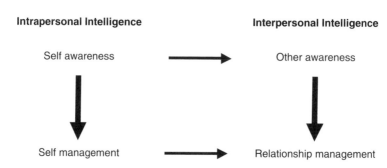

Figure 14.1 *Our model of emotional intelligence.*

self regard they can be clear which piece of negative feedback is something they can do something about, which is something to do with the individual and which to do with systems over which they have no control. A manager with good self regard will not get defensive with the appraisee but will be able to use, appreciate or discount appropriately the things they are being told.

Acceptance of another person is a personal attitude that will have a profound effect on the emotional experience of the interviewee. If they feel that they are being accepted for themselves and that it is only their actions that are being explored, then they are far less likely to be defensive, scared or angry.

Other awareness is obviously extremely important, as it helps the manager be empathic and tune into the interviewee, picking up any discomfort and helping them be as open as possible to the appraisal information. This is reinforced by the other scales of Invitation to Trust and Trust.

Goal directedness in conjunction with the other skills and attitudes helps the manager keep the interview on track and linked to the contract they made at the beginning concerning the aims of the session.

Finally, the skills of conflict management and a "better for both" attitude can be very valuable when an interviewee has become defensive and is responding antagonistically.

Managers and interviewees

We have found that assessing and training both managers and potential interviewees in the same skills and attitudes is critical for the appraisal process to be as effective as possible. This has reduced defensiveness, gone some way towards rebalancing the power differential in the process and speeded up the interviews.

Thinking of the typical stages of an appraisal system, you can see how emotional intelligence on the part of both the manager and the interviewee is helpful, particularly at stages 2, 3, 5 and 6.

Stage 1 – Identify criteria for assessment from job analysis, objectives, competency framework, etc.

Stage 2 – An appraisal report by the manager and sometimes by the appraisee.

Stage 3 – The appraisal interview for an exchange of views on performance.

Stage 4 – Review of the assessment by the appraiser's own boss.

Stage 5 – Action plans to achieve agreed improvements.
Stage 6 – Follow-up by monitoring the action plan.

Within organisations, appraisals are usually thought of in terms of being a system, but looked at another way they are about a process that takes place between two or more people and involves a relationship. In relationship management, a powerful feature within emotional intelligence development, we find that the capacity to address the emotional and practical ramifications of the process itself is extremely important in ensuring the success of both the process and the relationship. For instance, as the appraising manager, being able to introduce and explore with the appraisee what it means to each of you, how you both feel about it, what you both want out of it, how you see it potentially going wrong – and right – will be enormously helpful in setting up a dynamic human development process that really does build performance and liberate potential. Of course when appraisees are able to initiate and address these aspects too, the process becomes extraordinarily powerful. That such a powerful tool is so often seen as a chore and a bore by a third of the people who take part in it is a great waste. Many organisations need to undertake a thorough going review of their staff appraisal process in order to move towards effective performance management. Emotional intelligence assessment and development are an essential route to making appraisals better for all concerned.

Reference

Beckhard, R. and Harris, R. (1987) Organizational Transitions: Managing Complex Change (2nd ed.) Addison-Wesley: Reading MA.
McGregor, D. (2006) The Human Side of Enterprise, McGraw-Hill. First published in 1960.

15

EI in leadership

What is emotionally intelligent leadership?

As we know, our emotional intelligence is a combination of skills, attitudes and habits that we can develop to improve our own personal performance and our relationships with others. And high emotional intelligence has been shown to be a real indicator of performance in leadership. Indeed, Warren Bennis, the leadership guru, recognises the value of EI in leadership:

> *"In those fields I have studied, Emotional Intelligence is much more powerful than IQ in determining who emerges as a leader."*
>
> Warren Bennis On *Becoming a Leader*

Broadly, the history of the study of leadership seems to us a mess. We start with leadership as inborn, then leadership as character, then leadership as a behavioural tendency – none of which helps us towards a differentiated approach to leadership development. An advance was made soon after the Second World War with the introduction of the notion of different leadership styles: Lewin, Lippett and White's Autocratic / Democratic / Laissez-faire and Likert's Exploitative-authoritative / Benevolent-authoritative / Consultative / Participative. This analytic approach is reinforced by the notion of leadership as a bundle of competencies, which then allows for the notion of distributed leadership.

The increasing importance of leadership as we move to an economic structure based on the management of processes, rather than the transformation of objects, was articulated by emphasis on the distinctions between management and leadership and between authority and influence. More recently we have had particular visions of leadership such as Transformational leadership, Values-based leadership and the notion of the Leader as servant. The trouble with these, as with the earliest approaches, is that they are all partial. The rapid collapse of the Taliban showed the limitations of value-based leadership, and whereas some people in some situations will make the most of the leader as servant, there are other contexts where such an approach would be self-evidently disastrous, such as the military.

Still, now more than ever, leadership remains a crucial issue. And, as Warren Bennis makes clear, emotional intelligence has a lot to do with it. Daniel Goleman suggests that, whereas over a broad spectrum of jobs the variance in emotional intelligence accounts for twice as much of the variance in performance than does IQ, when you look at leadership jobs it is four times as much. Hence, in part, the fact that his article "What Makes a Leader?" in the *Harvard Business Review* of Nov–Dec 1998 attracted more demands for reprints than the HBR had ever had for an article before. Until, that is, they published his second article "Leadership That Gets Results" in the Mar–Apr 2000 edition, which even more people wanted a copy of!

The first of these articles makes the point that emotional intelligence is the sine qua non of leadership. "Effective leaders are alike in one crucial way: they all have a high degree of emotional intelligence." And he also rightly emphasises that "Emotional intelligence can be learned. The process is not easy. It takes time and commitment."

All unexceptionable, but it is the second article that really helps us to be specific about the question of the relationship of emotional intelligence and leadership and begins to suggest what we should do about it. In this article, Goleman's approach is a differentiated one: instead of treating "leadership" as an undifferentiated whole, he identifies six different leadership styles, which will be more or less effective according to the circumstances and the identity of the people being led. They are: Coercive, Authoritative, Affiliative, Democratic, Pacesetting and Coaching. He then reports on work by Hay/McBer which correlates these with their effect on aspects of the organisational climate that go with high performance, viz: Flexibility, Responsibility, Standards, Rewards, Clarity and Commitment, and derives an overall impact of each leadership style on the performance climate.

He also takes a differentiated approach to emotional intelligence, identifying which specific elements of EI are required to adopt effectively each of his leadership styles. This is important because emotional intelligence is not a unitary concept; it is shorthand for a collection of a number of independent, though related, attributes. The useful question to ask, therefore, is not "How emotionally intelligent am I?" but "What is my emotional intelligence profile?". In other words, which aspects come easily to me and which do I have more difficulty with? Not only will people have different profiles, but different jobs will have different ideal profiles, and the same job will have different ideal profiles in different situations. As Esther Orioli of Qmetrics puts it, "It's not how smart is this child, but how is this child smart?".

There is a problem with the model Daniel Goleman adopts in his second article. Two of the leadership styles (Coercive and Pacesetting) have a negative influence on the performance climate. Yet, he identifies specific emotional intelligence competencies as underlying each style. Since he starts from the premise that EI underlies leadership, how can it be that aspects of EI have a negative effect? The answer, in our view, is that those things he describes as underlying the Coercive and Pacesetting styles are not aspects of emotional intelligence at all. Goleman, under the influence of his former professor David McClelland, used to include motivation as one of the five main building blocks of emotional intelligence, but he has since, in our view rightly, dropped that. The two "EI competencies" he sees as underlying both the Coercive and the Pacesetting styles are Drive to Achieve and Initiative. We do not see those as being aspects of EI and therefore we are unsurprised to find that leadership styles incorporating these attributes are overall negatively correlated with performance. To see how the *is*™ scales with which you are now familiar map onto Goleman's leadership styles see Table 15.1. Of course different people will interpret these styles in different ways. For example, both the coercive and pace-setting styles ought ideally to demonstrate assertiveness, but will often rather be characterised by aggression.

The important point about Goleman's situational approach to leadership is that, while he shows that different styles need different elements of emotional intelligence and have differential effects on the performance climate, he acknowledges that even the ones which have an overall long-term

Table 15.1 *Leadership styles and related EI attributes.*

Style	Leader's modus operandi	Style in a phrase	Demonstrates these 'ie' elements	When the style works best
Coercive	Demands immediate compliance	"Do what I tell you"	Personal Power Goal Directedness Assertiveness	In a crisis, with problem employees, or to kick-start a turnaround
Authoritative	Mobilises people toward a vision	"Come with me"	Regard for Self and Others Personal Power Goal Directedness Balanced Outlook	When changes require a new vision, or when a clear direction is needed
Affiliative	Creates harmony and builds emotional bonds	"People come first"	Regard for Others Other Awareness Interdependence	To heal rifts in a team or to motivate people during stressful circumstances
Democratic	Forges consensus through participation	"What do you think?"	Regard for Self and Others Other Awareness Flexibility Interdependence	To build buy-in or consensus, or to get input from valuable employees
Pacesetting	Sets high standards for performance	"Do as I do now"	Personal Power Goal Directedness	To get quick results from a highly motivated and competent team
Coaching	Develops people for the future	"Try this"	Regard for Others Awareness of Others Flexibility	To help an employee improve performance or develop long-term strengths

negative effect on performance climate are the style of choice in particular situations. So, to be capable of being an effective leader in a whole range of situations, you need to have all the EI elements needed for each style, each of which is preferred for one situation or another.

The danger here is that we are back to saying leaders need to be maximally emotionally intelligent all round. This becomes so overgeneralised that we are back where we started – with a blunt instrument. But that is not the whole picture. There are also some metaqualities and attitudes that leaders need to have in order to be able to deploy the qualities Goleman has identified. These are best understood in terms of our overall EI model, depicted in Figure 14.1.

Leadership is obviously a subdivision of relationship management, but what is useful about this model in this context is that it shows us how relationship management depends on all the other main areas of emotional intelligence. Follow the causal arrows back and you will see that effective relationship management depends on both good other awareness and good self management. And both of these depend on good self awareness.

This is borne out by experience. When we use the Team Effectiveness questionnaire (te^{TM}), which asks team members to identify issues which are problematic to the functioning of their team, we often find that one of those identified as problematic is "The leadership in this team does not give a good example of how to manage your own feelings" – clearly a defect in self management. As an example of the fundamental importance of self awareness, consider the case of a senior manager in the food industry who thinks of himself as highly collaborative and collegial in his style. His subordinates, however, consider him highly directive and dictatorial. Even when he does say things which in terms of content are respectful and collaborative, these are belied by the way he says them and his incongruent body language. Yet he can't understand why his subordinates experience him the way they do. The problem that needs addressing here is one of relationship management, but no intervention addressing that directly is going to get off the ground until he has been helped to become more aware of himself, his attitudes and his behaviour. Only then can he begin to consider the impact of this on others (relationship management) and start to change what he does (self management). Self awareness is fundamental.

In order to be an effective leader in a variety of situations, you need:

1. To be able to identify the leadership style that is required by the person(s) you are to lead in each type of situation: for that you need *Other Awareness*.
2. To be willing to provide the appropriate style for a variety of people in a variety of situations: for that you need *Flexibility*, an aspect of self management.
3. To know whether you can effectively, and without too much personal cost, provide that style of leadership yourself, or whether you need to delegate a particular aspect: for that you need *Accurate Self Assessment*, otherwise known as Self Knowledge, which grows out of Self Awareness through the process of Reflective Learning.

To understand what is involved in all this we shall refer to individual scales of the Individual Effectiveness questionnaire (*ie*™) – see Part II of this book.

In order to be *other aware*, you have to have a high Regard for Others in general. We tend to think, because this has been the prevailing folk model of leadership in our culture, that effective leadership is all to do with self belief. And so, to a degree, it is: no-one is likely to be an effective leader if they do not have reasonably high Self Regard. But that is not enough: they need to believe not only in themselves but also in those whom it is their job to lead. This is brought home by the results of doing an exercise recommended by Qmetrics as part of the feedback process for the EQMap, which was generated in the leadership programme at Stanford University (Cooper and Sawaf, 1997). In order to convey their position that leadership is just a specific form of influence, respondents are asked to identify someone who has been particularly influential over them, in other words changed what they do, which is in a sense the role of the leader. And to identify what it was about this person and what they did that made the difference. Again and again, we find that the common factor in the stories this procedure evokes is that the leader believed in the person, often more than the person believed in themselves. "They believed I could do it, helped me to do it, and I did it." Effective leaders have high expectations of those they lead, not in a demanding way but in an encouraging way. The tricky thing about this is that calibrating your expectations is a constantly changing challenge. As people develop you need to expect more of them. If your expectations are too low, they miss out on the opportunity for challenge, growth and a sense of achievement and recognition. If your expectations are too high, the person is set up for a succession of failures and they may end up shrinking rather than growing. Accurate and subtle other awareness is obviously crucial here. With a high level of other awareness we shall be able to enlist their emotional engagement so that, as a leader, we can convince others that our way is the way to go.

This means we need to understand how someone is feeling about a given situation so that we can be sure they are comfortable with what is being asked of them, and so that we can help them move forward with commitment. If we try to coerce or be directive, yes we'll achieve short-term results but the likelihood is that the hard sell won't have been swallowed and we'll need to push for the same thing again and again further down the line.

Emotions are powerful things. Like it or not, emotions are involved in every single decision and action we take. If we don't acknowledge their importance within us, and within the people we live and work with, then we're missing a trick. The challenge, even in this enlightened age, is still the word "emotion" – many people would still rather just sweep these under the carpet!

Flexibility is, in some ways, more problematic as a concept. It was a popular psychological construct, as the opposite polarity to rigidity, in the 1950s, when the Frankfurt school of sociology in particular were attempting to understand the psychological underpinnings of fascism. Now it has come into the limelight again as a key element of emotional intelligence, particularly for leadership jobs. (It also has a more general application in that the level of flexibility tends to predict response to training and change interventions – the more flexible people are, the more use they are likely to make of training and the greater their response to change interventions.) However, when we talk about this in the educational sector, people's faces tend to fall. Our educational system is, it seems to us, ill designed for promoting and developing flexibility in its consumers, who will constitute the workforce of the future. This is even more true, alas, since the introduction of the National Curriculum. The first target for a teacher is to be in control of their class, and the simplest way to do that is to control reliably and predictably what all the pupils are doing, or supposed to be doing, all the time. This militates against their developing flexibility. All good teachers now prepare detailed and specific "lesson plans"; these have great virtues but they do not include the development of pupils' flexibility. The most obvious place, to our mind, where flexibility may be developed at school is on the team sports field, and also perhaps in such out-of-class activities as scouting.

So, a number of employees arrive in the workplace needing to have their flexibility developed. What we need to do to help them do that is something which we suspect many management teams, and many departments responsible for management training, do not know the answer to at present. What is clear from Goleman's work is that Authoritative, Affiliative and Democratic leadership styles increase flexibility, the Coaching style less so and the Coercive and Pacesetting styles actually have a negative effect on flexibility. Insofar as leadership development and succession planning is concerned, the clear consequence of the importance of flexibility is that there is a virtue in rotating high fliers and future leaders rapidly through a wide succession of jobs, not just to broaden their experience but also to develop their flexibility.

Accurate Self Assessment is the long-term correlate of Self Awareness, built up through the process of Reflective Learning. If you are in touch with yourself from minute to minute, you can build up an accurate picture of how you function over time. It is a crucial requirement of leadership and luckily what we need to do to develop it is fairly obvious. Organisations which seek to maximise the potential of their staff, and to be learning organisations, need to have climates in which feedback is readily and skillfully given and received downwards, sideways and upwards. Unfortunately, this often is not the case. Another of the items in the *i^{TM}* team questionnaire that frequently is seen as problematic is "In this team people don't seem to know how to relate to one another effectively, e.g. how to give and receive positive and negative feedback effectively and acceptably." Luckily, how to improve this situation is fairly clear: partly it is a question of skills training at giving and receiving positive and negative feedback (surprisingly, and sadly, one of the aspects the English are worst at is receiving positive feedback); partly it is a question of attitude development training to help people improve both their Self Regard and Regard for Others. In process terms, it is important to have an emotionally intelligent and effective appraisal system (see the previous chapter). And the need for accurate self assessment reinforces the value of 360° feedback procedures for aspects of emotional intelligence as for everything else.

So, what are the particular elements of emotional intelligence that are required for effective leadership? We have already seen that, in terms of the *i^{TM}*, all of the fundamental scales are, as you would expect, required:

1   Self Regard
2   Regard for Others
4   Self Awareness
5   Awareness of Others
17 Reflective Learning
18 Accurate Self Assessment

Of the more specific scales, which are important? Well, you can argue that they all are, but we have found that four in particular are crucial. *Flexibility* (Scale 9) we have already seen the importance of. *Goal Directedness*

(Scale 8) is also a requirement: after all, if you are going to be a leader you are going to be leading people to somewhere. *Personal Power* (Scale 7) – what the psychologists call locus of control, or talk of in terms of attribution theory – is also required because it is a self-fulfilling prophecy. If you believe that you are a victim and things happen to you, then so they do, but if you believe that you are "Master of my fate and captain of my soul", why then so you are and you have an impact on the world, rather than vice versa. Finally, leadership is an aspect of relationship management; it is about being influential within a series of personal relationships. Hence, *Personal Openness and Connectedness* (Scale 10) proves to be important: "the extent to which you make, and the ease with which you make, significant connections with other people". And if the connection is to be that of leader and follower then the leader will need to be completely trustworthy and have high integrity (Scale 11) – see our discussion on authentic leadership on page 212.

There is another lesson to be learned from a consideration of Goleman's work on leadership that gets results, and that is about the balancing act that leadership involves. If you look at what distinguishes the two leadership styles that have a negative effect on performance climate from those that have a positive effect, you find three related dimensions:

Product	vs.	Process
Task	vs.	Maintenance
Short term	vs.	Long term

The good manager, and still more the good leader, needs to keep in mind, to pay attention to and to juggle with both ends of these three polarities. The Coercive and Pacesetting leadership styles concentrate on Product to the exclusion of Process, on Task to the exclusion of Maintenance and on the Short term to the exclusion of the Long term. Hence, the long-term negative effect on performance, even paradoxically enough in the case of the Pacesetting style, which is, on the face of it, highly performance oriented.

But there are certain circumstances when it is right and proper, indeed crucially necessary, to concentrate on these: in a crisis, to kick start a turn-around, with problem employees (when the Coercive style may be needed) or to get quick results from a highly motivated and competent team (when the Pacesetting style may be needed). It is no good having a wonderfully developed and emotionally intelligent team if, meanwhile, the business has gone belly up.

Emotionally intelligent leadership, which is effective leadership, does not necessarily mean being all touchy and feely all the time. Rather it means being aware of yourself and others and the situation, knowing your strengths and relative weaknesses, being flexible and managing effectively your relationships with those you lead, while always staying goal directed.

Developing emotionally intelligent leadership

As with the propensity to act consistently with emotional intelligence, we believe most people have the potential to be a good leader too. A view shared by one of our clients, a Learning and Development Manager at one of the UK's largest financial services organisations, "We've got 2000 potential leaders working here . . ."

But how can we have this belief that most people have this potential? What stops *anyone* being a great leader?

As we have seen when we ask delegates on our training courses to name the qualities of someone who has influenced them greatly, or who they have experienced as a true leader, the majority will cite things like "He believed in me", "She values each person's contribution", "She's got a real belief and conviction", "He always follows through – does what he says he will do", etc. These are all about the attitudes of the leaders and the value they place on their people, and also on themselves (it's difficult to truly value others if you don't value yourself). And these are usually a mirror of the qualities by which the delegates themselves would like to be known for their own leadership – their own leadership values. And the great news is that, as most of us can develop these attitudes, so most of us can be good leaders!

In fact, as emotional intelligence requires the adoption of these same attitudes, as well as the same self management and relationship management skills that demonstrate effective leadership, we would go as far as to say that being a good leader requires emotional intelligence and being emotionally intelligent means that you will demonstrate good leadership – i.e. emotional intelligence and good leadership are mutually perpetuating, like one of Escher's drawings.

The important thing here is that whichever leadership model you sub-scribe to, emotional intelligence is going to be what makes the difference, because EI is present within every model of leadership that we have seen. Why? Because emotional intelligence is about self management and rela-tionship management and these are, of course, essential skills of a good leader and represented in various ways, with various labels, across the dif-ferent models.

Because we all have these skills to varying degrees, and all these skills are developable with the right interventions, then we can develop any or all aspects should we choose to do so. So what is the "right" intervention?

Underpinning all these self management and relationship management skills are some crucial attitudes. If these attitudes are not adopted, it will not be possible to act with emotional intelligence and therefore, in our view, it will be difficult to be a good, effective leader.

Well, first let us ask you this question: why should anyone follow you? With the decline of authority people now have much more of a choice of whether to follow a would-be leader, and more of an idea of what they want from a leader. If you want me to follow you, and to believe in your vision, I'll probably need some convincing!

So, when developing leaders in business, we need to start by helping people to develop their Self Regard, to value themselves and their own capa-bilities as a leader, and to then understand how their Regard for Others will impact on people's willingness to follow them. This is the uniqueness of our approach to leadership development.

Our emotional intelligence is the key factor that impacts our ability to be an inspirational leader. EI is a combination of skills, attitudes and habits that we can develop to improve our performance and our relationships with others. EI is about how we manage our personality.

For us, there is no great mystery about "what makes a good leader?" As we discussed at the beginning of this section, what matters is identifying what *stops* you from being a good leader.

Resonance – leading with feeling

At the Global Nexus conference on EI in June 2005, Daniel Goleman emphasised that leaders now need to look towards the relational side of leadership. At the same conference, his colleague Dr Annie McKee concluded that today's leader needs to be mindful, compassionate and hopeful.

We can have all the skills in the world, but if our underlying attitude towards ourselves and others is flawed, then we will not come across with the integrity and authenticity that is essential for today's leaders. Our integrity is determined by the degree to which our outward presentation is aligned with our inner thoughts and feelings. As Albert Mehrabian suggested in his research into how we respond to messages, the words we say may communicate only 7% of the message. The rest is delivered through our nonverbal communication. Human beings are highly sensitive to the energies they receive from other people – hence the undoubted importance of resonance. If we're saying one thing and our body is communicating something else, we'll be sussed out immediately. Equally, and again reinforced by TA theory, whichever message is ulterior (at the deeper level) will be the one that others will respond to. So, if we're not coherent, this will be bad news if we're needing to invite people to trust us enough to follow us.

With today's climate of accountability, leaders can no longer get away with the "JFDI" style of leadership. Today we have to understand the position from which we are evaluating ourselves and others in order to lead them. This evaluation involves our thinking and our feeling. So, leadership is no longer a case of mind over matter – today we need also to be able to lead with feeling.

Authentic leadership – being the change

Richard Harvey, a colleague of ours, has highlighted the crucial importance of leaders "walking their talk" during change: "Whatever attitudinal or behavioural changes you wish to see in your employees, it is essential that the organisational leaders act consistently as role models."

Here, we're now looking at what it means to "Be the Change" – why this is so essential and the challenges facing leaders in their own personal development if they are to achieve this.

Reactive vs. proactive change

First we need to make a distinction between the "push" of *reactive* change imposed by organisational necessity and the "pull" of *proactive* change made as a self development choice by individual leaders. There is a current consensus among both academics and practitioners of a need to move from *transactional leadership* – leadership through "command and control" and something that is *done* to people – to the current emphasis on *transformational leadership* – where leaders create the conditions through their behaviours and environmental influence to best free-up individual potential and contribution.

The following list of the factors generating the need for a shift from transactional to transformational leadership is very reminiscent of the list in Chapter 1 of the societal changes which are generating new organisational requirements dependent on emotional intelligence. Hardly surprising then that being a transformational leader turns out to involve being emotionally intelligent.

Factors driving the move from transactional to *transformational* leadership:

- Flattening of management structures
- Distributed leadership and decision-making
- Flexible contracts, project work, partnerships and alliances
- Legislation on behalf of workers
- Demanding expectations of generation x and y
  — the end of deference to authority figures
  — desire for variety, choice and flexibility: the end of the "job for life"
  — increased higher education
  — work/life balance
- Human capital – employees as investors of their knowledge and networks
- Recognition of the benefits of diversity and nonconformism, creativity and innovation, etc.
- The information age – easy access to information and IT
- The speed required to deal with complexity, e.g. globalisation
- Increasing customer demands and changing demographics

Organisations where the predominant and accepted leadership style is more transactional are likely to be those that are most out of step with the changing social and political environment in which they operate, and so increasingly out of step with changing customer needs. We would see these organisations as being low in collective EI.

In these organisations the need for a culture of transformational leadership is often only addressed as a *reactive* need to massive organisational change. Whatever structural changes are required can only be implemented successfully through people, and so without transformational leadership, change will be problematic.

In such situations, leaders often will not possess previous experience to draw on, or naturally possess the degree of flexibility and emotional resilience needed to separate their personal reactions from their professional responsibilities. These responsibilities include transforming their own behaviours and creating the conditions that will lead their people through their individual emotional responses to change. Some leaders will find themselves stuck, unable to do what is required. Others will be toxic to the organisation's progress; for example, they may take out their personal discomfort on their people. Leaders with the capability to lead radical change are rare and tend to be in great demand. Alan Leighton, for example – currently rolling out radical change at Royal Mail – is probably best remembered for his part in the turnaround of Asda in the 1990s.

But developing the capability for transformational leadership does not have to be as a reaction to organisational change. Ideally, the opportunity to "be the change" is self-generated – a *proactive* choice made by the leader, perhaps as a response to experiencing a career plateau or as a result of a realisation of a shift in attitudes after experiencing radical change in their personal lives. We see this as choosing to develop one's emotional intelligence: before transforming others, leaders must transform themselves.

Advice from a leadership guru

"You must be the change you wish to see in the world"

Mahatma Gandhi

This is an oft-quoted sentiment that now has sadly almost become a cliché – in danger of losing its impact because world leaders and development, training and change professionals alike (us included!) use it so often to illustrate a fundamental point.

To dilute the cliché, imagine Mahatma Gandhi talking to you now on a one-to-one basis, saying to you, "You must be the change you wish to see in the world". What does this really mean to you as an individual, as a leader? Be honest: are you really someone who has chosen to help others develop themselves? Or is leadership really an exercise in enhancing your ego? Do you wish others would be as visionary, as effective, as tolerant, as organised, as broad-minded, as committed to the cause as you? Do you see them as less than perfect, with room for improvement? If your answer is yes (and we defy anyone, except perhaps the likes of the Dalai Lama, to deny this, as we are only human after all!), then this is a barrier to modelling Gandhi's wisdom for yourself.

It is not about managing the change or making the change happen. What Gandhi meant by "being the change" is this:

> ". . . before we can expect changes in others, before we can truly endeavour to make a difference in this complex world, substantial change has to occur within us – as individuals. Too often we focus on external change while neglecting the necessity of examining our own hearts. Are we willing, through the process of critical self-examination, to experience our own personal transformation?" (Martin Luther King Symposium Planning Committee, 2003)

To understand ourselves requires introspection and being prepared to acknowledge parts of our self that we might prefer to ignore. A crucial quality of a transformational and emotionally intelligent leader is accurate self assessment and a willingness to receive honest feedback from others, as in 360° assessment. If we can't recognise our strengths and weaknesses, how can we expect others to do the same? And if we don't have this self knowledge, we cannot be authentic – rather we will attempt to cover up our perceived weaknesses, which will challenge our integrity. We will portray an image of who we think we should be as a leader, or what we think people want us to be. We need to be able to stand by our own principles and values. Equally, we also need to listen to and respect others' views and values so that we can lead for the good of the organisation, not just to increase our own power base. The process of reflective learning is essential for transformational personal change. Once we bring some new knowledge of our self, perhaps around our behaviours or our emotional responses, into our awareness, we then need to do something about it to develop as a leader and as a human being (Figure 15.1).

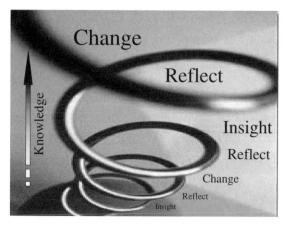

Figure 15.1 *Reflective learning helps to bring about transformational personal change.*

The challenge of personal change is being prepared to step out of our comfort zone – that safe, comfortable place where we think we know ourselves and can depend on our reactions and responses to our environment. As soon as we start to prod and probe, and destabilise what we thought to be true about ourselves, we delve into the realm of uncertainty – uncertainty of the validity of the behaviours we currently choose to display or the values we hold dear, of the attitudes that underpin our sense of self. But it is only through this uncertainty that we can come to discover our true self, the self that lies beneath our conditioned responses – the authentic self. And this takes perhaps the greatest courage of all – the courage to understand our thoughts and our feelings and how these shape the person we project to the world.

Being a role model

So, are you a transformational leader who has transformed yourself? Are you an exemplary role model, a living example of the kind of employee you wish everyone in your organisation could be, or of the kind of leader your training interventions advocate?

Indeed, why should anyone follow you? To be a transformational leader or change agent, you need to have healthy, emotionally intelligent attitudes.

Of course, leadership skills such as critical thinking, creativity and political astuteness are vital too, and it is often these skills that move us up the corporate ladder or lead us to management positions on change projects. And they are essential when leading change at any level. But it is the underlying attitudes to these skills that determine whether or not we actually inspire people and enable them to follow us.

Creativity, for example, requires flexibility of mind – to be open to new ideas, concepts or directions, without needing to control the outcome. "Man cannot discover new oceans unless he has the courage to lose sight of the shore" (André Gide). Political astuteness requires an awareness of others – to be able to understand where another is coming from, to recognise what their needs or issues are. But to be truly open to creativity, we have to embrace the fact that we may not have the answer and that someone else in our team could come up with the million-dollar creative solution. If we are in any way closing ourselves off to creative outlets because we are protecting our own positions we will limit our own creativity and disempower those around us who are willing and able to contribute.

Have a go at saying the following:

- I know I am creative.
- There is always a solution to a problem or challenge.
- I am the only person who can come up with good ideas in my team.
- I am the only person who should come up with good ideas in my team.
- As a team we are very creative and forward thinking.

Which of these statements do you believe?
Notice the feelings that arise within you when you make these statements.
Reflect on what comes into your awareness.

Equally, it is what we do with what we know about others' agendas and needs that marks the difference between being a trusted leader or not. It is not enough to seek people's views and opinions and give the impression that we have listened. We have to demonstrate that we value the needs of others and seek outcomes that will benefit everyone. So, political astuteness in transformational leadership terms requires integrity. We must invite people to trust us, so that they may become willing to put their trust in our vision and decisions.

Again, have a go at saying the following:

- I know how to really listen to people.
- I can always read between the lines of what someone is saying.
- I always take into account the needs of everyone involved in a decision.
- What I want is not always what's best for my organisation.
- People trust that I will do right by them.

Which of these statements do you believe?

Notice the feelings that arise within you when you make these statements.

Reflect on what comes into your awareness.

So, whether "being the change" is as a result of a reactive organisational "push" or of a proactive "pull", to seek to become a truly transformational leader, the journey is the same. You must look inside and seek personal meaning and transformation before you can truly be the change for others. However, the external imposition of the reactive "push" may not allow you the time and space required for the full journey of personal transformation.

So, if you or your clients have not experienced transformational change as yet, perhaps it's best to take the lead before circumstances outside your control remove that choice. To understand why this is going to be so important, we need to remember the predictions we mentioned earlier of leading business strategists such as Professor Richard Scase, Emeritus Professor of Organisational Behaviour at Kent University, and Dr Lynda Gratton, Professor of Management Practice at the London Business School.

The leaders of the future will need to be facilitators – leaders who enable others to develop their own leadership and potential. They will also be collaborative leaders, highly skilled in developing and sustaining mutually beneficial partnerships and able to influence and lead non-employees and stakeholders. These both require a new set of skills and attitudes for leadership – emotionally intelligent skills and attitudes. Being a role model of transformational leadership or "being the change" cannot be achieved without these.

Reflecting on your own leadership

This section provides a handful of exercises and prompts for reflection that will help you understand what kind of a leader you are and how you are currently using your emotional intelligence.

We suggest you write your reflections in a journal or in a Word document – something that you can add to easily should you choose to continue the process of reflective learning. These exercises can be continually revisited.

Leadership influence

In your journal, write down some thoughts on the following:

- Who is the person who has influenced you the most?
- What did this person do that touched you?
- What did it feel like to be with this person?
- What did you learn?

Now, in your journal, write down your thoughts on the following:

- Who have you touched?
- How have you touched others?
- How do you think others feel in your presence?

Leadership potential

Now take a look at your leadership potential:

- What do you value in a leader?
- What kind of a leader are you?

- How do you think others experience your leadership?
- How would you describe your current leadership performance?
- How can you aim to raise your leadership performance?

What's getting in your way?

Identify and seek to manage your leadership interferences:

- Explore your current performance and things you would like to change.
- Be honest about your current attitudes – which ones help and which ones hinder you?
- Identify the underlying limiting beliefs and outdated values that are inhibiting you as a leader.
- Rediscover your true positive beliefs about yourself and reaffirm values that are important to you now.
- Explore new attitudes and new ways of enhancing your leadership.

Reflective learning

How do you plan to raise your leadership performance even higher? Continually review:

- your potential;
- your goals;
- your values;
- how you are overcoming your interferences.

Value congruence

- What do you value in a leader?
- Which qualities do you want to develop as a leader?
- How do these sit with your organisation's values?

1. *Write down your values*.
   List the qualities that you would want to be known by as a leader.
   List the leaders you most respect (past and present, famous and not).
   What do they stand for, what beliefs did they have and show when

leading that you respect so much? These are likely to be the same beliefs and values you hold.

2. *Prioritise your values.*
   This may be difficult at first, but you can adjust the prioritisation as you discover more about who you are and what you stand for.

3. *Take your top three values.*
   Against each one describe how you currently express this value in your leadership.

4. *Develop your top three values.*
   Against each value now write down ways you can show the world more of this value.

5. *Remind yourself.*
   Before you next go into work, remind yourself of your core beliefs and values and how you experience and express these as you lead others. Write down three things that you will focus on daily which will bring you closer to your core values.

6. *Focus your attention on your values.*
   Don't think so much of what you need to do, focus more of your attention on your core values. With practice, you will find that improved performance as a leader will occur more effortlessly, as it will be driven from the depths of your soul rather than the forefront of your mind.

(Adapted from material produced by the Institute of Applied Sports Psychology.)

References

Bennis, W. (2003) *On Becoming a Leader*, revised edition, Random House.

Cooper, R.K. and Sawaf, A. (1997) *Executive EQ – Emotional Intelligence in Leadership and Organizations*, Perigee.

Goleman, D. (1998) "What Makes a Leader?", *Harvard Business Review*, Nov/Dec, 93–102.

Goleman, D. (2000) "Leadership that Gets Results", *Harvard Business Review*, Nov/Dec, 78–90.

Karseras, G. (2003) "Playing Your Values", Institute of Applied Sports Psychology.

Martin Luther King Symposium Planning Committee (2003) The University of Michigan's 16th observance of the life and contributions of the Rev. Dr Martin Luther King, Jr.

16

EI for teams

There is a fundamental point about teams that we need to bear in mind at all times when considering how they work, and in particular when seeking to identify what it is that differentiates high-performing from low-performing teams: teams are, or should be, greater than the sum of their parts. When we look at dysfunctional teams the problem almost always lies in how the various parts work together, rather than what the various parts are like. And "how the various parts work together" is very much a question of emotional intelligence.

The currently most popular model of team functioning is probably still Belbin® Team Roles. This is reminiscent of the instructions for assembling flatpack furniture: you get a list of parts required for the finished item (unfortunately, in the human case pictures are not included!), and then some instructions about how they are to fit together and so create the finished item. But human beings are not like furniture parts, fit for only one purpose. They are, or they can be, flexible, both in what they do and in how they relate to one another. Flexibility is a key aspect of emotional intelligence when it comes to team working. Indeed, you can argue that if you have a team composed of members who are high in flexibility then the Belbin® Team Roles model is not much help, because the members will alter their functioning to fit in with the requirements in this particular team and the propensities of the other members of the team. It is when a team is composed of members who are low in emotional intelligence, particularly who are inflexible, that the Team Roles model comes into its own. If people behave like furniture parts, comfortable in their roles and not wanting to develop and change, then the challenge is to help them move beyond this mindset if you want to raise the performance of the team.

The need for flexibility to allow the members of a team to adapt their functioning to one another is a particular example of the relevance to team functioning of the emotional intelligence of individual members. And when ideas about emotional intelligence first began to be applied to teams, in the 1990s, tests for measuring the emotional intelligence of teams tended to consist of measurements of the emotional intelligence of the individual members of the team. Then you got, at worst, a statement of the individual intelligence of the "average member", or at best a distribution pattern among the team members of the strengths and weaknesses in terms of the various elements of emotional intelligence. But this approach ignores what we started by saying was the most fundamental fact in this area: teams are more than the sum of their parts. Furniture parts work the same whichever particular piece of furniture they are being used to be part of, but human beings are responsive and interactive and they work differently in different teams.

If we are members of a team where the prevailing team culture or ethos is one of competition, of trying to grab the credit and shift the blame, then we will either find ourselves joining the process unwittingly, or withdrawing from the other team members or even leaving, or at the very least certainly not being able to share our vulnerabilities with others, float half-formed creative ideas, or ask for and get support from others. But if we are in a team where the prevailing team culture or ethos is one of collaboration, tolerance and mutual support, then we will most likely behave more openly and more effectively, although we are still the same person who could be closed, overindependent and overcompetitive in the first team. And for those who cannot adapt to an emotionally intelligent team environment, they will withdraw and probably eventually leave. So what matters here is clearly the team culture rather than the propensities of the individual members, and that is what is measured by our team measure of emotional intelligence the Team Effectiveness questionnaire ($\mathit{t3}^{™}$), which we explore below.

In terms of Timothy Gallwey's P = p − i formula, what we are dealing with here is not internal interferences, which differ from individual to individual, but external interferences. My propensity to behave with emotional intelligence in a team context will be determined not just by my personal interferences as measured by the $i3$™, but also by the external interferences as measured by the 43™. And the team itself will have its own external interferences, because it will be functioning in an environment largely determined by the organisation of which it forms a part: these are what our upcoming Organisational Effectiveness questionnaire will measure.

So, if the ethos of the team is the main thing which determines with how much emotional intelligence that team functions, and therefore how effectively it functions, what is it that determines the ethos of the team? There are at least four elements that are involved here:

1. The individual level of emotional intelligence of the members of the team
2. The level of emotional intelligence of the team leader
3. The environment, which is to say the emotional intelligence of the organisation of which the team forms a part, and
4. The history of the team, the team corollary of habit in an individual.

In practical terms what this means is that:

1. In a team which has problems with the emotional intelligence and effectiveness of its functioning, it may be helpful to measure both the team ethos with the 43™ and also the emotional intelligence of the individual members with the $i3$™, and to intervene at both levels.
2. One of the main functions of a team leader is to set the team ethos, and if you have an emotionally unintelligent team leader you are likely to get an emotionally unintelligent and ineffective team. One of the options in using the 43™ is to get a report comparing the leader's responses with those of the rest of the team, which would probably be useful in this context, as would the outcome of the leader's $i3$™. And there are questions in the 43™ which refer directly to the leader's style. It may be that EI development for the leader will result in EI development and greater effectiveness of the team.
3. To the degree that what goes on in the team is affected by what goes on outside the team in the organisation as a whole, these will be able to be identified with the Organisation Effectiveness questionnaire 43 and intervening at the organisation level, where necessary, will support interventions at the team level.

4. In some teams, unhealthy aspects of the team ethos are not due to any of the three factors we have already spelt out, but are leftovers from the team's history: for example, they may be due to limitations on the emotional intelligence of the first leader of the team when it was formed, who set the tone but has since moved on. So for teams as well as for individuals, the shift from unconscious incompetence through conscious incompetence and conscious competence to unconscious competence may need to be promoted by adopting a 21 day commitment to change and regularly reviewing progress.

The chief determinants of the level of performance, in teams as well as in individuals, are attitudinal. If people are emotionally intelligent, and in particular if they are high in flexibility, they will not always do their standard thing in every team setting but will have a range of behaviours to call on, will use their Awareness of Others to diagnose which particular way of working will be most needed in that particular team, and will adapt their behaviour accordingly.

But what if the emotional intelligence of the individuals has yet to be developed? Where do you start in developing sustainable quality performance in a team? First you need to be sure that you understand what the current attitudes of the team actually are. And this must not be confused with current outcomes, or even the behaviours of certain individuals. When you look at the emotional intelligence of a team, what you are really looking at is what is going on within the team and within the individual relationships within the team. A standard team development will take an external view of the team. It will tend to be focused on what the team is having to deal with, external factors such as policy, organisational culture and leadership styles. A good team development will also explore internal issues such as lack of trust and personality clashes. These, of course, are important, but addressing them on their own will not create a sustainable high team performance.

In our view what creates real synergy and cohesion within a team is not so much how the team deals with the outside world and the internal outcomes this generates – the outside world will always be there with its opportunities and its threats. But on what foundation is the team built? How does the team handle its internal world – what is actually going on within the team that may be hindering or helping its development and its performance?

The EI qualities of a high-performing team

The factors that differentiate effective, high-performing teams from their less effective and more poorly performing counterparts are seldom technical or skills related; they are seldom to do with knowledge or skills, but often to do with attitudes and habits. The mark of a high-performing team is that it is emotionally intelligent. And that is not just a question of being composed of emotionally intelligent members, though that obviously helps. Since we all of us behave differently in different teams, it is obviously more than that: it is about the team culture or ethos.

Time after time, when we work with teams on experiential programmes, the same learning outcomes present themselves: trust, effective communication, respect, etc. These are all related to the creation of true interdependence; and involve the belief by everyone in the team that the whole is greater than the sum of the parts, that by working together towards a common goal they can achieve far more than any one of them could achieve as an individual, and that they will be able at the same time to achieve their own goals too. In order to allow this interdependence, the team needs to have the trust, the respect, the open communication, etc. going on amongst its team members. It's easy to understand why this needs to be so, but far less easy to put into practice. To be in a team where this truly is a reality is rather special. For a team to reach this state, its internal world needs to be free of the interferences that inhibit this potential. Ultimately, it needs to dismantle any controlling or limiting individual egos which drain the energy of the team and which inhibit smooth-flowing communication and intent towards achieving agreed common goals.

So what do we mean by the term "an emotionally intelligent team"? What does it mean actually to live by emotionally intelligent team values?

Table 16.1 on the next page shows an example of a team whose members demonstrate high emotionally intelligent attitudes and behaviours. The high performance of this team is not just apparent through the breadth and depth of its success, but has also been fed back to them numerous times by various parties who have interacted with them and who have experienced the team's emotional intelligence for themselves.

Here are some of the beliefs the team identified that it holds about itself:

- leading, not conforming;
- warm, friendly and supporting;

- limitless potential;
- still open to learning;
- high-performing team;
- innovative and pioneering;
- facing an exciting and incredible future;
- enthused by development;
- a young butterfly.

This team culture is due in part to the regular reviews of its performance that the team engage in. This reflective learning process is an important part of the team's success and continued development.

Table 16.1 *An emotionally intelligent team.*

Motivation and commitment

Each person demonstrates strong loyalty and commitment to the team, because they see and trust how their own individual needs and goals can be met through focusing on the team's goals. The mood of the team is consistently positive and energetic.

Conflict handling

Conflicts of interest or view are challenged respectfully between its members, because no-one fears the process and everyone recognises that creativity and innovation are an outcome of expressions of differences.

Team climate

Each member of this team demonstrates continual care and appreciation for their team colleagues through positive and valued feedback, because they respect, value and accept each one as a person and for their individual contributions to the team.

Self management

Each person within the team is empathic and aware of the needs of their individual colleagues at any time, and will support them rather than put additional pressure upon them when they least need it.

Relationship management

The members of this team maintain healthy individual relationships with each other, which is demonstrated through the fun, support and spontaneity enjoyed by the team.

Openness of communication

This team engages in regular team and individual "check-ins". (A "check-in" is an emotionally intelligent process of sharing where you are at, at that point in time, whilst the other(s) listen without judging or responding until you have finished speaking). This enables each member of the team to explore with any other member their thinking, feeling and doing on a whole range of things.

Tolerance of differences

In this team it's the appreciation of everyone's differences that enables the team to engage in a wide range of activities, and to learn from each other and their individual knowledge and experiences.

The Team Effectiveness Questionnaire

te™

Building on the perception that the differentiator between high-performing and poorly performing, between emotionally intelligent and emotionally unintelligent, teams is the team culture or ethos, the TE or Team Effectiveness questionnaire is a diagnostic instrument designed not just as a cumulative profile of the individual members, but as a means of actually looking at what is going on within the team and how this may impair its functioning. Rather than a snapshot in time, a Polaroid, that many team-profiling tools provide, the *te*™ goes a bit deeper, like an endoscopy, looking down inside the team to see what's going on in there.

The value of this approach becomes apparent when the *te*™ results are fed back to a meeting of the whole team. Things which have been festering unaddressed are brought to the surface, differing and sometimes mutually exclusive perceptions of how the team works confront one another, and people soon move on to discussing what they want to change and how to set about changing it.

The Team Effectiveness questionnaire looks at the seven aspects of team behaviour listed below. These indicate the degree to which, in this team, members behave with emotional intelligence; they also suggest why they may do so at a less than ideal level.

A Motivation and Commitment
B Conflict Handling
C Team Climate
D Self Management
E Relationship Management
F Openness of Communication
G Tolerance of Differences

The good news is that all the aspects of emotional intelligence, because they are about practice more than about ability, are changeable and can be developed. Here we offer some suggestions for developing emotional intelligence in a team in each of the seven areas.

A Motivation and commitment

The extent to which people are motivated towards shared team goals rather than individual goals, and to which this motivation is enthusiastic and success oriented.

In order to be effective, individuals need to be motivated towards success in a positive, enthusiastic way, and the same is true of teams: it is hard for an individual to feel motivated if the overall climate is heavy, pessimistic or negative. Also, for a team to be successful, it is necessary that all members share a common goal and are motivated towards that goal, rather than each working at cross purposes for themselves. (This is not to say that people will not be different and have different ideas – see Tolerance of Differences below, nor that there will not be disagreements and conflict – see Conflict Handling.)

Developing motivation and commitment in the team

Express common purpose

Make sure that you all have a sense of the common identity of the team, a set of common values and a common purpose. If you do have, then make sure that they are regularly expressed and alluded to, so that they inform everybody's behaviour.

Challenge individualistic motivation

When you think one or more of your colleagues are following their own paths and that this is not for the good of the team, challenge them. Ask them how what they are doing is contributing towards the team goal. Make the same challenges to yourself when appropriate.

Raise the energy

Do what you can to raise the level of enthusiasm in the team. Be success oriented rather than problem oriented. Be optimistic rather than pessimistic. Have fun and let yourself get excited. Celebrate when you have a success.

B Conflict handling

How well the team acknowledges and expresses conflicts of interest or view between its members, and the degree to which they are then resolved productively and satisfactorily.

Individual members of a team are bound to have, to a greater or lesser degree, conflicts of interest about the aims of the team and what goes on in it, and also differences of view about what should be done. There are two ineffective ways of dealing with this. On the one hand, denial of conflict means that all, or some, of the members of the team may suppress their interests, their feelings and their views. This is not pleasant for them and not good for the team:

- because the team will be less creative;
- because the team is deprived of the information contained in the differences between its members (see Tolerance of Differences below);
- because the team members who suppress themselves to avoid conflict will be less well motivated.

On the other hand, there are teams where there is a lot of expressed conflict, which is handled in a way that:

- saps people's energy;
- makes it difficult for them to cooperate with one another;
- leaves some, if not all, of those involved feeling bad.

The secret is for people to stick with their interests and views and to express them, not necessarily as being incontrovertibly right but as being what they want or believe. And at the same time to accept others' expression of their interests and views, not as being right or wrong but as being what they want or believe. Then have a negotiation about the differences.

Developing effective conflict handling in the team

Learn to be assertive

Work out what you want and don't want and go for that, while at the same time respecting the other and their wants. Be creative to find solutions you can both live with.

When in conflict with another

Always stick to behaviour and getting what you want; don't attack them as a person. And don't accept attacks on you as a person.

Separate the content from the process

Be aware of the distinction between the *what* (what you are in disagreement about) and the *how* (how you are handling the disagreement between you, and the feelings it provokes). Deal with each separately.

C   Team climate

The extent to which the climate in the team is supportive of members and their self esteem.

Our sense of identity and of our own value is closely bound up with how our expressions of feeling are received and responded to. If our feelings are accepted and we are appreciated rather than criticised then:

* we feel better about ourselves and about those around us;
* we perform better;
* we communicate more;
* we cooperate more effectively.

Developing a favourable climate in the team

Praise and appreciation

Make sure that you regularly praise your colleagues for what they do and appreciate them for who they are. It doesn't have to be a big thing: making a nice cup of tea is worthy of appreciation as well as a significant piece of work. The secret is in the volume – create a climate of supportive response rather than silence or endless criticism. And make sure (you can ask!) that you get your fair share of praise and appreciation.

Negative feedback

When you don't like something a fellow team member does, make sure that you tell them your reaction to what they did without criticising them as a person. Be specific and make clear what you want them to do differently in the future, or what you are asking for by way of reparation for the past. Similarly, if you are criticised, don't accept criticism of yourself as a person, check with yourself whether you understand their negative response to what you have done and whether you are willing to do anything differently. (See pages 99–101 for detailed guidelines about receiving negative strokes).

Bear feeling responses in mind

In all your interactions with your colleagues, before you do or say anything, think about what their feeling reaction is likely to be. This doesn't mean "Never say anything that will upset anybody", but that you should be aware of the likely effect on them of what you say and do and so have chosen accordingly.

D Self management

The extent to which the team's culture supports people in managing themselves, and their energy, well.

In order to keep our energy up, we need

- to be optimistic;
- to have a realistic sense of our potential;
- to take steps to get what we need;
- to take time out to have fun and relax occasionally;
- to be resilient in the face of setbacks.

People vary individually in the degree to which they do these things, but such things are also much affected by the climate of the team we are in.

Developing self management in the team

Challenge and reframe pessimism

Whenever you or anyone else in the team speaks in a pessimistic or gloomy way, challenge it by putting an optimistic spin on the subject. (Though at the same time acknowledging their feelings and view.)

Personal power

Whenever anyone speaks in a way that conveys helplessness or blame of others, help yourself and others focus on the practical: "What can we do about this?".

Self care

Demonstrate in your own behaviour and be encouraging and supportive of others to take proper care of yourselves by:

- tuning in regularly to your body;
- making sure you eat, drink and rest regularly and well;
- having fun and relaxation as well as endless work.

E   Relationship management

How able members of the team are to relate effectively with one another.

Effective teams have members who don't just relate to one another in order to carry out the team task, but build mutually supportive and trusting relationships. They do this by being aware of, and attending to, their own and each other's feelings.

Developing effective relationship management in the team

Build relationships

Consciously invest time and effort to build relationships with your colleagues which are not narrowly confined to work interactions. Be interested in, and responsive to, their wants and feelings, interests and passions. And let them know about yours.

Build trust

Build others' trust in you

- by being reliable and doing what you say you will;
- by being responsive to and supportive of them;
- by letting them know your feelings.

Build your trust in others

- by letting yourself know when and why you don't trust them (that way your distrust will become limited and specific rather than undefined and wide-ranging);

- by letting them know too (in order that either they can explain their behaviour so that it no longer leaves you mistrustful, or that they have an opportunity to do it differently in the future);
- by checking out with them the validity of your assumptions about them;
- by experimenting with trusting them more.

Be "other aware"

Practise tuning in to what those around you are feeling by paying attention to their body language. Check out your assumptions about them by asking whether you are right.

F   Openness of communication

The extent to which people in the team feel free to talk to each other, in particular about feelings.

Communication in teams can be limited because not everybody talks or not everybody listens. Or because the talking and listening that is done is limited to certain thoughts and ideas and excludes, for example, talking

- about feelings;
- about vulnerabilities;
- about intuitions;
- about off-the-wall ideas.

Teams that avoid these subjects will be less cohesive, less flexible and less creative. They will also be less fun to be in.

Developing openness of communication in the team

Encourage expressions of feeling

When anyone in the team expresses a feeling, be accepting and express your acceptance. Don't criticise it (as being "silly" or "unjustified", for example) and don't offer reassurance (which conveys the message "Your feeling is unjustified: don't be so apprehensive, be more relaxed about it like me").

Instead,

- hear it;
- acknowledge it ("So you feel scared by this");
- validate it ("I can understand you feeling that").

Let yourself be known

If you are a person who tends to keep yourself to yourself, experiment with letting people know a bit more about you. Each day make sure you tell at least one other person at least one thing – a fact, an insecurity, an excitement – that you would normally keep to yourself.

Don't be critical of "work in progress"

Encourage others to express their hunches, their intuitions, their half-worked-out ideas. Respond with interest and enquiry rather than criticism or disapproval.

G   Tolerance of differences

The degree to which, in this team, people's differences, of all kinds, are tolerated, appreciated and made use of.

One of the strengths of team working, rather than individual working, is the range of different ideas, reactions, patterns and ways of being contained among its individual members. But this advantage is thrown away if there is a pattern in the team of insisting on one way of being, of thinking and of behaving, and of rejecting those who are different. Such teams are less creative and less flexible and also tend to be less cohesive and to work less well together.

Developing tolerance and valuing of differences in the team

Appreciate variety

Remember there is no one right way to be. Notice people's differences, appreciate them for their variety and consider how best each may contribute to the team effort.

Encourage different contributions

When colleagues

- express a different view from the team norm;
- have a different feeling response from the prevailing one; or
- act differently from the norm,

do not express amazement or disapproval – respond with interest and appreciation.

Understand others' positions

Make a conscious effort to understand where other people are coming from. Native American cultures used to say, "Judge no man until you have walked in his moccasins for many moons". Nowadays this is impractical, but we can make the effort to imagine how it is to be them, with their history, their thoughts and beliefs and their feelings. This kind of understanding usually leads to a greater degree of acceptance.

Example of the *ᴁ*™ in action

Here is an example of a team who used the Team Effectiveness questionnaire to help them identify the issues that were keeping them from achieving their potential.

Using the Performance = potential – interference formula, the team looked at where they were at the time (current performance) and where they were wanting to get to (potential). The *ᴁ*™ identified for them the issues (interferences) that they needed to address to ensure that they achieved this potential.

Six out of the top ten interferences for the team were in Scale A: Motivation and Commitment:

- there is not a strong feeling of being a "team" united by a common purpose;
- team members are more likely to bring others' motivation down than drive it forward;
- working in this team is not intrinsically fun or rewarding;

- team members tend to find problems and reasons why something will not work, which stifles progress;
- this team focuses on minimising problems rather than creating success;
- there is little sense of motivational leadership in this team.

As well as identifying individual behaviours that each team member then committed to change, the team created a set of new values, attitudes and habits to take them forward. These were each supported by a related action that ensured the new team climate was made real.

New value: RESPECT
New attitude: Respect each other, even when there's a problem
New habit: Help each other with mistakes.

New value: COMMITMENT
New attitude: Value the key performance indicators
New habit: Review against the indicators, celebrate and learn.

New value: OPEN, HONEST AND POSITIVE COMMUNICATION
New attitude: Have more courage to be open, honest and positive in our communications with each other
New habit: Speaking respectfully to each other.

New value: APPRECIATION
New attitude: We will appreciate each other more
New habit: Bringing success stories to the team briefings.

New value: SHARED OWNERSHIP
New attitude: Pulling together
New habit: Ask and be asked for help.

EI development for different kinds of teams

Different types of team will have differing EI development needs, not just because of their differing performance levels but because of the dynamic, structure and purpose of each team.

Here are some examples of different types of team and their diverse EI needs.

Sales teams

Sales teams are often not teams in the true sense: we define a team as a group of people who, at least sometimes, meet together and who share a common goal. The emphasis in a sales team is often very much on individual performance and targets, and support can be minimal because of everyone else in the team focusing on their individual targets too. Indeed, sometimes "fellow team members" are, in fact, the enemy: each individual's aim is to maximise their performance relative to colleagues so that they get a bigger share of the available bonus. If you really want a sales "team" (and you may not, but if not then the manager needs to be aware that he is not being asked to manage a true team), then the reward system must reflect this: at least in part use team-based, rather than individually based, commission / bonuses. Often, too, sales managers have become managers because they were good at sales, not necessarily because of their management or leadership capabilities.

EI development in sales teams then is often at an individual level, using the Individual Effectiveness questionnaire ($i\!s^{™}$) to help with individual sales performance. But by facilitating their EI development within the team situation, the team can support each other through buddying programmes. EI development for sales people will often focus on self confidence and relationship management.

Virtual or remote teams

Similar to sales teams, virtual or remote teams are often groups of individuals brought together under one manager for administrative purposes, rather than because they are a true team. As individuals they work in isolation, often from home or remote office locations. The challenge for these individuals is self management and self motivation, seeking support from other sources or providing self support that would otherwise be provided in a team environment.

Change teams

Change teams often work together or at least meet regularly in a team situation. Change teams are often transient, however, coming together for single projects. The EI challenge in working within a change team is two-fold.

First, there is the need to establish a good team dynamic quickly, so that the team can start performing effectively as soon as possible. This can be tackled, particularly if team members have worked together in other con-texts before and know one another, by completing the *ie*™ questionnaire as soon as the team is formed, rather than waiting for things to go wrong and then doing a post hoc analysis of why. When people join a team they will have some idea of what they think the team will be like and what its strengths and weaknesses will be. By completing the *ie*™ in terms of what they imagine will happen, possible pitfalls can be identified in advance and preventative action taken.

The second challenge is that individuals within the team are having to drive through change in departments or organisations and will likely meet with resistance from employees. Building rapport and developing influenc-ing skills are therefore key. These both require emotionally intelligent atti-tudes and skills.

Senior management teams

Top team dynamics are often quite challenging, with each member neces-sarily representing their own functional responsibilities. Equally, they need to recognise and buy into the common goals of the organisation. EI development for top teams often starts with a *ie*™ on an away-day to help the team sharpen its performance, and then continues with personal devel-opment based on responses to the Individual Effectiveness questionnaire (*ie*™) and executive coaching to look at specific issues such as leadership, assertiveness and tolerance of differences.

17

Assessing EI

The measurement of emotional intelligence has become a serious business, and significant numbers of people are recognising that EI measurement offers something more than the traditional psychometrics. As a result, there are now a number of EI profiling tools in the market place. So how do you select the one that's right for you and your business?

As with any psychometric measure, there are four initial requirements. It needs to:

1. *Discriminate* between respondents. In other words, it needs to allocate different scores to different people. It is no use having a ruler which tells you, of two sticks 80 cm and 120 cm long, "They are both about a metre long." There is one EI measure where everyone is clustered around the top end of most scales – not much use.
2. Be *Reliable*. In other words, measure consistently, so that a stick which is shown to be 80 cm long one day is also 80 cm long the next day, and two sticks of the same length get the same measurement. The requirement to give the same measure each time is not absolute, though. If what you are measuring is not fixed but changes over time, then if your measure gives the same score on both occasions it is likely to be inaccurate on at least one of them. Specifically, if the process of measurement affects what is being measured, as is the case with level of self knowledge and some

measures of EI, then you would not expect the same scores on test and on retest, and if you got them that might suggest that the test was inaccurate.

As well as reliability over time, which is measured by comparing the scores on test and on retest, there is also the question of whether a measure is consistently measuring one and the same thing; for example, are all the items in a scale measuring the same thing, do they generate related score levels? Here again, high reliability is not an unalloyed good, because there is a trade-off between the amount of information gathered and the level of reliability: a diagnostic test with very high reliability would probably supply too little information – see the discussion below about the distinction between assessment measures and development measures.

3. Be *valid*. In other words, not merely measuring something effectively and consistently, but measuring what it claims to be measuring. There are three main aspects to this. First, there is conceptual validity: does the measure grow out of, and is it well rooted in, a well-constructed, plausible, comprehensible and valid conceptual framework, or is it just a jumble of scales put together any old how? Second, there is predictive validity: if scores on the measure effectively predict some behaviour, then clearly they are measuring something relevant. Third, there is concurrent validity, which means that the spread of scores on this measure is similar to the spread of scores on another measure which is generally agreed to be measuring a particular variable. Apart from these three, there is also the question of face validity: regardless of whether it actually is valid or not, does it appear so to the respondent (and the prospective client user)? People will often be put off by something which appears weird or irrelevant, even if it actually works.

4. Be *useful*. This is a criterion which is often overlooked by psychometricians, but which is crucial. It is no use having a technically superb measure if the information it produces is no earthly use to anyone. So a measure may have high predictive validity, in that it effectively predicts a particular behaviour, but if that behaviour is of no interest to anyone, then the measure is useless. Since, as we have already seen, the components of emotional intelligence tend to be highly correlated with levels of job performance, EI measures are likely to prove extremely useful.

Turning from psychometric measures in general to measures of emotional intelligence in particular, to help you understand the differences between the different EI measurements, there are three things you need to consider when looking at which EI profiling tool is right for you:

- the difficulties inherent in measuring emotional intelligence;
- the history of EI measurement – how it has evolved;
- what you are going to use the measurement for.

The problems with EI measurement

First and foremost, what do we mean by emotional intelligence? Here's the first problem. There are as many definitions of EI as there are EI measurement tools, and different test designers favour different schools of thought.

Our view is that our EI is fundamentally about attitudes. It's the difference between on the one hand, knowing how you need to behave so as to demonstrate to yourself and others that you are assertive and then consciously trying to live up to that, and on the other having an inner belief and confidence that enables you to be naturally assertive. It (or the lack of it) is why, when you know all the ways to manage your time more effectively, you still procrastinate . . .

This view is different from the academic studies of the psychology of intelligence which see emotional intelligence as an ability or capacity (a skill or competence), whether it is practised or not.

This distinction has significant consequences for the process of measurement. If you are trying to measure an ability, you can set a series of test questions, mark them as right or wrong and extrapolate from these answers to grade people's ability – as IQ tests and some EI measures, such as the MSCEIT, do.

But if you are trying to measure or predict how people behave, you need to work out what it is that affects their tendency to behave in a particular way. In other words, you need to assess attitudes as well as competencies. The EQ Map from Essi Systems has a section entitled "Values and Attitudes", in contrast to Daniel Goleman's measure marketed by the Hay Group, which is called the ECI-360 or Emotional *Competence* Inventory, measuring competence-based (or skills-based) elements of EI rather than attitudinal ones.

The other category of EI measure which is aimed at predicting behaviour, rather than measuring capacity, is the group of measures which are based around personality – seeing personality and emotional intelligence as one and the same thing.

The presupposition here is that emotional intelligence is relatively fixed and unchanging, as is personality, which is derived from what is constant in people's behaviour over time. We, on the other hand, see all the different aspects of emotional intelligence as being changeable and developable, not fixed. This is another place where we find Timothy Gallwey's model relevant and helpful:

$$Performance = potential - interference$$

We believe that most people have the potential to behave with emotional intelligence, but that so much of the time we do not because of our interferences – internal interferences mostly resulting from false beliefs and limiting habits adopted (for what were then good reasons) in childhood and retained, unwittingly, in adulthood. The process of enabling someone to develop their emotional intelligence therefore consists in helping them to identify and dismantle these interferences.

So, for us, emotional intelligence is not a synonym for personality: it is about how we manage our personality.

Another particular difficulty with measuring emotional intelligence is "self awareness". Self awareness is the key attribute underpinning our emotional intelligence. The more aware we are of what is going on inside of us in emotional and hormonal terms, knowing what we need to do about that and then doing it, the more in control of our behaviours we can become. This directly impacts on our ability to self manage and on our awareness of others, of what's going on for them, and consequently on how well we manage our relationships within them.

This is shown in our model of emotional intelligence. Emotional intelligence is derived from two of the nine ways (so far researched) in which we can be intelligent – known as our multiple intelligences and identified by the Harvard educational psychologist Howard Gardner. These two intelligences are: our intrapersonal intelligence (how well we know and manage ourselves) and our interpersonal intelligence (how well we know others and manage our relationships with them).

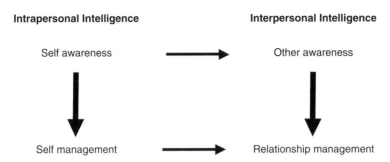

Figure 17.1 *For each intelligence, awareness leads to a category of effective management.*

Each of the two intelligences is composed first of an awareness and then a category of effective management, as shown in Figure 17.1.

As you can see from the causal arrows, our self awareness is needed to be truly aware of others (rather than projecting our assumptions on to them) and underpins our ability to be self managing. Awareness of others is clearly crucial for managing our relationships effectively, as is our responsibility for how we manage ourselves in our relationships.

So self awareness is in a sense the key element in our emotional intelligence, and is therefore a fundamental and crucial part of what needs to be measured. The trouble is that with most tests, self awareness is being presumed and relied on in the process. The difficulty with this is that if you ask someone who is very unselfaware about their level of self awareness, they will be unaware of their lack of self awareness and may answer truthfully (as it seems to them) that they are very self aware. Conversely, someone who is very self aware may be exquisitely aware of the limitations they have on their self awareness and represent themselves as less self aware than they truly are.

We'll look at how best to overcome this a little later, but first let's look at how the EI measurement industry has evolved.

Evolution of EI profiling

Shortly after the publication of Goleman's *Emotional Intelligence – Why it can matter more than IQ* in 1995, came the first generation of EI measures. These tests had two things in common: they were new tests specifically designed to measure emotional intelligence and all their scales were what are called "linear" scales.

Linear scales move from left to right with the notion that "more is better"; so the higher you score on any scale (the further to the right), the more emotionally intelligent you are perceived to be. This is fine for some EI attributes such as self awareness – you can't be too self aware. But what of scales such as Trust, or Outlook – when does trust become naïvety and gullibility, and optimism become seeing the world through rose-tinted glasses?

Next, we had the second generation of EI tests – which were the exact opposite of the first generation tests: they were adaptations of pre-existing personality tests and all their scales were "bipolar".

Bipolar scales show the scales being measured as two-ended; neither end of the scale is identified with emotional intelligence and usually the balanced place in the middle suggests itself as the most emotionally intelligent position. Again, as for the linear scales, this measurement is fine for some types of scale, but not for others. This time we can see the benefit of a balanced approach to Trust and Optimism, but it is not appropriate for Self Regard or Awareness of Others, of which surely you can't have too much?

There is one further problem with the bipolar scales often found in these EI tests. They still do not show the full picture for scales where "you can have too much of a good thing". For example, let's look at a scale for Emotional Expression and Control. A bipolar scale will suggest that if you score toward the right end of the scale, you are overcontrolled in your emotional expression rather than the balanced position of "free and in charge". And if you score to the left of the scale, you are undercontrolled. It makes sense that this is a bipolar scale most certainly. However, the way in which the score is normally calculated on these types of scale throws up an anomaly. Some people can score themselves high at both ends of the scale, i.e. swinging from being overcontrolled in their emotional expression until they "burst" and lose control, never really being free and in charge of their emotions – the balanced, emotionally intelligent position. The bipolar scale, however, would calculate that they were relatively "balanced", because the opposing behaviours would score high and low respectively and balance themselves out mathematically. So the bipolar would suggest that they were emotionally intelligent in the expression of their emotions, when in fact it couldn't be farther from the truth.

Obviously we need a new kind of scale, one that measures effectively the varying behaviours on a bipolar scale, distinguishing between the emotionally intelligent patterns in the middle and a mixture of the two extreme, emotionally unintelligent patterns. Such an animal has not been seen before, to our knowledge, in the field of psychometrics. We also need a test that is composed of a mixture of scales, some linear and some bipolar, to measure the mixture of linear and bipolar variables that emotional intelligence is composed of. This is unorthodox and superficially messy, which is probably why this, too, has never been done before.

Why are you measuring EI?

The other big issue about measuring emotional intelligence is what you are trying to use the measure for. Broadly speaking there are two reasons for measuring EI: to assess people (usually for recruitment or selection purposes) and to develop people. The criteria for choosing a measure for each of these purposes will be different.

To begin with, if you are choosing a measure for development purposes, it is important that the process of administering the measure, feeding the results back to the coachee and handling their responses to that should be a process which facilitates the development of EI in the coachee rather than the opposite.

The normal model of psychometric testing promotes, in our view, an emotionally *un*intelligent process, along the lines of a medical diagnosis and treatment. Here's what we mean. Below are three models of intervention. Which one to you seems to be the emotionally intelligent process?

The Medical Model
1. Diagnosis   (by doctor)
2. Selection of treatment   (by doctor)
3. Application of treatment   (by doctor)
4. Treatment consequence   (in patient)

The Medical Model in Testing
1. Diagnosis   (by test, interpreted by professional)
2. Selection of treatment   (by professional)
3. Application of treatment   (by professional)
4. Treatment consequence   (in profilee)

The Empowerment Model
1. Increase in self knowledge   (in coachee)
2. Selection of change plan   (by coachee)
3. Implementation of plan   (by coachee)
4. Chosen change achieved   (in coachee)

As we're sure you will agree, the first two models are "parental" or "authoritarian" in their approach, and the second model is unlikely to foster emotional intelligence in the profilee.

The person who feeds back the findings of the measure to any profilee/coachee needs not only to be knowledgeable about the measure and about emotional intelligence, but also needs to have good skills as a facilitator, needs to be emotionally intelligent themselves and needs to come from a position of non-judgement.

So what does an EI measure need to have in order to facilitate an empowering developmental process? It's all in the diagnosis. The test needs to convey as much information as possible so that the coachee can understand how their score was arrived at – i.e. the areas in which they scored themselves high and the areas, and reasons, for development. To this end, we have found that this information needs to include a copy of the questionnaire, individual scores for each question and a list of the items on which they scored low (in EI terms). Giving this information also has a significant impact on the issue of ownership.

In order to feed back a lot of information you need to have a lot of information, and this is not necessarily the case with tests designed for assessment purposes. The way in which these are often designed means that the mean score only conveys one piece of information. The score shows, for example, that the coachee is low on Goal Directedness, but does not explain which aspect(s) of Goal Directedness the coachee needs to develop. The score could have been brought down because the coachee has difficulty in knowing what they want and identifying their goals. Or it could be because they know what they want but distract themselves from going after it by paying attention instead to other people's needs. Or it could be because they know what they want but interrupt their progress towards it by distracting themselves by other short-term needs (like wanting a chocolate bar when their goal is to lose weight). For diagnostic and development purposes, assessment tools are therefore of little use.

Another important aspect that we mentioned just now is the issue of ownership. The test needs to provide the information in a way that the coachee can understand, take on board and make their own – otherwise their increase in self knowledge (stage 1 in the empowerment model) and consequently their ability to select an appropriate change strategy (stage 2) will be impaired. The difficulty here is that a lot of information and a lot of concepts are involved and some people may find it all overwhelming. What is important for this purpose, therefore, as well as inherently, is to have a clear and comprehensible conceptual model underlying the various scales and relating them to one another. And also not to have too many scales.

In our model there are two scales which, in combination, affect all the others. These are Self Regard, and Regard for Others. They correlate with the concept in Transactional Analysis of "I'm OK, You're OK". If the coachee is low in either of these it is most improbable that they will be able to behave with truly high emotional intelligence in any of the other respects which may be measured. We spell out the relationship between scores on these two scales and scores on the other scales, and that – as well as in our view being an appropriate representation of reality – allows people to have a simple structure which holds all the scales together. Similarly, the scores in the scales which measure awareness (Self Awareness and Awareness of Others) are likely to cause high and low scores in other scales – you need these awarenesses in order to be able to carry out the aspects of self management and relationship management measured by the other scales.

Setting out a clear and comprehensible conceptual model underlying the measure, and sharing full details of their responses and scores with the coachee, greatly enhances their ownership, both of their responses and the whole process of dealing with them. In TA terms it becomes an "I'm OK, You're OK" respectful process, and quite apart from any change strategies adopted will in itself be enhancing of emotional intelligence.

If these are the criteria for a development measure of EI, what of an assessment measure: how are the criteria different?

An effective EI development measure will constitute an effective intervention in and of itself, just taking it without getting feedback of the results. As and after they complete the measure, people tend to be stimulated and start thinking about and reacting to the issues raised. An effective measure will be addressing fundamental things about a person that cannot be brought into awareness and then just left hanging. For these reasons it would not be ethical to administer such a measure without offering the people who complete it the opportunity to discuss their results with an appropriately qualified person. Obviously, this means that it is a non-starter for many recruitment campaigns: the cost of providing to all applicants an exploration interview with an appropriately skilled person would be too great. From this point of view, what is required is an EI measure for assessment purposes in a format which does not in and of itself raise awareness. Not statements which need to be consciously processed, therefore, but something like checking a list of adjectives, which is the basis of our Potential Effectiveness (PE) measure. This is based on the same underlying model of EI as the $ie^{™}$, the one which is expounded in this book, and generates scores on the same scales, but because it is not in questionnaire format, composed of a series of grammatical and meaningful statements, it bypasses a lot of the respondent's cognitive processes and does not raise self knowledge as the $ie^{™}$ does. There is, therefore, no ethical obligation to give every respondent the opportunity of a feedback interview. On the other hand, if the respondent is successful in the preliminary recruitment process and comes to interview, their PE scores may provide useful guides for the interviewer and will provide an indication of what personal development the respondent may need to undertake.

The other issue which bedevils EI measures to be used for recruitment and selection is that of faking. In a development measure, you can point out to the coachee that the only person they are going to be conning if they give an artificially inflated view of their emotional intelligence is themselves. And you can tease out and explore the reality of the picture conveyed by the responses in the interviews which follow. With an assessment measure there may be no feedback process to allow a check-up. And most tests are designed in a way that makes it fairly clear which end of the scale is the "right" one – any EI measure of this common form is not going to be suitable for assessment purposes. Once again, this problem is well dealt with by the format of the Potential Effectiveness measure: a list of adjectives, checked quickly in a way which largely bypasses conscious thought.

So, does this mean that the kind of effective development measure we have discussed cannot be used at all for assessment purposes? For standard recruitment, yes. But for high-value posts, where the cost of bad judgement is great and it is worth spending a little on the recruitment process – such as the recruitment of graduates – then they can be used as part of an assessment-centre type of recruitment process, including EI exploration interviews, for shortlisted candidates. That way, you not only have a good idea of the successful candidates' development needs, but those that you turn down will be remarkably well disposed towards your company, because they will have had a useful development experience and will be able to use their increased self knowledge in the rest of their job-hunting.

So how can we overcome this problem of "faking" in a development, questionnaire-type measure? This also links to the self awareness issue we discussed earlier: how can you double-check this to ascertain the true level of self awareness?

Somehow we need to square the circle between providing some indirect validation of the self descriptions that most tests are composed of without incurring the time (and motivation) penalty of asking five or six other people, as well as the profilee, to complete the measure, as in a standard 360°.

The best way we have found to achieve this is to add an extra scale "Self-assessed EI" after all the others, consisting of one question related to each of the previous scales (or, for the bipolar scales, of the subscales measuring either end or the middle of the scale separately). This provides an "internal 360°", thus allowing a measurement of the Accuracy of self assessment, by comparing the answers in the Self-assessed EI scale to each corresponding scale.

This same final scale can also be amended slightly to create a simple and short 360° test. The beauty of this is that it takes just five minutes for each profiler to complete, compared with the usual 30 minutes per person for standard 360° questionnaires. Whilst the information output will not be as comprehensive, the essence of the issues will be highlighted, which is all that is needed in the hands of a proficient EI consultant. In turn, this saves the organisation an inordinate amount of time and money for the same outcome – an effective, insightful, EI-based 360° process.

Using an EI measure

This brings us finally to the appointment of an EI consultant. Most accredited EI consultants have experience with just one EI measure – the one in which they chose to become accredited. EI consultants that come to our three-day accreditation courses for our EI measures are also encouraged to further their professional development by undertaking an indepth study into EI through our nine-month Certificate in Applied Emotional Intelligence. One area studied during this programme by the EI consultants attending is the exploration of all of the major EI measures and conceptual models available in the marketplace. This not only widens their personal understanding of EI, but gives them a much broader knowledge of EI measurement, as well as its subsequent development. We strongly recommend that you select an EI practitioner to undertake your EI measurement who has this indepth knowledge and understanding.

So, to summarise, here are the key points that you need to be aware of when selecting your EI measure:

- Decide on the right definition of emotional intelligence for you – do you see it as to do with attitudes, competences or personality?
- Does the measure have a strong, comprehensible underlying conceptual model?
- How many scales are there, are they all given the same status or are they built upon the underlying model to demonstrate the interrelatedness of the individual scales?
- What kind of scales does the measure explore – linear, bipolar or a mixture of both for a clearer and deeper picture?
- What are you using the measure for – assessment or development?
- Are you in a position to provide a feedback session to each respondent?
- How does the measure validate self awareness and accuracy?
- Do you want a 360°?
- What knowledge do the accredited consultants of the measure have of other EI measures and applied EI?

The Individual Effectiveness questionnaire

Here are some bulleted summaries of the key differentiators of the *ie*™.
The characteristics of the *ie*™ are:

- It is theoretically based on a coherent EI model;
- It has linear and bipolar scales as appropriate;
- Bipolar scales have middle and both ends measured separately, thereby capturing more information;
- The scales are related to one another and to underlying connecting concepts;
- It has a speedily completed 360° element, internal and external;
- Feedback is as important as scoring.

It is a structure of 18 scales, grouped into:

- Life positions (Scales 1, 2) – linear,
  with a derivative Scale 3 (Scale 1 minus Scale 2) – bipolar;
- Awareness (Scales 4, 5) – linear;
- Self management (Scales 6, 7, 8, 9, 10, 11) – linear;
- Relationship management (Scales 12, 13, 14, 15, 16) – bipolar,
  with middle and both ends separately measured;
- Reflective learning (Scale 17) – linear.
- Self-assessed EI / Accuracy of self assessment (Scale 18) – hybrid.

The $iŝ^{™}$ linear scales are:

1   Self Regard
2   Regard for Others
4   Self Awareness
5   Other Awareness
6   Emotional Resilience
7   Personal Power
8   Goal Directedness
9   Flexibility
10 Personal Openness and Connectedness
11 Invitation to Trust
17 Reflective Learning.

The $iŝ^{™}$ bipolar scales are:

3   Relative Regard
12 Trust
    Mistrustful *through* Carefully Trusting *to* Overtrusting
13 Balanced Outlook
    Pessimistic *through* Realistically Optimistic *to* Overoptimistic
14 Emotional Expression and Control
    Undercontrolled *through* Free and In Charge *to* Overcontrolled
15 Conflict Handling (Assertiveness)
    Passive *through* Assertive *to* Aggressive
16 Interdependence
    Dependent *through* Interdependent *to* Overindependent.

The *æ*™ also has a hybrid scale:

18   Self Knowledge (Accuracy of self assessment).

This scale:

- has one item for each linear scale and for each subscale of the bipolar scales;
- on its own, measures Self-assessed EI;
- in comparison either with scores on the scales corresponding to the individual items, or with mean 360° scores, gives an indication of Accuracy of Self Assessment.

The *æ*™ unique qualities are:

- it has both bipolar and linear scales;
- the bipolar scales have both ends and middle separately measured in effect tripolar;
- it is diagnostic;
- the life positions;
- the underpinning model;
- it gives a brief 360°;
- its associated measures using the same model:

  Team measure *æ*™;
  Organisational measure (*æ*)*;
  Selection measure (Potential Effectiveness = PE)*.

  *Both planned for launch in 2006.

æ™ vs. other products

Here are some of the drawbacks we see to various other measures of EI:

- seeing EI as constitutional / fixed;
- the questionnaire is self-scored and totally fakeable;
- the scales include non-EI scales, e.g. happiness;
- some scales are combined scales, e.g. creativity, not pure EI scales;
- scales are treated in isolation and not related to one another to provide an overall picture;

- made-up scales, e.g. "leveraging ethnic diversity";
- odd clusters, e.g. Trust and Conscientiousness;
- all scales are at the same level with no regard for ontological levels (levels of "being");
- too few / too many scales;
- EI as one thing;
- cultural biases;
- failure of some scales to discriminate sufficiently between respondents: nearly everybody scores about the same.

Problems with measuring EI

Here's a quick checklist of potential problems in the measurement of emotional intelligence in terms of which you need to check out any test you are considering.

- Self awareness and self report
- The model: linear or bipolar?
- Cultural bias
- Relationships between scales
- The model of EI: fixed or fluid?
- Conceptual validity
- Fakeability.

Other schools of thought

In order to make clear the extent to which focusing on attitudes distinguishes our approach from that of others, and to give you some idea of where they are coming from, here are some alternative definitions.

Reuven BarOn's definition

BarOn is the designer of the EQ-i measure, one of the most popular. In his definition, "broadly speaking, emotional intelligence addresses the emotional, personal, social and survival dimensions of intelligence, which are often more important for daily functioning than the more traditional cognitive aspects of intelligence. Emotional intelligence is concerned with understanding oneself and others, relating to people and adapting to and coping with the immediate surroundings to be more successful in dealing with environmental demands.

Emotional intelligence is tactical (immediate functioning), while cognitive intelligence is strategic (long-term capacity). Emotional intelligence helps to predict success because it reflects how a person applies knowledge to the immediate situation. In a way, to measure emotional intelligence is to measure one's "common sense" and ability to get along in the world".

Daniel Goleman's definition (1997)

As well as being the Grand Young Man of emotional intelligence, Goleman was the designer of the ECI-360° measure. He defines EI as: "knowing what you are feeling and being able to handle those feelings without them having to swamp you; being able to motivate yourself to get jobs done, be creative and perform at your peak; and sensing what others are feeling, and handling relationships effectively.

Emotional intelligence is the capacity:

- for recognising our own feelings and those of others;
- for motivating ourselves;
- for managing emotions well in ourselves and in our relationships".

Martinez's definition

". . . an array of non-cognitive skills, capabilities and competencies that influence a person's ability to cope with environmental demands and pressures."
Martinez-Pons, 1997

Dulewicz and Higgs's definition

Vic Dulewicz and Malcolm Higgs of Henley Management College are the originators of the first British EI measure: the EIQ. Their definition is:

"Emotional Intelligence. This term refers to the overall concept as defined by Martinez and encompasses the concepts of Social Intelligence, Interpersonal Intelligence and Personal Intelligence."
Higgs and Dulewicz, 2002

Mayer and Salovey's definition (1997)

Jack Mayer and Peter Salovey were among the academic originators of the study of emotional intelligence and, with David Caruso, generated the MSCEIT – the Mayer Salovey Caruso Emotional Intelligence Test. In their view, "Emotional Intelligence is the ability to perceive emotions, to access and generate emotions so as to assist thought, to understand emotions and emotional knowledge and to reflectively regulate emotions so as to promote emotional and intellectual growth".

Working with other constructs

So far we have looked at the various components of emotional intelligence, which are measured by separate scales in the Individual Effectiveness questionnaire. Now we have identified what EI is composed of, the question arises: how does it relate to all the other psychological and management theories and approaches that people used before EI came on the scene ten years ago, and in many cases still do?

Self Regard

We have seen how fundamental self regard, or self esteem (same thing), is in determining the level of someone's emotional intelligence, and perhaps that concept is the one to start with. We see the relationship between emotional intelligence, self esteem and self confidence (the distinction here being that self esteem is how we feel about our being and self confidence is how we feel about our doing) as that summarised in Figure 17.2.

To be fully healthy (not just emotionally, but physically too), happy and successful we need to have high self esteem, high self confidence and high emotional intelligence, and of course these three variables tend to coincide to a considerable degree.

Self esteem, or self regard, we see as a prerequisite of emotional intelligence, and – in line with the Transactional Analysis model of the OK Corral – we see true self regard as carrying with it regard for others. Those who claim to have high self regard but who do not tend to regard others highly are probably denying and defending against an underlying feeling of low self regard.

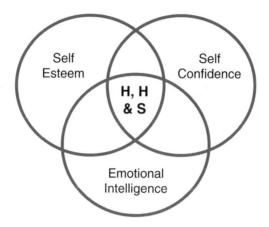

Figure 17.2 *The keys to health, happiness and success.*

One of the key features of EI is that all of its components are changeable and developable, and happily this applies too to the key underlying element of self esteem. The best way to have high self esteem is to choose the family you are born into well, so that you will emerge from childhood feeling good about yourself, but if you didn't manage to do that you can still alter your level of self esteem as an adult, by controlling the pattern of "stroking" that you receive and let in from yourself and others.

One of the common responses we get when we introduce people to emotional intelligence for the first time is, "I have done a lot of different bits of self development in my time, but EI seems to pull them all together and give them a structure." Apart from self esteem, which basically derives from the experience of being unconditionally accepted by others and which is a key prerequisite for emotional intelligence, many other important psychological concepts relating to the effectiveness of people's functioning in the world are subsumed within emotional intelligence and are given a coherent place within a structured framework by it.

Transactional Analysis (TA)

See the section "A word about Transactional Analysis (TA)" in Chapter 4.

"Intelligence"

Since EI has within its name the concept of intelligence, we should consider how the two concepts are related and how they differ. This is a bit tricky, because the normal understanding of the notion of intelligence has considerably changed over the last twenty-five years as a result of the work on multiple intelligences of Howard Gardner and his colleagues at Harvard. To oversimplify, a generation ago intelligence was conceived of largely as being one thing (what we now would call cognitive intelligence) and relatively fixed (probably largely inherited). Whereas now we see intelligences as being multiple and of different kinds. These are not just different realms of application for our underlying unitary intelligence, but are separate entities, which can vary separately (one being higher while another is lower) and which are located in different parts of the brain. Two of Gardner's original seven multiple intelligences were Intrapersonal Intelligence and Interpersonal Intelligence, and the combination of these two constitutes emotional intelligence. As well as being separate, these various intelligences are all seen as being open to development, rather than being fixed.

A number of EI theorists see emotional intelligence in terms of the old model of fixed cognitive intelligence, of which it forms a subsidiary part. We see it in terms of the new model of multiple intelligences, both its aspects being capable of development. There is probably an upper limit set by our inheritance, but in our view none of us gets near that because of our acquired psychological interferences, and so the existence of these inherited limits is largely of theoretical interest only. In practical terms, increasing our emotional intelligence involves identifying and dismantling, or at least managing, our interferences.

While that is the general picture, we have to acknowledge that the level of cognitive intelligence (logical-mathematical reasoning and facility with language) is capable of affecting the level of emotional intelligence, certainly at the extremes, in a limiting way. If EI involves thinking about feeling and we are limited in our capacity to think (say our IQ is below 80), then it is likely that this will affect our capacity to be emotionally intelligent.

"Emotions"

Traditionally, emotions were the Cinderella of psychological research and theorising. This was for two reasons. Partly, psychologists, like most academics, were brought up in the Cartesian tradition of "I think therefore I am", and they devalued the importance of feeling (largely female) as opposed to thinking (largely male). Partly, and this time more practically and defensibly, before the days of brain imaging it was difficult to operationalise feelings in physical terms and so conduct research into them. Nowadays, we are fortunate enough to be able to observe brain function in living human beings and to see what happens in the brain when they experience certain feelings. But, in addition to that, we have come to realise that feelings are not brain events, they are whole-body states mediated largely by hormones as well as neurons.

The consequences of this realisation are two-fold. First, and practically, it means that awareness – which is fundamental to emotional intelligence and is the prerequisite of self management and relationship management – means bodily awareness. Self awareness means being aware of what is going on in our body, what its significance is and what we need to do about it. Awareness of others means being aware of what is going on in their bodies, what significance that has for them and for us and our relationship management. Second, and more philosophically, it means that emotions just *are* (being the consequence of our heredity and our history, rather than being voluntary cognitive constructs) and therefore are to be accepted, rather than judged as good or bad. Hence, our Principle no. 6: "All emotions are self-justified, to be accepted and important."

"Gestalt"

The school of Gestalt Psychotherapy, founded by Fritz Perls, shares our emphasis on the bodily nature of emotions and of the importance of awareness. (A dictionary definition of gestalt: "(German) a form, shape pattern: organised whole or unit. Gestalt psychology, revolt from the atomistic outlook of the orthodox school, starts with the organised whole as something not a mere sum of the parts into which it can be logically analysed)." Many gestalt ways of working constitute effective interventions for the development of self awareness. A particular scale of the IEq, apart from Scales 4 and 5 Self Awareness and Awareness of Others, which has gestalt echoes is Scale 9 Flexibility, which is in effect measuring people's willingness to live with open gestalts.

"Personality"

Personality is, by definition, something relatively unchanging and enduring: it is an abstraction from the patterns of behaviour over time. (To what extent it is hereditary and fixed, and to what extent the result of very early learning and therefore potentially changeable, if with difficulty, will depend on where you stand in the heredity vs. environment debate.) EI, on the other hand, and all the things that compose it, are, as we have seen, changeable and developable. EI, therefore, is not, as some would have it, coterminous with personality, nor a set of personality traits. It is, rather, how effectively we manage our personality, given that it is what it is. The Myers–Briggs Type Inventory (MBTI), based on Jungian Analytical Psychology, is an example of a personality measure. A study of the links between the MBTI and the *i3*™ is presented at the end of this chapter.

Neurolinguistic Programming (NLP)

Fifteen years ago NLP was probably the psychological approach which found the greatest response in work organisations. In some ways it has close links with EI, and in others not. The distinction goes back to the origins of NLP. It was founded on the premise that successful therapists were successful not because of their theories about psychology but because of what they *did*, how they behaved, with their clients. A highly detailed analysis of the behaviours of some highly skilled therapists from different theoretical orientations generated some common patterns which were determined to be key. From the beginning, therefore, NLP has majored in technique and has tended to ignore theory, philosophy and ethics. Some of the techniques it has identified are extremely effective and can profitably be used in the process of facilitating EI development. The absence of an overarching theoretical approach, on the other hand, contrasts with our approach to EI, which manages to organise coherently a whole variety of different insights. Above all, the philosophical approach of NLP is, in EI terms, deficient. Whereas we come from a respectful empowering position, putting the client at the centre of their own development, many NLP techniques are done to the client (out of awareness) by the practitioner, rather than offered to the client to use on themselves. In TA terms this is Parent to Child, not Adult to Adult; it is not respectful and it is not empowering. Furthermore, NLP is open to being used manipulatively and exploitatively. That said, there are of course many excellent NLP practitioners who use NLP ethically.

Belbin® team roles

If the MBTI is the most popular way of categorising individuals in general, the Belbin® team roles provide the most popular way of categorising people's performance in team settings. For more about Belbin® team notes see Chapter 16.

Obviously, we could go on ad infinitum looking at the relationship between our approach to EI and various other psychological constructs and approaches. There is one more we need to look at, and then we hope we will have covered the most salient ones; the ones people are most interested in.

Motivation

One of the issues which those interested in the application of EI in organisations are often concerned with is motivation, but the relationship of motivation to emotional intelligence is not a simple one. Historically, it used to have a special place. Daniel Goleman was a student at Harvard of Professor David McClelland, who, as well as being the father of the competency movement (hence the ECI-360, the Emotional "Competence" Inventory), was a motivation guru and invented the idea of "nAch", the need for achievement. Consequently, Goleman's first model of EI was not the four part one which is now the same as ours, but had an additional fifth element: motivation. On reflection, he – in our view rightly – dropped that element.

Motivation does not appear explicitly in our model of emotional intelligence, nor is it measured directly by the Individual Effectiveness questionnaire. Of course, one crucial element is covered by Scale 8 Goal Directedness, which is definitely part of EI. Notions of Personal Power (Scale 7) are also involved: it is difficult to be highly motivated if you do not believe that what you do has much effect on the outcome. But there is more to motivation than that. Part of it appears to be constitutional: some people have higher levels of energy than others; some are fairly listless and some tend to be more active. This variation is not part of emotional intelligence; it seems relatively fixed rather than learned. EI comes into play when it comes to managing our energy levels, whatever they are.

The crucial question when exploring the relationship between motivation and EI is: where is the motivation coming from? Is the person driven or are they choosing to do what they do? Consider McClelland's concept of "need for achievement". Why do some people have this need? Because their OKness is conditional: "I am only OK if I am successful and seen to be successful". By definition, therefore, since Self Regard is the same as **un**conditional OKness, people with a high need for achievement are relatively low in Self Regard, the most fundamental of the elements of emotional intelligence. In TA terms, these people spend most of their time in conforming Adapted Child trying to fulfil the conditions of their OKness, obeying the demands of their internal Parent, rather than in Adult. They may be highly productive in the short term because they are so driven, but because they are not in Adult, their thinking and decision making will often be impaired, their lack of unconditional self regard will mean that they are likely not to be good at self management or to be emotionally resilient, they will be liable to burn out, to heart attacks, strokes and alcoholism, they are not likely to be creative and they are often not much fun to work alongside or under. In short, this is high motivation from a driven, emotionally unintelligent place, which can be quantitively productive in the short term but has lots of disadvantages, both for the individual and for the organisation, in the long term.

The more enlightened individuals will be aware that they also *need* to be emotionally intelligent, and will attempt to act with EI, putting additional pressure on themselves, and likely to be fairly unsuccessful at it too (because – given their underlying low Self Regard – their would-be emotionally intelligent behaviour is not rooted in and supported by the necessary attitudes).

Contrast this with people who are highly motivated in doing what they do, but who have a low need for achievement. (That is to say, they may have a strong desire to achieve a particular goal, or set of goals, which they have chosen, but they do not have a need to be seen as a high achiever per se.) They are self-motivated, they do what they do from choice not from need or from being driven: their OKness is unconditional. In TA terms, their motivation comes from Integrated Adult. The Adult is in charge, the goals are in line with the values held in Parent and the creativity, energy and enthusiasm of Free Child is engaged in the journey towards the goal. These people will be more creative and flexible, they will think better and make better decisions, they will take better care of themselves and not be liable to burn out or take to drink or become seriously ill. They will pace themselves better and may be less quantitatively productive than those with a high need for achievement in the short term, but over the long haul they will be a much more valuable asset to the organisation. And they will have a much more enjoyable time, as will those who work alongside them or for them. This is high motivation from a choiceful, emotionally intelligent place.

Linking the Emotional Intelligence framework with Jungian Typology

Reproduced by kind permission of Jo Maddocks C.Psychol

Introduction

Emotional intelligence (EI) is now an established concept that is frequently applied alongside type instruments for people development and change. Connections made between the two approaches have tended to look at the overlap between EI scales and type preferences (Pearman and Albritton, 1998; Higgs and Dulewicz, 2002), but no theoretical link explaining how they are related has been made between them. In this section I propose a theoretical link between the framework of EI and type dynamics and then go on to draw some practical implications.

The theoretical link

The EI framework, shown in Figure 17.3, consists of four parts: Self aware-ness (SA), Other awareness (OA), Self management (SM) and Relation-ship management (RM). The arrows indicate how they are related, with the cornerstone to EI being Self awareness. This framework is now largely con-sistent across EI theorists (Daniel Goleman, Reuven BarOn, Sparrow and Maddocks, etc.).

The framework may be separated left from right. On the left there is Intrapersonal EI, which is picking up what is going on inside of us (Self awareness) and doing what we need to do about it (Self management), and on the right is Interpersonal EI, which is picking up what is going on in other people and between people (Other awareness) and doing what we need to do about that (Relationship management).

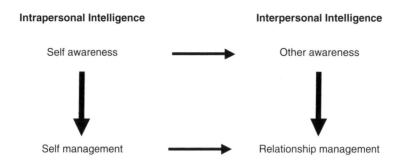

Figure 17.3 *The EI framework.*

In broad terms there are obvious similarities here to the Extraverted–Introverted attitudes of Type theory. Introverts are more oriented towards the left side (intrapersonal EI) and extraverts to the right side (interpersonal EI).

The second way in which the EI framework may be divided is by top and bottom. At the top we have the two Awareness parts (Self and Other awareness) and on the bottom we have the Management parts (Self and Relationship management).

Again, there are clear similarities here with the Jungian Functions. The Perceiving functions are related to the top half of how we take information in (Awareness) and the Judging functions are related to the bottom half of how we decide and act upon our perception (Management).

Having made these conceptual links it is possible to assign the eight Jungian preferences within the EI framework, as illustrated below.

EI components:	Intrapersonal Intelligence	Interpersonal Intelligence
Jungian Attitudes:	Introversion	Extraversion
EI Processes:	Self awareness	Other awareness
Jungian Perceiving	*Introverted Sensing*	*Extraverted Sensing*
Functions:	*Introverted iNtuition*	*Extraverted iNtuition*
EI Processes:	Self management	Relationship management
Jungian Judging	*Introverted Thinking*	*Extraverted Thinking*
Functions:	*Introverted Feeling*	*Extraverted Feeling*

For example, Introverted Sensing would lie "top" (Perceiving function) "left" (Introverted attitude) under the "Self awareness" part of the EI framework.

Defining Emotional Intelligence

Although there is broad agreement on the framework of emotional intelligence (shown above), there is less consensus about the definition. Our definition is:

> "EI is the habitual practice of using thinking about feeling and feeling about thinking when choosing what to do."

The extent to which we have this habit is determined largely by our internal interferences, which are beliefs and attitudes largely left over from our childhood. (NB the terms Thinking, Feelings, Intuition and Attitudes used to describe EI here are not meant in the Jungian sense).

The process by which we practise *"Thinking about feeling"* may take several steps:

1. Noticing feelings   e.g. *Tummy tingle*
2. Paying attention to them   *"My tummy tingles!"*
3. Giving them significance   *"I feel anxious"*
4. Thinking about them   *"This happens when I meet people"*
5. Taking them into account in   *"I will breathe deeply"*
   deciding how to act.

This applies both to one's own feelings and those of others.

"Feeling about thinking" refers to using our intuitive bodily sense to advise our thinking, e.g. when we do something because it seems logically right, yet our body tells us it feels wrong.

Much of the popularity in EI has come about from the advances in brain science. For example, there is strong evidence that feelings precede and largely determine our cognitive thinking, rather than the assumed opinion that thinking leads feeling. In turn, feelings are largely determined by our attitudes, which may better be described as "metaphorical patterns" within the limbic brain that, when matched with a given stimulus, create an emotion / feeling or expectation.

Attitudes are therefore the core to how we feel, think and behave. We have identified 8 core humanistic attitudes which are pre-determinants of emotional intelligence and fit well within the philosophy of Type theory. Our view is that individuals who hold these attitudes will more easily develop their EI and capitalise on the strengths of their Type.

If we are to assume this link exists between EI and Type theory, what then are the practical implications? To answer this question we need to understand how EI and Type differ and that we are not just replicating one theory with a different nomenclature. EI differs from Type theory in two fundamental ways:

1. Type is entirely fixed, EI is changeable.
2. Type is a preference, EI is a competence.

Difference 1: Type theory assumes that a person's type preferences are innate and do not change. EI theories describe it as consisting of attitudes, habits and skills which are acquired and therefore changeable.

Difference 2: Type theory provides a model for understanding individual differences, it does not suggest that any particular type is better or more competent than another type. EI on the other hand does emphasise the difference between better and worse scale scores, reflecting more or less adaptive ways of responding to oneself and the world.

The practical implications

There are two ways of considering the relationship between EI and Type: firstly that Type will influence development of EI and secondly that EI will influence the development of Type.

We would suggest that Type and EI are interdependent, that EI influences the effectiveness with which Type is applied and Type influences the ease with which different aspects of EI are learned. We can now go on to consider both of these hypotheses.

Hypothesis 1: Personality type influences how we develop our EI

One way to explore this relationship would be to see if Type dynamics predicts an order of strengths in the corresponding parts of the EI framework. For example, an INFP would have the following order of strengths in EI:

Dynamic	Type preference	EI link
Dominant	Introverted Feeling	Self management
Auxiliary	Extraverted iNtuition	Other awareness
Tertiary	Introverted Sensing	Self awareness
Inferior	Extraverted Thinking	Relationship management

Table 17.1 shows the dynamic order and link to EI for each of the personality types.

Table 17.1 *Linking type and EI.*

EI pattern	Dom	Aux	Ter	Inf	Type
EI 1:	SA	RM	SM	OA	I–J
Jungian Si/Ni	Te/Fe	Ti/Fi	Se/Ne		
EI 2:	SM	OA	SA	RM	I–P
Jungian Ti/Fi	Se/Ne	Si/Ni	Te/Fe		
EI 3:	OA	SM	RM	SA	E–P
Jungian Se/Fe	Ti/Fi	Te/Fe	Si/Ni		
EI 4:	RM	SA	OA	SM	E–J
Jungian Te/Fe	Si/Ni	Se/Ne	Ti/Fi		

Incidentally, we can see from this analysis that the dominant and auxiliary of each type link to both an Awareness and Management part, as well as to an Intrapersonal and Interpersonal part of the EI framework.

The implication here is that by using Type dynamics we can identify how easy or difficult it may be for an individual to develop their EI competence. Knowledge of Type would therefore be a useful tool for those seeking to develop their EI.

To provide an example of how this table may be interpreted, consider the profile of an ISTP, who, from the table, may score High (SM–Self management) High (OA–Other awareness) Low (SA–Self awareness) Low (RM–Relationship management). This may be interpreted as follows.

High Self management but lower Self awareness indicates this person may follow a set of automatic habits and attitudes in their life which, on the surface, are quite effective, but in the longer run may not meet the individual's real needs. Such as, meeting others' expectations of them rather than being in touch with their own wants. In Type terms this person may not be using their Introverted Sensing and Intuition sufficiently to have an accurate sense of what is important to them.

High Other awareness and low Relationship Management indicate that this person is aware of others and their relationships but does not act upon this awareness. There are several possible reasons for this, such as having an overly suspicious view of others (their Other awareness may, in fact, be distorted), having a lack of social confidence and poor basic interpersonal skills. Through the Type lens, this person may not be applying their Extraverted Feeling to help support them in managing their relationships.

Their high Self Management and low Relationship Management suggests they may be more effective at managing themselves than their relationships, which may reflect an underpinning attitude of high Self Regard and lower Regard for Others (I+ U–).

EI interpretations are more evaluative than for Type and therefore provide a different set of interpretations to be explored with the client.

Hypothesis 2: EI influences how we apply and develop our personality type

Based on the links made between the EI framework and Type theory, and the differences between Type and EI, we would assert that EI is about *how effectively we learn to apply our personality type*. For example, an emotionally intelligent introvert would have developed the attitudes, skills and habits to be interpersonally effective, i.e. to use their less preferred extraverted attitude. Equally, an emotionally *un*intelligent introvert may have poor interpersonal behaviour, i.e. underdeveloped extravert attitudes. The proposal here is that to be a fully functioning personality we must apply emotional intelligence. One reason that EI enables Type development is because for each Type preference there are several aspects of emotional intelligence that relate to it. For example, Introverted Thinking, which links to the self management part of EI, may include:

- motivating yourself;
- emotional resilience;
- inner confidence;
- managing your emotions.

Being able to measure these aspects of EI alongside a person's type preference gives the user more options for what and how to develop their type.

The second main benefit of using EI alongside Type is that it provides a measure of performance which helps us identify how effectively a person is using their personality type. Because we have made links between the two models, it is now possible to help the Type user to see how effectively they are applying each of their Type preferences and how to make improvements in this.

Here is an example of how an individual's EI profile (from the *ie*™ questionnaire) may be used to inform their type development:

An ESFP client reported a specific concern that she lacked assertiveness. The EI profile identified three particularly low scores on: Personal Power (the degree to which she is in charge of and takes responsibility for her outcomes in life), Goal Directedness (the degree to which she relates her own behaviour to long-term goals) and Self Awareness (the degree to which she is in touch with her body, her feelings and her intuition).

From this we identified specific objectives and strategies to improve her assertiveness including:

- *Self Awareness: turning into her feelings, e.g. when she feels "no" when she says "yes"*
- *Goal Directedness: developing impulse control, knowing what she wants, having clear intentions and not being distracted.*
- *Personal Power: learning to ask for what she wants.*

The client also used two of her high-scoring scales as a resource, e.g.

- *Flexibility: trying out different approaches and giving it a go.*
- *Personal Openness: seeking support from others to meet her objectives.*

The purpose of EI intervention is usually to help individuals become more aware of their emotional state, to identify unhelpful attitudes and adopt new habits of behaviour. Combined with an understanding of Type, clients can better understand why they may typically feel and behave as they do.

Conclusion

From our premise of the EI framework, we have overlaid the Jungian Type preferences and shown how Type dynamics may indicate a possible order of strength in the four parts of EI. We then identified two basic differences between both approaches: that EI is about competence and not preference, and EI is changeable not fixed. This led us to explore two hypotheses of how EI and Type are interdependent and provide a more powerful approach for change when used together than in isolation. In sum, emotional intelligence is the practice of managing and guiding our personality to be both personally and interpersonally effective.

Appendix
Examples of related aspects of EI to the eight Jungian preferences

Introverted Sensing

Link to the EI framework: Self Awareness
Examples of related aspects of EI:

- self awareness: body awareness;
- noticing your state (wants, likes, needs);
- being aware of your thoughts;
- reflection on past experience;
- knowing your wants, likes and needs;
- stored inner impressions and self knowledge;
- kinaesthetic learning – physical ability.

Introverted Intuition

Link to the EI framework: Self Awareness
Examples of related aspects of EI:

- reflective learning;
- making sense of accumulated moments of experience;
- inferring from experiences;
- understanding self wants and needs;
- reflection and drawing out insights;

- self insight – about inner purpose and identity;
- spiritual awareness;
- intuition and prediction about own future.

Extraverted Sensing

Link to the EI framework: Other Awareness
Examples of related aspects of EI:

- other awareness;
- noticing body language, voice, mannerisms and posture in others;
- hearing and listening accurately – keen observers;
- noticing interaction, behaviour and responses;
- accurate perception of others;
- being present in the moment – seeing the reality, as things are;
- attention to details, immediate focus.

Extraverted Intuition

Link to the EI framework: Other Awareness
Examples of related aspects of EI:

- reflective learning – usually happens after the event;
- seeing patterns and tendencies;
- making inferences;
- detecting and intuiting nuances about people and situation;
- inferring how person is probably feeling;
- getting meaning on complexities of human behaviour and interpersonal relationships;
- seeing beyond the obvious explanation.

Introverted Thinking

Link to the EI framework: Self Management
Examples of related aspects of EI:

- cortical and logical analysis of how to behave;
- can step outside of inner feelings to "think about feelings";

- Emotional Resilience – being firm minded;
- Goal Directedness – prioritising;
- emotional self regulation;
- consistency, sense of fairness, right and wrong;
- accepting responsibility, self determined to make things happen.

Introverted Feeling

Link to the EI framework: Self Management
Examples of related aspects of EI:

- congruity, walking your talk, integrity;
- holding clear inner principles and values;
- seeking harmony between inner and outer life;
- sense of personal identity;
- doing what is intrinsically important;
- meeting own expectations of self, values driven;
- sense of inner purpose;
- inner belief and strength of conviction.

Extraverted Thinking

Link to the EI framework: Relationship Management
Examples of related aspects of EI:

- motivating others through demonstrating drive;
- influencer providing convincing reason;
- clarity of communication – concise, businesslike and logical;
- natural organiser of people and things;
- decisive in taking action. Target and goal focused;
- leadership characteristics, e.g. taking charge and directive;
- will deal with conflict confidently and assertively.

Extraverted Feeling

Link to the EI framework: Relationship Management
Examples of related aspects of EI:

- empathiser – put self in others' shoes;
- interested in others;
- expressing and sharing feelings, wants, likes, etc.;
- may enjoy coaching and supporting others;
- making contacts, building relationships, developing close relationships;
- passionate, emotional expression;
- interdependence, team working.

References

Goleman, D. (1995) *Emotional Intelligence: Why it can matter more than IQ*, Bantam Books.
Higgs, M. and Dulewicz, V. (2002) *Making Sense of Emotional Intelligence*, NFER.
Martinez-Pons, M. (1997) "The relation of emotional intelligence with selected areas of personal functioning", *Imagination, Cognition and Personality*, **17**, 3–13.
Pearman, R. and Albritton, S. (1998) *I'm Not Crazy, I'm Just Not You: Real meaning of the 16 personality types*, Davies-Black Publishing.

ie and the ie logo, te and the te logo, and oe and the oe logo are trademarks of JCA (Occupational Psychologists) Limited. JCA reserves all rights and is the exclusive worldwide publisher www.ie-te.co.uk.

18

The EI practitioner

Creating emotionally intelligent learning interventions

Why most development training doesn't work

When you think of how much is spent on "management development", "leadership development" and similar courses, the notion that most development training just doesn't work is a fairly radical suggestion. It implies that British business is throwing away many hundreds of millions of pounds each year. Why on earth would that happen?

As we discussed in Chapter 4 there are four determinants of the quality of human performance in any role and at any task:

> Knowledge
> Attitudes
> Skills
> Habits

Each of these needs to be right to generate effective performance.

As we have said, when we introduce the KASH model to employees of business and government organisations and then ask them, "Which of these does your organisation address in its training provision?", the answer is almost invariably, "Entirely knowledge and skills. Attitudes and habits are not addressed at all." So then we push, and say, "OK, that may be true for training overall, but what about development training specifically?" And still the answer comes back, "Entirely knowledge and skills. Attitudes and habits are not addressed at all."

We have already seen that each of the four KASH elements needs to be right in order for performance to be optimised. Therefore, ignoring two of the four elements means that you are bound not to get to where you want to get to. Unless you are dealing only with people whose attitudes and habits are ideal before you start and who are deficient only in the necessary knowledge and skills, which is very rarely the case.

So why on earth do the designers and deliverers of development training shoot themselves in the foot in this way, condemned before they start to fail to reach their training objectives? On the face of it, it seems daft. What can be the cause of this fundamental aberration? We believe that there are eight main reasons.

1. *An overly cognitive and mechanistic view of human nature.*
   In other words, the prevailing view of what determines human behaviour is not based on the KASH model, but is cognitive behavioural in nature: if people know what they need to know and have acquired the necessary skills, then they will automatically behave as required. The significance of attitudes and habits (and feelings) is entirely overlooked.

2. *Habit: this is what people have traditionally focused on.*
   This is how we were trained / developed and if, as a result, we are now senior enough to be taking decisions about the format of development training, then clearly this was the right way to do it and is what the next generation needs too.

3. *Difficulties of measurement.*
   Until recently people have not been able to identify the relevant attitudes or to measure them, but you can give someone an exam to test their knowledge or a test to evaluate their skills. Measurement allows you to decide where your training should begin and helps you find out where it has taken the trainees to at the end.

4. *Moral scruples about judging, and intervening to change people's attitudes.*
   There is a radical and libertarian streak in many of us which is not comfortable with the notion of employers evaluating their employees' beliefs and attitudes, still less requiring them to alter their beliefs and attitudes

and to hold particular ones prescribed by the employer. And yet, when in 2004 certain police cadets were shown to be racist, there was general agreement that they should be expelled from the force, that being racist was not compatible with being a fair-minded police officer. So at some level we do recognise that attitudes are relevant to job performance and a legitimate concern of management.

5. *Ease of intervention.*

You can give someone a book or a manual to increase their knowledge or a training course to develop their skills. But people don't know about facilitating people to change their attitudes if they wish to do so, and they know that changing habits takes a long time. Furthermore, you can try to inject knowledge and skills into someone, but changing attitudes and habits can only be done by the person themselves. Skilled facilitation rather than straightforward instruction is therefore required.

6. *Desire for control.*

One of the corollaries of the fact that changing attitudes and habits can only be done by the person themselves is that the outcome of the development process is up to them, and out of the control of the development trainers. This can be uncomfortable for those who like to be in control.

7. *Succumbing to senior management time pressure.*

Changing one's attitudes or one's habits tends not to be an instantaneous affair. Both tend to take longer than the acquisition of knowledge or skills. (To change one item of habitual behaviour, to change the unconscious "default setting", can take three weaks or more – not surprising when you consider that we have probably been behaving in this habitual way since we were seven or so.) Any development process that addresses attitudes and habits is therefore likely to take longer than one that confines itself to inculcating knowledge and skills. But we all want quick results, and it takes some courage in a Learning and Development Manager to say to his or her seniors, "Yes, I can do something in a fortnight or so, but it will be a waste of your money because it won't actually do the business, and if you want an intervention which has a reasonable chance of achieving what you want, then you will be looking at something which is going to take three months and more."

8. *Misguided economising.*

Development programmes which address attitudes and habits as well as knowledge and skills usually cost more, for four reasons:

- It is not a question of attitudes and habits *instead of* knowledge and skills, but of attitudes and habits *as well as* knowledge and skills. You are going to be doing something additional rather than something alternative, and that is going to have cost implications.
- As we have just seen, it is going to take longer, and that means it is going to be more expensive.
- As we saw in point 5 above, you are going to need skilled facilitators rather than trainers, and they take longer to develop and therefore cost more.
- Because the identity of the attitudes and the habits that need changing varies from person to person, much of your intervention will need to be individually based rather than group based, and will therefore be more expensive.

The problem is that spending £x on something that doesn't work rather than £2x on something that does work is a rotten way to save money. What you are doing instead is throwing it away. Luckily, addressing attitudes and habits as well as knowledge and skills is going to have a significant and measurable effect on performance, and therefore the extra expenditure is easier to justify.

Having reviewed these eight reasons, it seems a bit more understandable that so much development training should be of a format that is bound not to work. But what do we need to do now to alter this state of affairs? How do you design development training that does work?

If we are to set about designing development programmes that do work, then we need first to identify which of these eight "reasons" are just explanations and which are, to a degree, justifications and need addressing. We believe that with numbers 1, 2, 6, 7 and 8 we can take the attitude, "This is misguided. Do it differently." But numbers 3, 4 and 5 contain elements that need addressing and providing for in any future programmes. Let us take them one by one.

(3) Difficulties of measurement

We suggested above that "until recently people have not been able to identify the relevant attitudes or to measure them". There is an implication there that something has happened recently which means that this is no longer the case. What is that?

For us, it is the advent of the notion of emotional intelligence, the increasing realisation of the significant correlations between levels of emotional intelligence and levels of performance and the availability of well-designed measures of emotional intelligence. Now we are the first to acknowledge that for many of the promoters of EI it has nothing to do with attitudes, but at the Centre for Applied Emotional Intelligence, as this book has made clear, we see the main determinants of emotional intelligence as being attitudinal in nature. Following Timothy Gallwey, we believe that

$$Performance = potential - interference$$

and that all human beings, bar the brain damaged and the psychotic, are capable of acting with emotional intelligence. Most of the time, of course, we do not, because of our internal interferences, which are misguided beliefs and attitudes adopted in childhood but surviving unproductively into adulthood.

Measuring someone's emotional intelligence, therefore, is – or ought to be – tantamount to identifying the extent and nature of their interferences; certainly that is what is done by the $ie^{™}$ Individual Effectiveness questionnaire, the measure which this book has explored.

The attitudes which have the most profound effect on performance are those measured by the first two scales of the $ie^{™}$ Self Regard (same as self esteem) and Regard for Others, which together define what Transactional Analysis refers to as a "life position". Somebody's life position tends to affect all other aspects of emotional intelligence. In addition, at the Centre for Applied Emotional Intelligence we have identified eight attitudes which constitute a mindset conducive to emotional intelligence – see the Eight Principles of EI in Chapter 4. The $ie^{™}$ does not measure them directly, but exploring someone's $ie^{™}$ responses helps to identify which principles they find it most difficult to adhere to and when.

It is, therefore, no longer the case that we do not know what attitudes are conducive to effective performance, nor that we do not know how to find out where people stand on them.

(4) Moral scruples about judging, and intervening to change, people's attitudes

Such scruples we often encounter when people are introduced to the eight principles of emotional intelligence, but they tend to be resolved when we are clear about the eight principles' ontological status; in other words, what they are and what they aren't.

1. They are not descriptive: we do not suggest that people habitually behave in a manner that conforms to the principles. On the contrary, because we all have our interferences, and because the norms of the culture we live in are, on the whole, incompatible with the principles, a lot of the time we don't.
2. They are not prescriptive: we do not suggest that people *ought* to sub-scribe to these principles. People are entitled to believe whatever they want to believe and to hold whatever attitudes they wish.
3. They are correlational.

We observe three connections between holding the principles and acting with emotional intelligence:

1. To the extent that you subscribe to the principles, you will find it easy to behave with emotional intelligence, i.e. to be good at self management and relationship management. Hence, you are likely to be happier, healthier and more successful.
2. To the extent that you do not subscribe to the principles, you will find it difficult to behave with emotional intelligence.
3. Whenever someone behaves in an emotionally unintelligent way, it will always be found on examination that they have breached one or more of these principles.

We are not, therefore, in the business of intervening to change people's attitudes. Rather, what we do is to help people recognise the attitudes they hold and point out the connection between those attitudes and behaving with emotional intelligence, which leads to effective self management and relationship management and therefore to high performance, and in the long run promotes health, happiness and success. The degree to which they then choose to set about changing their attitudes, and the extent to which they allow themselves to choose their behaviour in accordance with the new attitudes, is entirely up to them. Their autonomy is respected. Indeed, their autonomy in psychotherapeutic terms is enhanced, because they are making conscious choices rather than behaving in a driven or habitually uncon-scious way.

(5) Ease of intervention

As we pointed out above, "you can try to inject knowledge and skills into someone, but changing attitudes and habits can only be done by the person themselves. Skilled facilitation rather than straightforward instruction is therefore required." And, "because the identity of the attitudes and the habits that need changing varies from person to person, much of your intervention will need to be individually based rather than group based". Also, "changing one's attitudes or one's habits tends not to be an instantaneous affair. Both tend to take longer than the acquisition of knowledge or skills." The necessary interventions will, therefore, be staff intensive in terms of numbers as well as of quality. Not all organisations will have the necessary numbers of skilled staff in post at the moment to start addressing, with their own resources, attitudes and habits as well as knowledge and skills.

At the Centre for Applied Emotional Intelligence we attempt to address this issue in two ways. First, we recognise that not all the support that individuals will need over time to help them go through the lengthy process of changing attitudes and habits without falling by the wayside (think of New Year's resolutions!) needs to be highly skilled and professional. So, after the initial exploration of their *is*™ results with a professional and their making a 21-day commitment to change a particular item of behaviour relating to the particular aspect of EI which they wish to develop, we ask them to choose a buddy to support them through the process. This can be their spouse, a colleague, a friend – it doesn't matter as long as it is someone whom they trust and with whom they feel free to be open. The buddy is given a copy of the 21-day commitment and the two make contact regularly through that period to support the habit changer and to help iron out any difficulties which may arise.

The buddying system to a degree reduces the amount of professional help required for habit change, but there will still be a requirement for skilled professional input into the programme of attitude and habit change. So the Centre has, for five years, been running the only training course in the world (so far as we know) for professional EI practitioners, an action learning based course running over nine months. This allows large organisations to develop the necessary skills in house by sending their own specialists on this course, and also has generated a body of skilled consultants who can support smaller organisations to address attitudes and habits in their development programmes and therefore to have a much greater chance of a successful outcome.

An executive coaching programme based around emotional intelligence development and starting from the respondent's *ie*™ results is a singularly effective intervention. So, another strategy for building the necessary skills base is for those organisations which already use coaches to get them accredited in the use of the *ie*™.

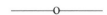

There is no longer any excuse for focusing development programmes on knowledge and skills alone and failing to incorporate attitude change and habit change. Learning and development managers now need to be brave enough to stand up to their senior management and be frank: effective development which addresses all four of the KASH elements is more expensive and will take longer, but it works and it is now do-able. Whereas development programmes focusing on knowledge and skills alone are cheaper and quicker, but don't really work (as we see from the recurrent "transfer of training" problem) and therefore are an extravagance. In that, to an extent, they represent money thrown away.

Experiential learning

With advances in developmental thinking, encompassing the concepts of multiple intelligences, heart / brain learning and particularly emotional intelligence, we're able to create a new effective breed of development training. Deeper understanding of how we learn, what makes us tick, how our emotions (like it or not) are intrinsic to our decision-making, has led to a change in the way training programmes need to be structured. The immediacy of personal learning in an engaging experiential environment makes its validity as a development training medium suddenly so much more apparent.

The personal learning process is accelerated through experiential learning – learning by doing – as described by Kolb's learning cycle (Figure 18.1 on the following page).

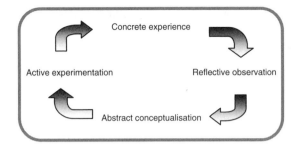

Figure 18.1 *Kolb's learning cycle.*
Source: Kolb (1984). Reproduced by permission.

An "experiential learning cycle" is a means of representing sequences in experiential learning. The stages of a learning cycle can be:

- managed by a facilitator;
- self-managed;
- "unmanaged", in the sense that learning from experience is a normal everyday process for most people.

"I hear, I forget; I see, I remember; I do, I understand."
Chinese proverb

Experiential learning facilitates emotional learning because:

- we can understand how our behaviour is an expression of our emotions;
- we can experience how our emotions cannot be separated from the body or the mind;
- we are able to recognise how moods are created and how they can be managed;
- we can build our self esteem and regard for others.

This requires the creation of stimulating learning experiences using a range of development tools and challenges. By using real challenges in real situations in real time, experiential learning creates the ideal environment in which to practise and develop new personal attitudes, skills and habits.

Experiential learning and, in particular, experiential learning incorporating aspects of the outdoors, with highly skilled EI facilitators promotes personal growth. Giges and Rosenfeld's model of personal growth suggests that:

> "*Personal growth* can be viewed as making new connections in any of several directions:
>
> *upward* to achieve one's full potential;
> *outward* to make contact and encounter others;
> *inward* to increase our awareness of who we are and what we want, need, sense, feel, think and do; and
> *downward* to touch earth, to be grounded and to connect."
>
> (Giges and Rosenfeld 1976)

This model suggests that an individual grows as they explore their potential, their relationships with others, their self knowledge and their connection with the environment – all of which are experienced through an outdoor experiential learning programme.

How the outdoor environment accelerates learning

We have found that experiential learning in the outdoors is highly conducive to immediate personal growth spurts. This vastly under-rated medium is viewed by most either in trepidation, recalling the images of people being forced to swim beneath a boat in a freezing Scottish loch, or as a bit of a "jolly" – great fun, but where's the business relevance in a pile of rope, planks and barrels? Of course, as with most things, the memory remains whilst the reality moves on.

First and foremost, the outdoors creates a "neutral" environment – away from offices and hotel conference rooms. It is a great leveller – and immediately reduces, and has the potential to eliminate, hierarchy – each person can come into their own.

Immediately we can identify people's different attitudes towards the unknown, change, comfort and security, and facing irrational fears.

For many it provides new and unexplored experiences. It can be challenging but ultimately should always be positive for real learning to stay with you.

The outdoor challenge provides an opportunity to re-experience particular emotional situations in a different context. We can experience a different outcome. We can develop our presence – presence of mind. "*Yes this is reminding me of a bad experience, but actually is it the same?*"

The outdoor challenge also requires us to deal with the combination of feeling and logical thinking – dealing with fear and working out what to do next. This demonstrates how emotions can inhibit, and indeed enhance, logic and action. *"What's the worst that can happen here?"*

The outdoors takes us away from the context of our everyday lives, so that we can explore our emotions and our potential in a safe, natural and neutral environment.

At the same time, for any organisation to justify sending employees away from the workplace, the outdoor experience needs to be practical and relevant. It is also important to make the learning relevant to the needs of the group or individual by relating issues and key learning points directly back to the workplace or appropriate "real life" situations. It needs to:

- have practical scenarios with learning which is directly transferable to the workplace;
- be in real time, requiring planning, teamwork and leadership;
- have real challenges exploring beliefs, behaviours and emotions.

The perfect combination

The experiential challenges themselves need to sit within a developmental framework to enable learning to be explored, reflected upon and taken forward. Through our own continuous research and exploration we find that emotional intelligence always sits at the heart of any personal development issue.

In an experiential context, Tim Gallwey's simple formula for increasing performance by managing, and ultimately dismantling, interferences is revealing. By combining the exploration of emotional intelligence with the opportunity for experiential learning, ideally with outdoor components, we create programmes that facilitate true personal learning. This has a direct impact on an individual's future performance and effectiveness. Using the $P = p - i$ formula for reviewing experiential challenges, we help people develop themselves in terms of their emotional learning, achieving more of their potential and enhancing relationships with others. The formula works just as well on macro levels with a team, a department or, indeed, a whole organisation. Table 18.1 shows an example of how it can be used in an experiential review of a team task.

Table 18.1 *Using Gallwey's formula to review a team task.*

	TASK	TEAM	INDIVIDUAL
PERFORMANCE	What did the team actually achieve?	How well did you relate to each other as a team?	How well did your individual effectiveness contribute to the team?
POTENTIAL	What was the potential? Objectives, ideal, etc.	What additional qualities could the team have demonstrated?	What more could you have done as individuals to help the team achieve its potential?
INTERFERENCE	What got in the way of achieving optimal task performance?	What inhibited the team from working together at your optimum?	What were you feeling or saying to yourself that inhibited your own performance?
IMPROVING PERFORMANCE	How would you undertake the task differently next time?	What have you learned about the team's relationships that you will take forward?	What have you learned about yourself in this exercise?

The role of action learning

The process of action learning, too, is an emotionally intelligent one. It is the perfect follow-through for EI-based experiential learning, to enable learning to continue and develop within the group. According to Joanna Kozubska of the IMC Association, it enables the group to:

- work out what needs to be done (the learning);
- implement their learning;
- learn through a social process with and from each other, in a learning set group;
- help each other to learn rather than being taught;
- identify, recognise and review what has been learned.

Action learning is a process of taking self responsibility for learning with support from the group. Together, learners or delegates can work out what their individual interferences are by creating clarity around what everyone is trying to do, working out what is stopping each person from moving forward, finding strategies for working through blocks and gaining support from each other, the learning set tutors and personal contacts.

Being an emotionally intelligent EI consultant

There are plenty of articles and books about being an effective organisational consultant. We concentrate here specifically on the dos and don'ts of being a consultant specialising in emotional intelligence. In our view there are two big extra problems over and above those of consultants in general: people's, including clients', expectations are higher and it is very tempting, but fatal, to oversell what you can offer.

First, the issue of expectations. Like people who take on any consultant, what the clients of EI consultants are really interested in in the long run is whether you produce the goods, whether you are able to generate the kinds of change in their organisation that they are looking for, and thus increase their organisational effectiveness and – in the case of a commercial organisation – profitability, in the direction and to the extent that they hope. It takes a while, however, to work out whether you are going to be able to deliver. Meanwhile, they will very quickly be able to assess whether, in their dealings with you, they experience you as emotionally intelligent. And that will be another one of their expectations, even if not explicitly expressed as such. So, quite rightly, it is important that process matches content, and that not only does the EI consultant help generate emotionally intelligent working in the organisation and facilitate the development of the emotional intelligence of the members of the organisation, but also that he/she acts with emotional intelligence personally while doing so. Hence, in part, the importance in the training process of EI consultants of not only learning about EI and how to promote it, but also of enhancing their own emotional intelligence. However, it is not only a question of being seen to be emotionally intelligent, you actually have to be emotionally intelligent too. Just as you can't teach someone French if you don't speak French yourself, neither can you foster emotional intelligence if you aren't reasonably emotionally intelligent yourself.

Next, the other side of expectations: the danger of EI consultants overinflating themselves by overselling what they can offer. This is very tempting because what is on offer is indeed very powerful. In part because of the combination of numbers 2 and 4 of our five crucial attributes of emotional intelligence (see Chapter 3):

2. EI predicts performance.
4. EI is changeable and developable.

Since all consultancy clients are seeking to improve the performance of their organisation, and of its members, that means that what EI has to offer is the holy grail: something which affects performance across the board *and* which can be changed and developed.

That, in a nutshell, is the key to what EI consultancy has to offer in terms of content. But it also has something unique to offer in terms of process.

We have seen that any programme of change which is aimed at enhancing performance levels needs to address Knowledge **and** Attitudes **and** Skills **and** Habits. But that is not what happens. The vast majority of organisational change programmes focus almost entirely on knowledge and skills and ignore attitudes and habits. This is why so many developmental training programmes have only limited success.

EI consultants, on the other hand, are aware of the importance of attitudes (both Self Regard and Regard for Others and the eight Principles of Emotional Intelligence) and habits; they have the knowledge and skills (and the attitudes and habits!) to tackle them; and they address their efforts largely to these aspects. Consequently, not only is EI-based consultancy setting out to change things which have a determining effect on performance level, but it sets out to do so in a way that will work.

However, and this is where the danger of overselling comes in, there are two serious drawbacks about trying to change attitudes and habits.

1. It takes time. Many of the emotional and personal habits that are the likeliest candidates for change will have been in place since childhood and cannot be changed overnight, whereas you can impart knowledge and skills much more rapidly. As a rule of thumb, we take it that to change one piece of habitual behaviour (with its attendant feeling and thinking) will take about three weeks of repetition of the new behaviour: that will be enough to "change the default setting" (in IT terms) so that the new behaviour is unconscious and automatic, just as the old one

was. During the three weeks of changeover, particularly at the beginning, the new behaviour will seem strange and artificial, and, far from being unconscious, it will need attention and energy, so only one piece of behaviour change can be tackled at a time. And, of course, a given aspect of our emotional intelligence may be expressed in a variety of behaviours, some of which will each need to be addressed separately. People will vary in the time they take to make significant changes: some will "see the light" and change rapidly, others will be unconsciously resistant and will have to work doggedly through a series of behaviour changes.

2. This brings us on to the second drawback. Changing attitudes and habits is entirely dependent on the readiness and willingness of the person concerned. Any training in this area needs to be facilitative rather than instructional in nature. And the motivation of the person concerned is much more likely to be enhanced by one-to-one individually aligned interventions which allow for the development of rapport, rather than by group work. For this reason, and because everybody is different and will need to do different things and have different input to help them in the process of developing their emotional intelligence, one-to-one work, such as a coaching relationship, is likely to feature somewhere in the process. The implication for the art of EI consultancy is that skilful facilitation and coaching need to be part of the toolkit.

Consultancy clients, and we acknowledge that this is a little unfair on some of the more sophisticated ones, tend to want guaranteed results and to want them by yesterday. The temptation is to respond to what they want, offer guarantees where none are possible and to agree to an unrealistic timescale. It is important to bear in mind what we have been looking at and to take into account that:

1. Changing attitudes and habits takes time.
2. You can take a horse to water but you can't make it drink. However skilled the consultant is as a facilitator, some people will choose not to change in the direction the organisation would like. Guarantees of specific outcomes in particular cases are therefore not possible.
3. One-to-one work will probably be needed, and this is relatively time-consuming and relatively expensive compared with group training.

It follows that introducing emotional intelligence in a systematic way to an organisation is not a quick or a cheap fix. But the benefits are likely to be across the board and substantial.

One aspect of EI consultancy which we have not touched on yet is measurement. This is pretty crucial, as it allows us to assess what needs to be done, to intervene in an appropriately directed way and to measure progress / achievement. Our ability to do this is based on the first and third of the five crucial attributes of emotional intelligence which are:

1. EI is multifaceted.
3. EI is measurable.

Process must match content and it is fortunate that in the Individual Effectiveness questionnaire (ie^{TM}) and the Team Effectiveness questionnaire (te^{TM}) we have measures which lend themselves to being used in an empowering way, rather than involving the belittling process of most psychometric testing. They both, too, have the advantage that merely completing the questionnaire is an intervention in itself, in that it invites the respondents to consider the issues being explored. Feeding back results and exploring them with the respondents develops the process. Team responses to discussion of te^{TM} results tend to be very productive in terms of identifying what the necessary interventions are, and of generating willingness to undertake them. Probably a skilled team consultant could gather the same information over three days of interviews, but the use of the te^{TM} saves both consultant time and management time. Exploration of ie^{TM} results at least allows an individual to focus their self-development energies, and at best it can prove a life-changing experience, profoundly deepening the individual's self knowledge and self acceptance.

A word here about using the 360° version of the ie^{TM}. Because the ie^{TM} 360° version is abbreviated and not time consuming, it can routinely be used to validate the ie^{TM} itself. From the consultant's point of view this is a relief, because it provides the easiest way of dealing with the potentially most difficult kind of individual respondent. We have noticed the importance of Self Regard within EI as a whole, and the most tricky set of responses come from those who have an underlying, if unconscious and unadmitted, sense of low Self Regard, but who cloak this by adopting the "I'm OK, You're Not OK" life position. This will usually be apparent to the consultant, despite their high score on Self Regard, because their Regard for Others, and consequently their Relative Regard, will be low. Such people, however, tend to be pretty defended and to be resistant to taking in negative feedback from others. Nonetheless, it will be difficult for them to deny the reality of a 360° which is at variance with their own self assessment in Scale 18, and this may provide the impetus for them to reconsider their view of themselves. It is particularly important in such cases that respondents to the 360° are reassured before they complete it that their responses will be anonymous and not identifiable to them, and that all attempts by the ratee to discover how individual raters assessed them are resisted.

One question which EI consultants in particular have to address is whether to go into a particular organisation explicitly flying the banner of "Emotional Intelligence", or whether to offer generic performance improvement in terms of self management and relationship management. It is hard to lay down general rules about this: it is up to the skill of the consultant and his/her knowledge of the particular circumstances. What is more important is that the work gets done, rather than the particular name it is initiated under.

An issue which EI consultants share with management consultants in general is where to start; what level to go in at. There is a particular difficulty here in that senior management will often assume that they are emotionally intelligent (because they are senior) and that the interventions need to be directed further down the hierarchy, towards middle and junior management. The more they believe this, the less it is likely to be true! It is usually best to start at the top if you have the "in" to do so. If not, it is often helpful to start a pilot scheme in a particular corner of the organisation: if all goes well, the success of that will be the basis for spreading EI promotion more widely.

EI consultants need to bear in mind the three levels at which one can assess the level of functioning in terms of emotional intelligence, and at which one can intervene: individual, team (including leadership) and organisation. There is an almost infinite variety of ways in which intervening at these three levels can be related and programmed. Often, one level will enhance the other. For example, doing a *te*™ on a board of directors first will often lead to suggestions that each should do the *ie*™, and then when the board-level interventions have been completed, they will likely want to address the extent to which the whole organisation is run in an emotionally intelligent way. Conversely, one can start by having team members each complete an *i3*™ and often that will lead to a suggestion that they should then complete a *i3*™ on the team as a whole. Again, there are no hard and fast rules: it is down to the skill of the consultant to respond to the inclination of the client and the particular circumstances of the organisation.

In terms of defining the focus of a piece of EI consultancy, it is a common pattern that the client presents with a problem of relationships (e.g., "Sales and Accounts are at war") with the expectation that the interventions will be at the inter-group relationship level. Often, however, it is important to bear in mind the direction of the causal arrows in our four-part model (see page 241). The symptoms may be at the Relationship Management level, but in order to deal with them it is often necessary to address Self Management, Awareness of Others and indeed Self Awareness, from which everything else springs.

Finally, a reminder and a word of warning. The last of our five crucial attributes of emotional intelligence is:

5. EI is an aspect of the whole person.

What this means is that it is not a bolt-on addition. If someone changes the level of their functioning in terms of emotional intelligence, they themselves are changed, both at home and at work, at weekends as well as 9–5. Furthermore, feelings are a core part of our identity and something we tend to feel pretty tender about. It therefore behoves all EI consultants to work in a respectful and professionally careful manner, to facilitate the respondent to go where they want to go and not to instruct them as to where to go.

In order to be able to do this, since the consultant is being paid by the organisation, not the individual respondent, it is important to be very clear about the elements of this three-cornered contract before the work begins, so that each party knows where they stand, for example in regard to confidentiality.

The process of helping people enhance their emotional intelligence can be an exciting and a moving one, and in the process respondents may share things, and themselves, with the consultant in a way that it is a privilege to receive. The only down side of this is that occasionally in the process individual respondents may go through a period of emotional distress and/or may discover that they need professional help to sort themselves out. This does not mean that an EI consultant needs to be a trained psychotherapist. What they do need is

1. To be able to recognise when they are reaching the limits of their competency and they need to refer on.
2. To know who to refer the client to, or at least how to find out.
3. To be able to handle the process of referral professionally.

Until that point, they just need to remember that they don't have to fix anything, they just have to be there for the client. Active empathic listening, which they do need to have in their toolkit, will do the business. After all, that is probably what the trained psychotherapist would be doing too!

CAEI code of ethics

Professional practitioners of emotional intelligence concepts, frameworks, methods, techniques, models and processes are committed to achieving the highest standards of professionalism in their work.

Their work involves supporting personal development and improving work-related performance in individuals, teams and organisations. To this end they are committed to following and developing best practice procedures in this field. They seek to:

- constantly improve their own performance and results;
- adhere to proper conduct regarding confidentiality;
- act in an accountable way with their colleagues and clients;
- make clear, concise, legal and psychological contracts with their colleagues and clients;
- commit to a lifetime of learning;
- continually develop their own skills, knowledge, habits and attitudes in emotional intelligence and related fields.

When undertaking research or contractual work in this field they will take care to:

- plan appropriately;
- consider the professional context, cultural environment, ethics and legal requirements;
- have conceptual frameworks from which they can operate to make personal development a cohesive and integrated experience for learners;
- make regular and relevant self assessments;
- make regular and relevant evaluations of ongoing projects with individuals, teams or organisations;
- create a programme for development and evaluate it regularly with participants and peers;
- ensure they have the personal and organisational resources necessary to allow them to fulfil their contractual obligations;
- prepare the groups, individuals or organisations involved in a responsible way;
- take active steps to keep abreast of trends or create them.

Regarding their performance in the measurement and/or application of emotional intelligence, they will commit to having high levels of:

- self knowledge;
- emotional competencies;
- personal adaptability;
- knowledge concerning emotional conditions and dynamics in individuals and teams.

They will operate in ways that create mutual benefit by being:

- collaborative;
- creative;
- open to diversity and difference;
- accepting;
- respectfully challenging;
- open to feedback.

They will structure and manage development programmes in ways that:

- create trust;
- promote mutual benefit and respect;

- demonstrate acceptance and support, both of individuals and the organisations they work for.

They will have the practice of self reflection and will undertake this in their professional work too, through processes such as:

- review interviews;
- focus groups;
- questionnaires;
- peer supervision;
- mentoring arrangements with experienced senior practitioners.

They will undertake rigorous evaluation of their programmes and be prepared to correct programmes that have not added value or created the return on investment that was outlined in the initial contract.

AppliedEI™

AppliedEI™ represents our approach to EI development – the importance of attitudes in the development of EI – and this underpins the ethos and the work of the Centre for Applied Emotional Intelligence. The CAEI promotes high performance and personal success through:

- learning to manage yourself and your personality effectively;
- learning to manage your relationships effectively; and
- acceptance of self and others.

AppliedEI™ is a registered trade mark. It describes our approach to EI development and is a kitemark awarded to graduates of our Certificate in Applied Emotional Intelligence who continue to demonstrate ongoing EI practitionership and CPD. Wherever you see this mark, you can be assured that the practitioner or training organisation subscribes to the CAEI standards in EI development and has undertaken indepth training with us.

Why is AppliedEI™ important?

EI should be part of the organisational culture – emotionally intelligent behaviour throughout an organisation will directly impact on the working environment. A lack of organisational EI will affect employee health and morale, key indicators being absenteeism, high turnover and work-related stress.

Since emotional intelligence is about *how we manage* our personality, AppliedEI™, or knowing how to put EI into practice, is essential for effective leadership, for transforming team and organisational culture, in fact for any job where individuals have a lot of interaction with others or where the individual has to manage his/herself.

So, AppliedEI™ defines our approach to developing transformational leadership, high-performing teams and personal effectiveness within organisations. The CAEI facilitates this through its flexible range of EI training and development products and services offered through its training partners. We can either work with you to design and implement effective EI development programmes specific to your needs, or run "Train the Trainer" programmes to provide your organisation with people who have the necessary attitudes and skills to implement long-term EI strategies.

Emotionally intelligent practices

Contracting

In Chapter 4 we suggested that being emotionally intelligent was equivalent in TA terms to being in Integrated Adult. TA lays great emphasis on the need for careful and explicit contracting, because that is an effective way to ensure that people are relating Adult to Adult and not Parent to Child. Precisely the same considerations apply to working in the field of emotional intelligence, and therefore practitioners need to be scrupulous about their contracting.

Eric Berne, the originator of TA, suggested that there are three levels of contracting:

- the administrative level;
- the professional level;
- the psychological level (often but unhelpfully left implicit).

Contracts involving organisations can be three- or four-cornered too – stakeholders may include the practitioner, the client organisation (e.g. represented by HR), the individual being coached and potentially the individual's manager. The practitioner needs to be aware of the complexity of the issues with a multi-cornered contract and to be explicit, clarifying any conflicting assumptions and expectations.

Depending on the number of corners to the contract, the administrative contract may be simple or complex. The more complex administrative level may include:

- relevant laws/directives and policies in the organisation;
- purpose – duties, roles and responsibilities of each person;
- finance;
- personnel – who is supplying what resource?
- facilities – room(s), uninterrupted time, administrative support;
- equipment;
- notes and record-keeping procedures;
- monitoring and evaluation processes;
- referring on to other professionals/groups/people.

The professional contract clearly states the limits and potential reaches of the work, specifying goals and tasks. Again, the more complex contract may include the following elements at the professional level:

- purpose/goals;
- benefits and limitations;
- accountability and competence;
- responsibility;
- insurance cover;
- confidentiality.

The psychological contract identifies the hopes, fears and expectations of the client based on assumptions or previous experiences. Possible positive and negative outcomes need to be considered too.

ROTI

And finally we have ROTI – the return on training investment.

The aim of an EI development programme is to move individuals from performing with interferences to performing without interferences. The amount of dismantling of interferences will depend on the objectives of the programme, the length of the programme and the buy-in from the individual participants.

Using the Kirkpatrick four-step model (1975), an evaluation plan for an EI development programme may look something like that shown in Table 18.2.

Table 18.2 *An evaluation plan for an EI development programme.*

Evaluation	Components
Level 1	What the participants thought of the programme Continual feedback during programme
Level 2	The change in knowledge, skills and attitude with respect to the training objectives Using internal performance appraisal framework to benchmark Individual assessment of personal interferences to be dismantled — skills/knowledge gaps from performance appraisal — attitudinal development needs from EI profiling Demonstrating new knowledge, skills and attitudes on the job Delegate group vs. hidden control group
Level 3	How behaviour has changed and is sustained over time Using internal competency framework to benchmark Ownership of behavioural change and self assessment through learning log Before and after EI self assessment and 360° feedback Delegate group vs. hidden control group
Level 4	Bottom line contribution – costs, quality, ROI Dependent on training objectives ROI – costs recouped Improvement to service and / or performance Delegate group vs. hidden control group

In summary, an evaluation process is likely to incorporate:

- continual delegate feedback during the programme;
- internal performance appraisal or leadership competency framework for benchmarking;
- individual assessment of personal interferences to be dismantled;
- before and after EI self assessment and 360° feedback;
- self assessment and reflective learning through learning logs;
- delegate group vs. hidden control group;
- calculation of the ROI;

- the amount of costs recouped;
- increase in organisation performance or improvement to service.

We are confident that any EI training intervention based on the model we have outlined in this book will generate a more than satisfactory return on training investment. More generally, we hope that the contents of this book will have enabled and encouraged its readers to develop aspects of their own emotional intelligence and that of the teams and organisations of which they are members. We invite readers to contact the Centre for Applied Emotional Intelligence and/or its partners to help further this process. The necessary contact details can be found in the Appendix.

Reference

Giges, B. and Rosenfeld, E. (1976) *The Intensive Group Experience*, edited by Rosenbaum, M. and Snadowsky, A., The Free Press.

Kirkpatrick, D. (1975) *Evaluating Training Programs*, ASTD.

Kolb, D.A. (1984) *Experiential Learning: Experience as the source of learning and development*, Prentice-Hall.

Kozubska, J. (1999) "What is Action Learning?" IMC Association.

Appendix: Contact information

The CAEI

The contents of this book represent the ethos of the Centre for Applied Emotional Intelligence (CAEI).

The CAEI has a register of qualified practitioners, available on request, and provides:

- CAEI Certificate in Applied Emotional Intelligence;
- consultancy in AppliedEI™;
- keynotes and seminars;
- AppliedEI™ development training;
- Applied EI – the ezine.

Contact:

Tim Sparrow or Amanda Knight
Centre for Applied Emotional Intelligence

Tel: +44 (0)1242 282907

Email Tim: tim@appliedei.co.uk
Email Amanda: amanda@appliedei.co.uk

Web: www.emotionalintelligence.co.uk

To subscribe to our free monthly ezine email: ezine@appliedei.co.uk

Our Aims

The CAEI is a charitable trust which is established:

(i) to promote the understanding of, and the development of, emotional intelligence among members of the general population, and of organisations, and hence to enhance the health, happiness and success of those involved, and (ii) to this end to promote ethical and professional practice in the effective development of emotional intelligence, and (iii) to promote research into the application of emotional intelligence, and the role played by attitudes in determining emotional intelligence, and (iv) to promote the availability of emotional intelligence development to disadvantaged categories of people and individuals who would particularly profit from it and who would otherwise not have access to it or be able to afford it.

To this end it collaborates with the following organisations.

The CAEI's strategic partners

Activate Training – for outdoor experiential development training
Contact:

> Matt King
> Activate Training
>
> Tel: +44 (0)1590 688011
> Email: matt@activate-training.co.uk
> Web: www.activate-training.co.uk

JCA (Occupational Psychologists) Ltd – for EI diagnostic tools
Contact:

> Jo Maddocks
> JCA (Occupational Psychologists) Ltd
>
> Tel: +44 (0)1242 239238
> Email: jo@jca.biz
> Web: www.ie-te.co.uk

Minds4Success Limited – for individual development
Contact:

> Marilyn Latcham
> Minds4Success Limited
>
> Tel: +44 (0)1202 742162
> Email: marilyn@minds4success.co.uk
> Web: www.minds4success.co.uk

Other Contact:

> Dr Alexandra Concorde
> The Concorde Initiative
>
> Tel: 0870 345 2255
> Email: service@the-concorde-initiative.com
> Web: www.the-concorde-initiative.com

Further reading

Bennis, W. (2003) *On Becoming a Leader*, revised edition, Random House.

Bowes, M. (2006) *me + you = 100 Ways to Work Out a Formula for Success in Your Personal and Professional Relationships*, Trafford Publishing.

Childre, D. and Martin, H. (2000) *The HeartMath Solution*, HarperSanFrancisco.

Csikszentmihali, M. (1996) *Flow: The Psychology of Optimal Experience*, Harper & Row.

Damasio, A.R. (2005) *Descartes' Error: Emotion, Reason and the Human Brain*, Penguin.

Gallwey, W.T. (1986) *The Inner Game of Tennis*, Pan.

Gallwey, W.T. (2000) *The Inner Game of Work*, Random House.

Gardner, H. (1983/1993) *Frames of Mind*, Fontana.

Goleman, D. (1995) *Emotional Intelligence: Why it can matter more than IQ*, Bantam Books.

Goleman, D. (2004) *Destructive Emotions*, Bloomsbury.

Holmes, R. and Holmes, J. (1999) *The Good Mood Guide: How to Embrace your Pain and Face your Fears*, Orion.

James, M. and Jongeward, D. (1996) *Born to Win – Transactional Analysis with Gestalt Experiments*, Da Capo Press.

Joines, V. and Stewart, I. (2002) *Personality Adaptations: A New Guide to Human Understanding in Psychotherapy and Counselling*, Lifespace Publishing.

Pert, C.B. (1997) *Molecules of Emotion*, Prentice-Hall.

Senge, P., Jaworski, J., Scharmer, C.O. and Flowers, B.S. (2005) *Presence: Exploring Profound Change in People, Organizations and Society*, Nicholas Brearley Publishing.

Stewart, I. and Joines, V. (1987) *TA Today: A new introduction to transactional analysis*, Lifespace Publishing.

Ware, P. (1983) "Personality Adaptations", *Transactional Analysis Journal*, **13**(1), 11–19.

Index

Index compiled by Terry Halliday